THOSE PEOPLE

CONTRIBUTIONS IN SOCIOLOGY

Series Editor: Don Martindale

New Perspectives on Organization Theory: An Empirical
Reconsideration of the Marxian and Classical Analyses
William L. Zwerman

Garrison Community: A Study of an Overseas
American Military Colony
Charlotte Wolf

Small town and the Nation: The Conflict
of Local and Translocal Forces
Don Martindale and R. Galen Hanson

The Social Shaping of Science: Institutions,
Ideology, and Careers in Science
Roger G. Krohn

Commitment to Deviance: The Nonprofessional
Criminal in the Community
Robert A. Stebbins

Capitalists Without Capitalism: The Jains of India
and the Quakers of the West
Balwant Nevaskar

Black Belonging: A Study of the Social Correlates
of Work Relations Among Negroes
Jack C. Ross and Raymond H. Wheeler

The School Managers: Power and Conflict
in American Public Education
Donald J. McCarty and Charles E. Ramsey

The Social Dimensions of Mental Illness,
Alcoholism, and Drug Dependence
Don Martindale and Edith Martindale

THOSE PEOPLE

The Subculture of a Housing Project
(Ces Gens-Là)

by Colette Pétonnet

Translated by Rita Smidt

CONTRIBUTIONS IN SOCIOLOGY, NO. 10

GREENWOOD PRESS, INC.
Westport, Connecticut · London, England

Library of Congress Cataloging in Publication Data

Pétonnet, Colette.
Those People.

(Contributions in sociology, no. 10)
Bibliography: p.
1. France—Social conditions—Case studies.
2. Public housing—France—Case studies. 3. Poor—
France—Case studies. I. Title.
HN425.5.P3513   309.1′ 44   72-825
ISBN 0-8371-6393-5

Library of Congress Catalog Card Number: 72–825
ISBN: 0–8371–6393–5
Translation first published in 1973

Greenwood Press, Inc.
Publishing Division
51 Riverside Avenue, Westport, Connecticut 06880
Printed in the United States of America

Contents

List of Tables

Foreword to the Translation

The author of *Those People* presents us with a significant contribution to the literature bearing upon the culture of poverty. The anthropological literature in this area of studies of the urban poor in industrialized nations has been written largely by United States anthropologists, although Oscar Lewis conducted major work along this line in Mexico and Puerto Rico. This study from France enables us to broaden our comparative perspective on a field that is currently the focus of much scholarly controversy.

Colette Pétonnet received her B.A. in psychology at the University of Paris in 1953. During this period of study, she worked for three years in a home for delinquent children. Next, she worked in Morocco for several years, first in government educational programs in the slums of Casablanca and then later for the Ministry of Youth, when she worked on problems of juvenile delinquency. This foreign experience led her into studies in social anthropology. *Those People* grew

out of her doctoral dissertation in that field. Since 1968 she
has been with the CNRS (National Center for Scientific
Research).

With this background of psychology and social anthropology
and experience in working on the problems of youth, Mlle.
Pétonnet was able to immerse herself in the lives of the people
of the public-housing project. She speaks with the authority
of a participant observer, presenting us with a remarkably com-
prehensive picture of economic resources, family life, boys'
gangs, the use of space and time, and values and beliefs of
the project residents.

We find the housing project isolated from the mainstream
of French life. The residents must go outside for education,
shopping, entertainment, and political participation. Project
residents appear to be looked down upon by those of higher
social status and greater economic resources. Yet this isolation
does not seem to have produced internal cohesion among project residents. The groupings that have arisen appear to be
based upon propinquity in residence for the adults and upon
peer group membership for the young people. The residents
feel subordinated by the outside world, but appear to take
no organized steps to better their position.

We are presented with a picture of people who are struggling
to hold their own and are not going anywhere. They work
for small gains rather than major changes. School is regarded
as a place to learn to read and write, and many people see
no need for education beyond that point. They do not recognize
the connection, at least for themselves, of education with the
ability to cope with more complex problems and therefore
to gain higher paying and higher prestige positions. The reading skill they acquire in school is little practiced in the home.
If you already have learned to read, why should you bother
reading at home?

Television is such a prominent part of life for nearly everybody in the project that we wonder how people lived in these
situations before TV. Television seems to provide a vicarious
escape from the constraints of the immediate and limited surroundings.

What light does the study throw upon the question of the "culture of poverty"? Indeed, is it useful to think in terms of such a culture of poverty? This study illustrates some of the possibilities and also some of the limitations of research guided by this concept.

While the housing project is composed of people of several distinct ethnic groups, Pétonnet finds similarities as well as differences in culture. In other words, there seem to be some general conditions of living in the housing project that reduce the differences due to ethnic group membership. But at this point, we are faced with a question that this study does not answer. Do the common elements noted by the author arise because the subjects of study are poor people, or do they arise because of the peculiar circumstances of poor people living in a large public-housing project?

We would assume that some of the common elements arise out of the life situation the residents share—low education, low income, low-skilled jobs—and the features that generally accompany these conditions. On the other hand, we would expect that some of these common elements would derive from the peculiar situation of the large housing project. Until we have comparable studies of residents in working-class neighborhoods in a large city in France, we will not be able to sort out the special characteristics that arise out of the housing project and those that are common to lower-class people.

The problem of interpreting the residents' relations with the outside world also points to the need for comparative studies. The housing project appears to be isolated from the city of which it is nominally a part. The residents appear dependent and alienated from the larger society. They seem to feel that they have no control over the political decisions that affect their fate. Since France is known for the centralization of its governmental structures, would we expect that poor people everywhere in France feel that they have little impact upon the decision-making process at the community level? Or is this sense of powerlessness and alienation particularly associated with life in the public-housing project? Questions such as these can only be answered after research into the lives of people at the same socio-economic level but living in neighborhoods of large cities rather than in the governmentally contrived environment of the housing project.

This suggests a general orientation to the question of the culture of poverty. If that term is to be used as a guide to research, we must recognize that it is useless to try to prove that there is or there is not a culture of poverty. When we find some common elements forming a characteristic pattern of behavior, attitude, and belief, we nevertheless still need to find the elements of the environment that have produced these responses.

It is characteristic of a good study that it raises more questions than it answers. Colette Pétonnet has given us a penetrating view into the lives of a segment of the French working class. The view presented here will take on still more meaning as the author and her colleagues undertake further studies of working-class life in other environments in France.

WILLIAM FOOTE WHYTE

Preface

It has been quite a long time since sociologists like Gustav Schmoller (1838–1917) showed that the type of dwelling has much more sociohistoric importance than other factors that were once considered dominant, such as race. More recently, Brazilian sociologist Gilberto Freyre has devoted three of his most important works to studying the social history of the home in order to reveal through it the private story, the marital and family life, of almost all Brazilians. Naturally, there is a dialectic between the nature of the apartment and the structure of the family living in it. But it is no doubt less the family that creates its home than the home that shapes the relationships between husband and wife, parents and children, and family and neighbors, as well as the nature of the bonds that extend into the street. The street is most often just the inverse image of the home, and its dual, antithetical aspect (the fact that it is both frightening and enticing) cannot be understood unless one has first considered "the house" or "the apartment."

To be sure, a certain number of analyses of some current types of housing, from slums or shantytowns to apartment complexes, are now available in France, in particular the works of Chombard de Lauwe's group and others. Apparently the transitional housing project had still escaped the sociologist's attention, however, and we must thank Colette Pétonnet for now giving us an exciting book, admirably conceived and written, on this subject. But we must go further; we must congratulate her for having applied the methods of ethnology to this subject, by living in the project she describes, and by using participant–observer and sustained interview techniques over many hours and seasons. This makes the La Halle project come alive before us, with its gossip in the hallways, its dramas or its festive moments, the secret rites in the cellars, and the adventures of the young in the surrounding "bush." Here the "house" is not just the apartment; it is also the hallway, the stairway, the cellars, or the courtyard, with each subgroup, sex group, or age group having its own domain, which it shapes and is shaped by.

The transitional housing project is intended to educate and form new habits in a population of the ill-housed, pending their relocation in apartment complexes. This results in the heterogeneous character of this population: North Africans, foreigners, and nationals who are encamped but not integrated into the larger society. But relocation is long in coming and by living together, these ethnic subgroups end up "secreting" a relatively homogeneous culture. (Like that of *Children of Sanchez,* it is a "culture of poverty" or, if you prefer, a "marginal" culture, but with special traits compared to the one Oscar Lewis studied.) And this is where we see the full advantage of that ethnological method that Colette Pétonnet handles with such assurance. She makes us grasp the nature of this culture, just as she makes us grasp the process of its formation, its defense mechanisms against the alien world surrounding it, and, consequently, its simultaneous institutionalization and fluidity. Here, fortunately, we go beyond the balance-sheets of classical sociology, the procrustean bed imposed on the facts by the tyranny of questionnaires; subtle analysis triumphs at last over punched cards!

One will certainly read with excitement this whole set of analyses defining a stagnant, segregated population; its spatial and temporal frameworks (not as perceived from outside but as experienced by the group in the form of qualitative places loaded with affective meaning, or in the form of temporality); its exchange mechanisms (trading of gossip among the neighbors, as well as gifts and sexual benefits between gang members); its mechanisms for selecting from among all the influences that come from the larger society—penetrating the project walls through radio, television, and contact with school-mates and later with pals at the factory—keeping only those that fit with the culture of the group and rejecting all others; and finally its mixing of cultural traits. Some of these traits are brought from North Africa, others from Jewish ghettoes, and still others from the French countryside. They are main-tained for a short while in the refuge of a few apartments and are then eroded by conflicts and exchanges, the slow disin-tegration of the "sacred," and the disorganization imposed by the ecological milieu, interpersonal relations, family forms, and finally the rupture with the nucleus of traditions, which is the village for the Frenchmen and the shantytown for the foreigners.

As we read, the transitional housing project is reconstructed in our minds and begins to live in us. Colette Pétonnet has torn us from our own world to make us participate too. She is to be thanked for it; this book of science is also a human book—a book of love.

ROGER BASTIDE

Translator's Note

I wish to acknowledge the help given me by Dominique Michaelson, Danielle Marinet, Jacqueline Laufer, and several others. Without their explanations of many ordinary facts of life in France today, as well as more technical matters, this translation would have remained far less understandable for the American reader.

RITA SMIDT

Introduction

The problems posed by present-day urbanization and the new form of habitat in groups of buildings and apartment complexes have already been studied at length by the group on social ethnology directed by Ph. Chombard de Lauwe[1] among others, while the ill-housed are the subject of Andrée Michel's thesis.[2] But little work has yet been devoted to the transitional housing projects specifically intended for occupants from the large city slums, and this is the gap that we intend to try to fill here.

For the past fifteen years or so, the public authorities of a zone of great urban concentration[3] have assigned certain sums for the construction of substandard buildings. This construction makes it possible to offer a suitable apartment at a modest rent to families presently crammed into a single room or to occupants of condemned buildings. The administrative history of the transitional projects will be examined in chapter 2. Here, we shall mention only the essential fact that determines their originality, namely, that the residents must live

in the project just temporarily. In principle, after a trial period
of one to three years, these residents should be eligible for
the HLM [moderate-rent public housing], which provides
greater comfort at higher rent, but they may also be subject
to eviction for not paying the rent or for "misbehavior." The
transitional projects thus appear at first glance to be
heterogeneous, involuntary agglomerates of people living in
an interim situation.

The project that concerns us is implanted in a commune*
containing three such projects. One of them stands at the end
of an apartment complex and is not autonomous. The other
two are joined side by side. The older of these, built in 1957,
has already deteriorated more, is hostile, and seemed more
difficult to penetrate. The other, built more recently and with
more definite boundaries, had less obviously hostile residents;
it seemed more interesting to us, and that is why we have
chosen it. We shall call it "La Halle."

What is striking from the outset is that it looks like a blind
alley at the end of the inhabited world, a closed-off space
in which a mixed population finds itself fortuitously side by
side. But from the beginning of the study, we realized that
the project cannot be defined as just a heterogeneous agglomerate. In fact, the people take root in the space made available
to them and take over favorite spots according to age and sex;
they maintain interpersonal relations; and they live out their
sojourn in a particular way. The project forms a group.
Moreover, it forms a special group created by its members'
awareness of their rejection by society, the constraints they
endure, and the insecurity caused by an uncertain future.

The municipality, which would like to pride itself on being
an expanding city, in fact has difficulty tolerating the people
of La Halle and seeks a way to get rid of them in other places.
Teachers and government employees call them *"those*

---

*A commune is roughly the size of a large village or several smaller ones
and has its own officials, budget, etc., but, like other levels of government,
it is responsible to and dependent on the central government.—R.S.

people," "misfits," and "antisocial," while other townfolk use more colorful terms. The tradesmen who exploit the ignorance of the adults and the café owners who shut their doors to the adolescents from the project call them "Mafia," "Chicago," "dregs," and "lower depths." One cannot help thinking of the appellations "barbarians" and "savages" generally used by Eugéne Sue and Victor Hugo, revived by Balzac and analyzed by Louis Chevalier, who thus describes the population pushed back toward the southern outskirts during the last century:

> Stranded there is the least developed part of the population, the least specialized and least exacting manpower.... It is like the end of the world, a strange country, reached at length only by dirt paths, that is frightening.[4]

Although society today sets aside places to live for some of them, the reasons why it still rejects its "savages" have scarcely changed since Proudhon's time. These reasons are contained in a passage from *La Guerre et La Paix* which we quote because, if all the value judgments in it are carefully suppressed, it can be taken as a working hypothesis precisely on the system of values.

> Pauperism is characterized by the "slow starvation" of which Fourier spoke, starvation of every moment, the whole year, a whole lifetime, starvation which does not kill in a day but which is composed of all the privations [and] regrets that ceaselessly undermine the body, ruin the mind, demoralize the conscience, deteriorate the races, [and] engender all the ills and vices: drunkenness ... and envy, distaste for work and thrift, baseness of soul, indelicacy of conscience, coarseness of manners, laziness, mendicity, prostitution and theft.[5]

There is only a difference of degree between Proudhon's unfortunates and the occupants of our project. Lumped together under the same scorn and sadly surprised by the names they are called, the residents of La Halle have no alternative but to recognize themselves as the group they form in relation to the outside world. They quickly define the territory belonging to them and refer to themselves as "we in La Halle." The children fight any outside group; as is common in villages, they defend their membership in "their project."

But the group also arises from constraint and insecurity. Subjected to "public charity," the residents have had to accept the housing offered to them in the project because refusal would mean losing any hope of leaving the slums. Another constraint is that they are considered merely occupants; they pay an occupant's fee, which is turned over to the general tax collector. If they are adjudged bad tenants by the caretaker or the manager, they are evicted. But even while living under that threat, their hopes of leaving the project through a promotion to better housing are maintained by the government. So they settle down temporarily, with the feeling of living through a transitional period that makes them inferior. Moreover, their hope of promotion decreases from year to year because the HLM companies do not put up enough new buildings, and the population stagnates despite "skimming off" by the government. Some manage to leave by their own means, but none of them can settle down in the present knowing what the future holds. None can feel secure. Among those remaining, evictions reinforce the feeling of belonging to a special group.

This special group is made up of three main ethnic groups (Arabs, Jews, and underprivileged French) against whom society practices a certain amount of racism. We can assume that the feeling of rejection will produce antagonism that will be expressed in aggressive behavior and coherence of group feelings, and we may ask whether the various systems of values would not be inclined to polarize around values belonging to the group. In other words, because of the relative isolation of the La Halle project from society, is it not secreting its own subculture?

It is from this perspective that the present research is oriented. The first part will deal with the ecological framework, the second will study family structure and life, and the third will circumscribe the subculture more narrowly through social relations, the concept of time and space, acquisition and use of information, and the system of values.

NOTES

[1]Ph. Chombard de Lauwe, *Famille et Habitation*, vols. I–II.

[2]A. Michel, *Famille, Industrialisation, Logement.*

[3]The city in question will be kept anonymous throughout this work. For greater convenience, we shall call it "the city."

[4]L. Chevalier, *Classes Laborieuses et Classes Dangereuses à Paris Pendant la Première Moitié du XIXe Siecle*, p. 82.

[5]Proudhon, *La Guerre et La Paix* (Paris: Marcel Rivière, 1927), p. 136.

Part I

THE CONTEXTS OF LIFE
IN LA HALLE

1

The Physical Context

The Commune

The commune in which we find the project under study is located ten miles from the city, on its southeastern edge. Still rustic until recent years, it has seen the rapid disappearance of its wheat fields, its truck farms, and part of its vacant land. Expansion is in full swing, and the district around it, which is in the midst of a population explosion, will grow by 500,000 inhabitants in twenty years.

The population of the commune is distributed in clearly defined areas. The earlier residents occupy the town and old homes surrounded by gardens. New people who have moved in live either in scattered residences, ranging from luxury apartment houses to housing projects, or in the apartment complex on the hill. This complex was built for 50,000 occupants; it is beginning to be self-sufficient as installation of facilities is completed.

The census is always inexact for the commune's continually

3

increasing population, which has grown from 13,000 inhabitants just after World War II to 50,000 in 1965. Two hundred
thousand inhabitants are anticipated by 1980.

The commune has no public offices to date and has been
administered from the capital of the canton.* It is crossed by
two highways, and has no industry. It is in this commune,
with its juxtaposed populations, that three transitional projects
were built at three separate times over the past eleven years.
We shall study La Halle, the most recent project.

The Project

The traveler getting off the bus at the town church sets off
on foot on a very busy highway lined by private houses and
enclosures. He must walk for ten minutes along a dirt path
before reaching the traffic light at the bend, which marks the
intersection with the access road to the project. No habitation
can be seen beyond this point; a gray, nondescript plain
stretches out to a horizon barred by factory chimneys and gas-
storage tanks. To the left, some six-sided gray structures with
pointed roofs stand with their backs to the road. This is the
project. You must first cross a hundred yards between a curb
dampened in winter by vapor from cars being refueled, and
a high, wide white building protected by a thick grill. At the
corner of the recessed ground floor of this building are some
shops: a grocery, a cleaner, and a drugstore.

Women carrying shopping baskets and men dangling loaves
of bread walk carelessly in the middle of the road, as heedless
of the cars as the children following them. They are very much
at home. Passing cars can belong only in the project or be
going there, so they are not dangerous.

At the end of the road skirting the back of one of the gray
blocks, some children in mud-spattered shoes are coming home
from school. The road is passable only by foot because it has

---

*A canton is comprised of several communes and is roughly equivalent
to an American county.—R.S.

become more and more broken up. The school buildings and the apartment complex can be reached by taking this road past some overgrown gardens.

Where is the entrance? Is it by the curb flanked by a yellow wood barracks labeled "Supermarket"? No, for that way you come up against a low wall straddled by some adolescents trying to have a quiet smoke. You must go through a large space, almost a gateway, between the end of one building where the caretaker keeps watch and another with a flight of steps and a boarded-up window. The latter is an abandoned store; originally it was the only market opened for the residents' shopping, but it was ruined in 1965 by competition from the supermarket. You then enter an interior space bounded by two parallel, elongated four-story buildings with small, symmetrical yellow openings that have no outside blinds or shutters. Up a flight of stairs, a dozen doors open on this inner courtyard. You have the impression of entering private property rather than a village. One does not come to La Halle; one enters it. The side of the first building touches the narrow enclosing wall scaled by the children. The second is separated from the wall by a large space, which is reserved for the games of the younger children, judging from the merry-go-round and slide put at their disposal. This space is backed up on one side by a "youth club" and is extended on the other by a vaulted passage that joins the La Halle project to the first building of the neighboring Le Pas project. Le Pas is also turned toward its inner courtyard, which is reached by the passage. The lodge of the second caretaker is situated here. He is an elderly man who often scolds the disobedient boys breaking rules—against digging holes, rummaging in the garbage cans, dragging old cartons and rags around, playing in the cellars, and fighting—whose merits only he appreciates.

The courtyard, bounded by straight, parallel sidewalks at the foot of the buildings, is paved along a narrow perimeter and rises in the center in a large elongated oval circled by a cement border and planted with a few high-perched lights and some plane trees that have not yet had time to grow very much. Here and there some cement benches invite you to sit down, but the space is somewhat cluttered by cars, which are too numerous for the parking area provided at the entrance.

Cars are normally parked as close to home as possible, so they are brought into the courtyard instead of being left on the road behind the first building. The area intended for parking quickly became a garbage dump, but the project is so arranged that the residents are not at all concerned about it. The cars, about fifty in all, are lined up on the courtyard curb despite the sharp edge of the border. They are safer here; outside, they would be subject to the depredations of the children who play around them and are just waiting until no one is looking to play in them. The smaller cars are new; they are all clean and are washed often. The others—large old cars or faded delivery trucks—are breaking down although they are often repaired.

On arriving, one is struck by the difference in appearance between the clean interior, watched over without respite by the caretaker, broom and shovel in hand, and the smelly exterior, full of all kinds of refuse—household rubbish surreptitiously thrown out of kitchen windows—with blue stains from empty milk cartons floating on the surface. The rear of the first building is used as a dumping ground because the caretaker cannot be everywhere at once, but also because the edge of the public road is no longer part of the village. The best proof of this is that the rear of the opposite building is kept clean because the enclosing wall is a few yards behind it; the space in between is integrated into his jurisdiction and as such is better supervised by the caretaker.

Some men are riding home on motorcycles from work; they slow down, climb the sidewalk, and disappear along the front of the building on a ramp covered by a grill, one of the entrances to the basement. They come out on a square space that continues on either side in a long, dimly lit corridor going past the individual cellars, each barred by a gate. This corridor runs all along the building, making a sort of tunnel with exits on each side of an open space containing two flights of stairs.

It is very dark in the unlit individual cellars; a flashlight can pick out strange objects lying on a dusty floor. Many cellars can no longer be locked and are almost empty; others contain piles of mattresses and nondescript debris. You come up with your legs covered with fleas, but this in no way prevents the children from going there to play.

Children are everywhere, wherever you look, sitting with dangling legs on the gray garbage cans lined up in fours and crouching on the five steps that lead to the stairwell door of iron and barred translucent glass. The aluminum letters designating the stairwell, from A to M, are nailed to the outside right corner of the door; the B has fallen off and the D has been nailed back on backwards.

The individual wooden mailboxes are on the same level, behind the stairwell door. They are a luxury. Other projects do not have any; instead, the caretaker draws squares corresponding to the door numbers on a large board visible to the outside, and every morning he marks the squares of those who have received mail. At La Halle everyone has his own key, but the mailboxes are not completely intact—more than one lock has been broken—and they are so small that the mail sometimes sticks out of the slot and can be pulled through it. Above the boxes in H stairwell, someone has posted a hand-written notice: "Making pee-pee in the stairwell is forbidden."

Depending on the size of the apartments, each landing has two or three plain doors, each with a peephole and a winding bell.

Each stairwell has a particular visage, language, and odor, as well as reputation. Although they are all alike—the walls covered with fine gravel halfway up and painted beige above—there are attractive and grim ones, noisy and silent, eloquent and mute, happy and sad, cold and hot, clothed and naked, inhabited and deserted. There are those that have not stirred since the beginning, where the doors have remained light green and you never meet anyone; those that flaunt in graffiti their clandestine love affairs, their occupants' pride, and their children's insults; those with carefully kept door mats; those whose doors bear no names; those that throb with bursts of Arab music, reveal the envenomed quarrels, and leak out the laughter of girls being teased; those that smell of burnt olive oil or the persistent odor of urine, or like the back of a Magrab alley; those bearing witness to the life within, whose doors have been violently repainted in violet; those where all the mud from every foot, orange peels, crusts of bread, greasy papers, and doll legs remain all week; and those that finally disclose the white color of the concrete when they are washed. And then we must not forget those with growling dogs, gigantic or pug-size; those where stray cats run out; and those with a glacial draft coming steadily from air vents now permanently broken. Stagnating in almost all of them is a bitter, indefinable, constant musty smell: the odor of the project.

The apartments are decent and relatively comfortable. Each door opens on the beginning of a hallway. One yard in, there is an opening on one side but no door, so you enter straight into the square living room. This room is broken up by two windows and two doors going to the bedrooms, making it difficult to furnish. The hall continues, leading to one, two, or three small bedrooms, depending on the apartment. The square kitchen is too small to eat in but large enough to work in. The gas water heater is not provided by the public authorities but the connections are arranged so that it has only to be put in place to furnish hot water in the kitchen and bathroom, which is equipped with a sink and a slipper-bath* with faucet and shower head. There is a built-in fuel storage tank in the entrance to the water closet. The problem of floor covering has been resolved by using small red tiles that are easily cleaned with a wet rag. The heater is set into the wall of the hall; it is sufficient to heat the whole apartment by means of heating vents placed near the ceiling. The fuel supply comes from a central tank and is regulated electrically so there is no effort involved for the housewife.

When you have gone through the apartment, taken a good look at the sufficiently large and light rooms, and admired the oil heating system, you are ready to exclaim that this type

---

*This type of bathtub is not generally found in the U.S. It is a short tub, with one end raised, so the bather is in a sitting rather than prone position.—R.S.

of moderate-rent housing is almost perfect. You then realize that the whole building vibrates from the noise of other people and that there is no garbage disposal or clothes dryer in the kitchen. The lack of garbage disposals is a lesser evil because there are generally enough children available to empty the garbage. But no clothes dryer, when the washing machine in a family of eight is running twice a week! The tenants are forbidden to hang laundry from the windows so as not to spoil the project's appearance. Although this rule is often broken, the only remaining solution is to hang lines in the already overtaxed bathroom or to clutter up the hall with chairs holding wet laundry in front of the stove. The building regulations stipulate that a garbage disposal and clothes dryer are not compulsory.

Obviously, the project is easy to praise in comparison with dwellings these people have previously known. Besides, it is not they who complain. They have always been used to seeing laundry everlastingly hung above their heads or drying before the fire, except perhaps for those who had the advantage of a corner of a courtyard or garden in the suburbs. Yet would it not have been better to offer them completely comfortable housing that posed no further material problems?

The apartments are functional only: there is no closet, no storage space, no nook available to the children or the handyman husband. Five apartments are occupied by social services and a doctor, so social-service facilities and some medical supervision have been provided, although the PMI[1] applies only to children under six and the doctor is free to choose his clientele. But there was no thought given to collective facilities. The club, built on private initiative, has just two rooms to hold the hordes of children of all ages. There is neither day nursery nor lounge, nor any kind of common room for meeting, instruction, or relaxation.

Two parallel gray blocks facing an inner space, a closed-off village with no public places, café, church, houses, or streets, the project turns its back to the outside world. Yet its horizon is vast and open. At its feet spread immense vacant lots, still partly planted in 1964; this land has been set aside for construction. The children have made it their favorite play-ground; they haul out old mattresses and build strange scaffolds there. Despite this, the view from the windows is not at all unpleasant. On the other side of the access road, behind a thick and indestructible but not impassable grill, there is the broad, quiet green interval of a hospital's pavilions and gardens. In the background, the apartment complex twinkles at night with all its lights, which caused one woman to say, "At night you'd think you were in a fashionable neighborhood."

The air is brisk and wholesome, with no smoke. It gets quite cold since the wind is quickly changed into a draft in the courtyard, but in general it is healthy.

It takes just an hour to reach the city by bus during the day, but you must allow an hour and three-quarters during the rush hours. The city is not so far off as it is difficult to reach, and the town too is far away when you have to go on foot to the post office, town hall, or church, or to buy something besides food. A quarter of an hour seems long and boring when you have to walk along a road with no stores or anything of interest.

The apartment complex is not any closer, but the street with the bus line to it can be reached by a shortcut. It is well equipped, with two or three stores of every kind, including deluxe shops for leather goods and jewelry, beauty salons, etc. In addition, two richly stocked supermarkets share a large clientele. But the complex probably looks too futuristic to those who are already nostalgic for "real streets" and who seek the familiar and reassuring appearance of their old neighborhood for shopping.

La Halle residents, therefore, prefer to go to the town, but it offers little. That is why the apartment complex is acquiring some autonomy by setting up its own facilities. Government offices and public utilities have not yet moved in, so for every procedure concerning taxes or the electric and gas companies, residents must go to the capital of the next canton. This canton is adjacent to the town but is not linked to it by any common transportation line. To walk there takes an hour.

What is available in the center of the town? Just one not very lively business street, lined with low, old-fashioned houses, where everything is dead between noon and 2:00. It has one variety store and three cafés (two of these are quite old-fashioned and do not even serve sandwiches) around a tiny turn-of-the-century town hall, a church at the corner, a new post office, and an old movie theater. A few outdoor restaurants on the river bank come to life on Saturday, but there is no swimming in winter. There is nothing much in the town beyond the strictly mundane.

Employment opportunities are particularly scarce. There are a few modest businesses and a few small workshops, such as electrical assembly, yogurt-making, and pharmaceutical packaging, which employ mostly women. On the other hand, a large hospital offers a complete gamut of medical care. Old-fashioned and poor as it is, the town makes it possible for the men and women of the project to do their shopping freely, to loiter in front of some shop window full of trifles, or to have a drink or a cigarette.

We must not forget the open market.* It is highly prized by all because, in addition to bringing back the pleasures of noise, color, quantity, and choice and the chance to steep themselves in an old and well-loved atmosphere, it allows them to be individuals among so many others like themselves, unidentified in a crowd. When project residents must give a name and address for a large or major purchase in the permanent shops on the business street, they are spotted as belonging to La Halle. This problem does not arise in the project, as long as they stay among their own and do not cross the border. The border is simply the road.

The barracks we mentioned stand on the same side of the road as the project. Hardly anyone but the project residents goes there. They buy all their food there, including bread. The products are good and sensibly priced, and fruits and vegetables are sold to large families in cases of five or six

---

*Temporary stalls, usually set up once a week in each neighborhood.—R.S.

kilograms at wholesale prices. But the improvised arrangements, the rude shelves, the wine cask, the rough floor, the bare walls, the inadequate lighting, the absence of any advertising and the two simplified counters that provide a narrow exit show the intention to create a market meant exclusively for a disfavored clientele.[2]

Sometimes the project housewives go across the street to the butcher or grocer in the white building, and of course they go to the druggist to avoid "going up to town." Surrounded by barriers and symbolically called "the domain," this building allows only one of each kind of shop. When they have the chance, the owners take advantage of the lack of competition to deliver, along with the merchandise, a few acerbic reflections on the composition and mentality of that undesirable neighboring population. The housewives come home furious, swearing they will not go there any more. They often make their husbands do the shopping at work or, if they have free time, they go to the city to do it themselves. For the rest, they make do with the barracks.

In short, then, the project looks like a relatively isolated hamlet, far from the town and the apartment complex, and its outward life bears no resemblance to the deserted atmosphere of bedroom communities.

Administered by the commune and an office of the prefecture that handles this locality, the project does not constitute an administrative unit in itself. It is how La Halle appears physically and, on first approach, in its relations with the outside world, that make it a social group on this first, ecological level and enable us to study it as such.

NOTES

[1]Mother and child care clinic.
[2]The market was improved at the end of 1966.

2

The Historic and Administrative Context

Administrative Background

As we shall try to show, the administrative background of La Halle is connected to general history and to the particular history of its residents.

The transitional housing projects, also called buildings of social transition or relocation centers, are designed for a small number of people who presently live in rented rooms and unsanitary or condemned dwellings and who can expect to be assigned housing if they meet certain conditions. The first of these conditions is to be listed in the departmental* housing service's central card file for the ill-housed, where applications are processed and priorities are assigned by machine.

As the name "transitional project" indicates, this relocation is temporary. In the minds of its originators, it was a matter

---

*A department is roughly equivalent to an American state.—R.S.

of rehabituating families to living decently and then, if the trial was judged conclusive, to propose them to the HLM by putting their names on a so-called housing promotion list. They are supposed to have a chance to be permanently relocated at the end of three years, but in reality, since the HLM does not construct enough new buildings or sets the rents too high, they stay where they are or leave by their own means.

There are eighteen transitional projects in the city's suburbs, but these buildings are not qualitatively equal. They range from emergency barracks built in 1954 that are still in use, to the "almost HLM" type like La Halle, built more recently according to higher standards. However, the standards are still low enough that this housing can have the advantage of lower rents. For instance, the land must not cost more than 50F per square meter, which is why these buildings are always on the distant periphery of the city. The La Halle project was built on land sold at cost by Public Assistance, which had acquired immense land reserves during the nineteenth century. A three-room apartment cost 35,000F. These relocation centers can be placed under departmental authority but even if they are municipal, like La Halle, they are built under state supervision using sums allocated for this purpose by the general council.*

Since building codes are defined by law, the minimum standards published by the official journal (i.e., the minimum-regulations manual) are chosen. Materials are selected in terms of greatest durability at the lowest price. It is difficult to resolve the problems of interior fittings such as doors, flooring, and heating. To be solid, doors must be expensive. La Halle's doors are laminated, and they undergo frequent repairs.

Construction is relatively rapid, taking from eighteen months to two years. The 180 apartments in La Halle were begun in December 1959 and were open for occupancy in February 1962, after completion of the access roads to the interior and

---

*An elective body with representatives from each canton, which apportions the budget of the department.—R.S.

the parking space. The municipality was left with the responsibility for the exterior road, which was not paved until August 1964. The project is composed as follows:

Number of Rooms	Number of Units
2	10
3	60
4	56
5	36
6	18

The occupants of La Halle, like those of other transitional projects, are not officially tenants. They have just an occupancy permit and pay an occupant's fee instead of rent. The absence of any lease or contract gives the government the right to evict the occupant, who has no protection. There is no reciprocity of rights.

The Treasurer* collects the fees which management calculates on the following basis. The cost of the loans is spread out over forty-five years and the annual loan amortization is based on an interest rate of 6.88 percent, to which 1 percent is added for management expenses. This payment, divided by the corrected total area, gives the basic cost per square meter. Then maintenance costs are calculated and added.

The problem of dividing the cost of water and heating among residents is hard to resolve. Billing at the end of the heating season is impossible, because the fuel is centrally stored and the meters do not provide an accurate reading. In fact, until 1966 the meters recorded the consumption of electricity by the pump but not fuel consumption. Other meters have been installed since then, but the residents put them out of order. Water billing is done quarterly. The cost in the first two years was so high that the central meter had to be replaced by individual meters; the cost then decreased by one-third.

Each week the manager inspects the project to see that it

---

*This is equivalent to the Secretary of the Treasury in the United States.—R.S.

is clean and in good order, and to call needed repairs to the attention of a local business. He is reluctant to report minor repairs, hoping that the residents themselves will make them. His testimony counts in proposed promotions or evictions. Evictions are ordered by the court, principally for nonpayment of rent but also for "misbehavior." The evicted families are degraded and relocated less comfortably in old barracks projects. Experience shows that these families have no further chance to rise.

History of the Residents

The project does not really have a history or a past yet because it has only been in existence since 1962. Within two months' time, 176 families moved in. The majority of these families are still there today, at the end of 1966.

Their origins are different but they have in common a similar recent past that is relatively easy to reconstruct. Whether they came from North Africa, Sicily, or Brittany, the men fled from low-wage areas to seek work in the city. Skilled or unskilled, it is not their professional qualifications that differentiate them from those born in the city region. Europeans and Jews who left North Africa when it became independent are part of this same social class of wage earners and workmen. We are therefore dealing with a population that is ethnically heterogeneous but relatively homogeneous economically.

Those who fled North Africa at the time of independence were already married before they came to France. The other couples met by chance in the streets, "at the bar downstairs of Mom's," or "standing in line at Social Security." Having all come from large or broken families, they found themselves alone at a young age and were in a hurry to find a mate to escape the family atmosphere or loneliness. The following really sums up how many households in La Halle came together: "I didn't know where to go. He asked me if I was alone. He said, 'Me, too,' so we got together."

All of them had previously known profound poverty, physical or emotional or both. They had been orphans or had been detested, beaten, abandoned, or turned over to unscrupulous

adults in houses of correction.[1] They had endured overcrowding, slums, poverty, alcoholism, illness, and being sent to work
too soon. None of them talks voluntarily about his parents
or his childhood. It would be tiresome to multiply the evidence. However, let us cite three cases taken at random.

—Mrs. P., thirty-four, left school at ten to take care of her
alcoholic mother whom she used to pick up from the floor,
dead drunk. Her older siblings having disappeared, she was
left alone at sixteen and married at seventeen.

—Mr. F., thirty-seven, an early orphan, was not brought up
by anyone. At sixteen, tired of begging his keep, he came
to the city by himself from his native Kabylia.* He then became
familiar with the struggle for work, temporary community shel-
ters, park benches, and hunger.

—Mr. J., forty, from Normandy, was placed in a foster home
because his mother put alcohol in his bottle, but the farmer
who was responsible for raising him sent him to the fields
instead of to school. At seventeen, he was returned to his
parents, for whom he went to work until called up for military
service.

Three other case histories dictated by their subjects will
be found in the appendix. Together with the preceding examples they show that the people of La Halle, although of different
ethnic origins, have hard or painful childhoods in common.

Their recent past is even more alike. After their marriage
or arrival in France, the couples looked for housing, but with
neither money nor help they could find only furnished rooms
or garrets. Let us remember that furnished rooms are expensive[2] and that rearranging the furniture or bringing in one's
own is prohibited. Then the chilren were born, completing
the overcrowding in the tiny room, or else the apartment hotel
did not allow babies and the parents were evicted and obliged
to wander from one lodging to another, often separated, until
they found a place to live. This might have been in a building
slated for demolition, and in that case they became squatters.
Some succeeded in finding a kitchenette apartment and, happy
to be independent, they stayed there with their children.

*The Kabyles are a Berber tribe of North Africa.—R.S.

Others rented a two-room apartment, where seven children were packed in horizontally or vertically. Still others took shelter with relatives or friends or even employers.

All of them have lived in uncomfortable conditions for several years. One woman tells how she thought she would "go crazy because for twelve years I had to move the youngest child's cradle from in front of the buffet every time I needed a fork." At another house, people lived in a six-square-yard maid's room without running water. All of them had to climb over the nearer beds to reach the farther ones, or sleep four children to a bed.

The population of the project is divided into two almost equal groups, one from the suburbs (46.4 percent) and the other from the city (53.6 percent). In the suburbs where it is easier to find small apartments, the first group occupied apartments with one or two rooms plus kitchen in tumbledown eighteenth-century buildings. Of the second group, 24 percent had rooms in residential neighborhoods, while 76 percent lived in unhealthy tenements in decrepit or overpopulated neighborhoods. The families sheltered by others also came from poor neighboorhoods. The Jews and Arabs took refuge in certain streets or blocks of houses where many of their coreligionists live. The squatters or unauthorized occupants who lived in abandoned barracks or other vacated buildings represented about 6 percent of the total population. The government's selection criteria, which we shall look into further on, explain the small number of families (just six) from the shantytowns.

All these families came to La Halle at the same time and the majority settled down in a normal, habitable space for the first time in their lives.

NOTES

[1]Let us recall that the reform dates only from 1945. [This reform established reformatories for children, in place of prisons, where they are taught a trade; the child is kept there until age twenty-one or, if released earlier, he is on parole until that age.—R.S.]

[2]150F–300F in 1964.

3

The Demographic Context

It is difficult to take a population census of La Halle and examine its characteristics in detail because the information collected in government files is incomplete. Mostly dating from 1962, the year when people first moved in, this information has not been corrected if the family's situation has changed. Births and deaths are noted irregularly, and the records are not kept up to date. A count was taken in June 1964, but it cannot give an exact picture of the present population because two years' difference has changed the profile of age categories far too much. Moreover, the numbers were given in totals with no distribution by sex.

Changes in the Population

In 1964 the project numbered 1,034 residents: 327 adults and 707 children. Using the record book that the caretaker is supposed to keep up to date, we counted only 670 children in

June 1965. We counted again in June 1966 but, as in the preceding year, it was impossible to obtain exact information on the
number and age of the recently born, who were sometimes
mentioned simply as babies. This was the demographic situation in June 1966:

	Male	*Female*	*Total*
Adults over 18	160	172	332
Children 0–18	325	346	671
Total population	485	518	1,003

These figures do not take into account the families secretly
lodged by others; we can estimate that there are about twenty
of these.

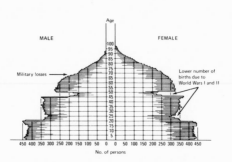

Table 1
Distribution of French Population,
January 1, 1967

SOURCE: L'Institut National de la Statistique et des Etudes Economiques

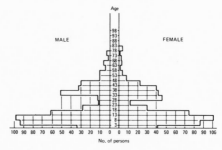

Table 2
Composition of the Population of La Halle,
1966

NOTE: The count is approximate for those under age three.

The Age Pyramid

We can make some useful distinctions by examining the population pyramid and its variations. We immediately notice that the pyramid reveals the artificial composition of La Halle's population. The striking feature is the sharp disproportion between people ages twenty-three to twenty-eight and those under twenty or over thirty. In other words, there is almost no one between the older generation and its offspring. The eleven men and twelve women of the twenty-three to twenty-eight age bracket principally represent the oldest children of the oldest families, who stayed with their parents even after marrying. There are few people over thirty coming in because several years' wait is often necessary after being listed in the central card file.

The pyramid is a good illustration of the department's relocation formula. The fact that the largest group of adults is between thirty and forty-five years old is an effect of that formula, and it in turn affects the number of births. Most of the children are between eight and thirteen years old.

The number born in these last three years has decreased by half in comparison with the preceding bracket, although some are the product of the second generation. This would tend to prove that a large part of the population had already reached the end of its child-bearing years at the time of relocation and that it is consequently stagnating. Since the young adults leave to live elsewhere, the population will steadily shrink if the project is allowed to age without artificially renewing the number of young households.

Among the children as among the adults, the feminine sex predominates. In the twenty-eight to thirty-three age bracket, there are many more women than men (forty-six women to twelve men). This is the optimum age of the project women's sexual lives but either their mate is older, as the larger number of men in the bracket just above indicates, or else they are single or divorced and have no legal spouse (see chapter 6). In that case, their temporary companion is not carried on any register.

The number of households of old people is among the most limited. People around age fifty were rarely relocated. So few old people live in the project that their distribution by sex has no significance.

Changes in Population

Births have exceeded deaths by more than ten to one over the four-year period. The population is young and relatively healthy. In fact, there have been just ten deaths since the beginning of the project: two aged grandmothers and a forty-year-old woman, four men between fifty-five and sixty, a thirty-year-old man who died accidentally, a thirty-five-year-old man who died of illness, and one adolescent. No children have died and mortality at birth is nil.

Population movement caused by successive relocations is small. There have been thirty-five departures and arrivals, but it should be noted that fifteen apartments have each undergone three successive occupancies. Of the thirty-five departures, nine evictions have actually been carried out and ten are presently in progress. We do not know how many departures are due to final relocation in HLM; all who can do so leave by their own means.

About 140 families have been living in La Halle since the beginning. Available apartments often stand empty for several months. When a resident is serving a prison term, his apartment cannot be assigned before he is freed even if it is vacant (we know of two examples of this kind). On the average, the number of households varies between 170 and 175. (For the composition and number of households, see chapter 6.)

In 1962, the households were divided up as follows:

Number of children per household	0	1	2	3	4	5	6	7	8	9	10	11
Number of households	3	17	31	23	30	21	17	10	10	4	2	2

Obviously, this table no longer corresponds to reality in 1966. The number of households with one, two, or three children has certainly changed, and some large families have grown smaller due to the departure of the older children. Since the government prohibits exchanging apartments within the project, younger households with children born after they moved in are threatened by overcrowding, while some families are beginning to find their apartments too large. The present distribution of families no longer corresponds to the initial standards in some cases because there has not been enough population movement.

Ethnic Composition

The population is divided into three main groups: those from North Africa, metropolitans [those from France], and foreigners.

Table 3

Ethnic Composition (by couples)

Total Population

North African	33
Mixed French-Arab	17
Metropolitan	83
Foreign	10
Mixed French-foreign	13
Total	156[1]

North Africans and Mixed French-Arab Couples

JEWS	
Tunisian	7
Algerian	7
Moroccan	1
Total	15
ARABS	
Algerian (Arab)	11
Algerian (Kabyle)	1
Tunisian	2
Total	14

Table 3 *(continued)*

EUROPEANS
  Italian   2
  Spanish   2
  Total   4

MIXED
  Franco-Algerian   9
  Franco-Kabyle   5
  Franco-Tunisian   3
  Total   17

[1]This total does not take into account fourteen single women, divorced or widowed, whose possible companion is not included.

More than half the metropolitan French come from around the city while the others come from all over the country. Their attitudes and behavior hardly seem to be influenced by what province or what part of the country they came from, as we shall see in parts II and III.

The foreigners are few in number, of diverse origins, and largely assimilated to the metropolitans.

Family composition and number of children are the same in the project as in the rest of France. (Studies on the family in France give an average of three children per household.) From the standpoint of ethnic distribution, however, we find that 12 percent are Moslems, clearly a higher percentage than the figures reported by the National Institute for Demographic Studies (1.3 percent according to the 1962 general population census of the Paris area), and 54 percent of the Moslem households are of mixed ethnic background. This very high proportion of both Moslem and mixed households is probably one of the factors that make La Halle a special group.

4

The Economic Context

The economic criteria that govern the choice of residents and their range of occupations, changes in jobs over time and space, and sources of income will give us the main constant features of the economic context in La Halle.

Economic Criteria for Residents

The housing office estimates that 40,000 people live in fringe areas of the region around the city, in shantytowns and various slums. Not all of them are listed in the central card file because many are unaware of its existence, but the allocation board has many more applicants than available accommodations and can therefore choose its tenants. It studies 1,000 files to select 100, sorting them out according to urgency and seniority of registration and serving the occupants of condemned buildings first as far as possible. But the government takes account of income above all. In order to be assigned housing, a family must prove it has an income that is too modest for an HLM rent but regular enough that the management service will be assured of receiving the fee. That is why many in the project are government employees. Though their wages may be very modest, they are also secure and stable, whereas it is never certain that the laborer will have steady employment even if his pay is higher. The periodic regularity of allowances and pensions also gives a guarantee to the government, which insists on the specification that this population not represent the lowest economic stratum of society. Despite these precautions in choosing the residents, twenty-three families (of whom nineteen are French) are delinquent in their rent at present.

Here is a sample fee for a six-room apartment:

Rent	115.18F
Maintenance	22.12
Heat	75.00
Water	5.00
Total	217.30F

The tenants have the advantage of the housing allowance. The rent for a five-room apartment in the neighboring apartment complex goes up to 500F.

Range of Occupations

Generally, just the men work. Since jobs are scarce in the commune, most of the women have stopped working entirely since moving in; there are only about 25 of them working at any given time. The women go to work in response to certain special conditions: temporary or lasting break-up of the household, temporary stop in the man's work (including those stops caused by misunderstandings with his employer), insufficient income, or temporary aggravation of financial difficulties. The women work too irregularly for detailed analysis, but they are generally unskilled. It should be noted that of the three women office workers, two are foreigners (Dutch and Italian).

Table 4

Men's Jobs

Government employees	32
Skilled (mechanics, electricians, plumbers, metalworkers)	19
Semiskilled (automotive workers)	15
Unskilled	15
Masons	11
Truck drivers	11
Packers and stock clerks	9
Office workers	5
Pensioned for disability	14

NOTE: In addition, there are 3 painters, 3 carpenters, 2 waiters, 4 salesmen, 2 butchers, 1 shoemaker, 1 fishmonger, 1 crane operator, 1 geologist's assistant, 1 translator, 1 furniture mover, 1 poultryman, 1 demolition worker, and 1 assistant IBM operator.

We must analyze the jobs of the thirty-two government employees in finer detail.

Table 5

Government Employees' Jobs

Medical attendants or stretcher-bearers	9
Park maintenance (prefectural)	5
Garbage collectors (municipal)	9
Road repairmen (municipal)	3
Janitors	4
Bus conductor	1
Watchman (international organization)	1

Table 6
Occupations by Ethnic Group[1]

	Metropolitans	Arabs	Jews	Foreigners	Total
Government employees					
Medical attendants	9				9
Garbage collectors	4	5			9
Miscellaneous	11	1	2		14
Unskilled	13	2			15
Semiskilled	5	9		1	15
Skilled	12	3	4		19
Masons	5	2		4	11
Packers and					
stock clerks	7	2			9
Truck drivers	8	2		1	11
Office workers	2		3[2]		5
Pensioned for					
disability	8	3	1	2	14
Total	84	29	10	8	131

[1]Not included in this table are the various occupations listed in the note to Table 4, which are divided among the Jews, metropolitans, and foreigners.

[2]The three Jewish office workers are bank clerks.

Table 7

Women's Jobs

Nurses' aides	9
Domestics	4
Office workers	3
Waitresses, school lunchroom	2
Stock clerks	2
Cable welder	1
Pensioned for disability	4

Table 4 gives a general idea of jobs at La Halle. We immediately notice the large number of government employees (about 20 percent) and laborers. Table 5 shows the different kinds of government wage earners. But Table 6 gives much more information. The mass of metropolitans fall in the unskilled columns (government employees, laborers, stock clerks and truck drivers), while the Jews and foreigners are practically excluded from them. The latter follow trades, some of which require more skill. Among the Jews we find a foreman and a typographer, and three of them are intelligent enough to be bank clerks.

The Arabs have tried to acquire some vocational skill. Five are skilled workmen: a lathe operator, a roofer, a plumber, and two masons. The others fall principally among the semi-skilled (automotive workers). For the Arabs, being a garbage collector represents admission to official ranks and gives them the opportunity to make use of things they find, whereas for the metropolitans it represents an inferior status.

The metropolitans make up the majority of unskilled workers, as is shown in the following table in percentages.

	Unskilled	Disabled
Metropolitans	62.0%	8.0%
Arabs	46.0	10.3
Jews	13.0	6.6
Foreigners	8.0	14.0

Changes in Jobs over Time and Space

The location and duration of work varies in all groups but it is not possible to estimate its fluctuations quantitatively. Any figure would be applicable for just that moment in time.

Changes in Space

These changes principally affect the laborers and stock clerks. The mobile laborers change jobs for various reasons when

they realize that their job is uninteresting, or if the distance
tires them, or if they have a chance to be hired elsewhere
at higher wages. In addition, they are the first to bear the
brunt of economic fluctuations, for they are dismissed when
production declines. One sees a veritable rotation of unskilled
manpower. Stock clerks would tend to be more stable, but
proneness to fatigue crops up rather quickly in heavy stock
work.

The truck drivers drive delivery vans rather than heavy
trucks. They too do not hesitate to change employers or jobs
whenever they can expect a raise in wages somewhere else.
For instance, one former driver became a gas station attendant.

Changes over Time

The men generally do not stay unemployed for long between
jobs, especially if their departure was premeditated. They go
out looking systematically for two or three days unless they
are waiting for a "pal's promise" to be carried out, although
they may find a small, temporary job if there is too long a
delay. There is no rule at La Halle concerning work stoppages,
which remain unregulated. It can be estimated, however, that
unemployment is at most partial but not regular.

Nonemployment, like the actual time of work, varies from
a few days, or even a few hours, to (more rarely) a year. For
example, the same man may put in sixty hours a week for
six months, then suddenly change jobs and take a day off on
Saturday. He may also have worked for the same company
for fifteen years, but if he is dismissed he may remain unemployed for a year. Those who are paid by the hour put in
the maximum amount of overtime and their workday is often
much more than eight hours.

Other causes of work stoppages over time are work-
connected accidents, illness, and, for the masons, winter and
inclement weather. Long and final work stoppages are caused
by "going on disability." Contrary to common opinion, the
doctor asserts that he has to insist on the men taking a rest
and that the percentage who apply for medical benefits without

real reason is infinitesimal. The same individuals are always involved and they come from all groups. The Arabs sometimes complain of strange symptoms that are impossible either to diagnose or call fake.

Work-connected accidents are frequent but most often are confined to injuries to the hands and do not involve long work stoppages.

Disability pensions are proportional to the degree of disability, and even for the highest category they are equivalent to just a low wage (500F a month). Even if their disability category prohibits it, under penalty of the pension's being taken away, the disabled work from time to time depending on the state of their health. But they have great difficulty finding work and give it up as soon as they get tired. Here are examples of three known cases.

—A man afflicted with hip trouble has been washing cars for two months, after three years of not working.

—An epileptic has been cleaning offices at night since he was dismissed from his position as a factory stock clerk. He is presently looking for "another little job" to help with household expenses.

—A former mechanic, who is allergic to oil and seriously ill, made several attempts to work before agreeing to remain idle.

So the figure of fourteen disabled men in Table 4 does not necessarily correspond to the number of men permanently out of work.

Being unskilled is the cause and effect of fluctuations in time and space among the workers of La Halle. These fluctuations are impossible to quantify; they usually range from no work to sixty hours' work per week.

Sources of Income and Wealth

Depending on the type of job, the pay period varies from hourly wages received each week to monthly wages. The wage total is irregular and partly depends on the amount of overtime.

All the workers are on wages, which fluctuate between 500F

and 1,500F a month. The majority earn between 500F and 1,000F. Family and housing allowances must be added to wages, as well as possible temporary charitable donations and benefits or pensions coupled with wages (see chapter 7 on the budget).

At La Halle, the distribution of goods is not necessarily proportional to total income. It also depends on the degree of pressure felt by the individual, and fluctuations in income affect food more than goods. Fifty cars in the parking area is not significant if you take account of the age of the secondhand cars and their low purchase price (100F–2,000F). About twenty-five of the cars are new, but we must not forget the discount of about 1,000F that automobile manufacturers give their employees, enabling them to change cars every year. One can count nearly as many refrigerators and television sets as families. Outward signs of wealth will be set forth in detail in the course of various chapters (especially chapter 7) but we can say here that the most comfortable and the poorest families differ from each other less in quantity of goods than in size of financial deficit.

In this chapter we have called attention to two characteristics: the modesty of income and the fact that all these occupations are in the unskilled or less-skilled category. It is clear that these special economic conditions contribute a certain aspect to a social group like La Halle, but that is not enough to explain its cultural life.

5

The Ethnocultural Context

We must again define the groups appearing in chapter 3, this
time not because of their origin but because they exist as cultural groups within the project.

Foreigners

The foreigners do not really form a group. Few in number,
very diverse, and often married to a French spouse, they bend
all their efforts toward rapid assimilation. Their standard of
living is relatively better than that of the others, and their
respectability is uncontested. They live rather withdrawn to
themselves and take little interest in life in the project. Others
do not know them well. We might have expected the Italians
to form a subgroup, but they have not because differences
in customs and dialect separate the Milanese from the Cala-
brians and Sardinians. The men have struck up friendships

with compatriots outside the project, but the women complain of loneliness.

The foreigners are thus an amorphous and unfamiliar group, and they do not belong to or oppose any other group. They form personal relationships with other project residents for whom they have some affinity and not preferentially according to nationality. We shall therefore not devote any special study to them.

Europeans from North Africa ("Pied-Noirs")

Pied-Noirs make up only four families who do not know each other, but it is interesting to briefly consider their particular case. They are not disturbed by the project's cosmopolitan character, to which they are accustomed, but it pains them to find themselves on an equal footing with the Arabs and Jews. They fear being mixed up with those groups because they "feel somewhat African," so they keep apart. This does not prevent them from helping a "clean, civilized" Arab, due to old habits of coexistence.

They are no closer to the metropolitans because a class phenomenon comes into play. Artisans and skilled workmen in North Africa, they know themselves to be inferior to civil servants and colonists. But they have discovered classes in the project that they consider inferior to themselves, for moral and not economic reasons.

The Pied-Noir cells form few and scrupulously chosen individual relationships, take an identical attitude toward Arabs and Jews, and live withdrawn to themselves, shielded by the family structure they have preserved. On the other hand, they belong to the widespread group of "repatriates" who support their efforts to adapt to the larger society. We shall only cite the Pied-Noirs individually in the following chapters.

The Metropolitans

The metropolitans form the largest and most disparate group, composed for the most part of Frenchmen born around the city or in other provinces, but who have hardly any more ties to their original milieu. A collection of rootless individuals, it is a group without structure, traditions, or cohesion, and is defined instead by negative comparison with the project's other social groups.

As we have seen in the preceding chapter, it is in this group that the poorest people are most numerous. Those who slip down to the lowest level after a "slow process of pauperization"[1] are metropolitans.[2] All the residents of La Halle previously lived in overcrowded conditions, but the case of the metropolitans is more dramatic because, unlike the North Africans, they have no original community to refer back to. They are individuals of no importance submerged in the mass of society, to which they belong with some feeling of insecurity and inferiority because it often judges them with less understanding than it offers to foreigners. They greatly resent the segregation practiced on the project. They are cut off from the world, having no "relationship" to it in the common sense of the term, and they suffer from loneliness.

They may seem different from each other at first sight but these differences hardly stand up under closer observation. A brief incursion into two families will show that this is easy to prove.

Mrs. G.'s apartment is kept very clean with an obvious decorative intention carried out in the wallpaper with its studied detail, the curtains, and the shiny waxed floors. The children are well dressed, and Mrs. G., an elegant woman, is careful not to let her hairdo get mussed. She is married to a skilled worker who earns about 1,500F a month.

Mrs. W. resembles Toulouse-Lautrec's "La Goulue." She puts up her hair any old way and conceals the fact that she is getting fat under a nondescript, pleated, black shirtwaist dress that she wears at night as well as during the day under a coat. Her bed is covered with a gray bedspread full of dog hairs. Three dogs and two cats clutter up the apartment entrance. The heating system is out of order, the water heater does not work any more, and the sink faucet can only be turned on with a monkey wrench. The wallpaper is held up by thumbtacks. The curtains are dirty, as are the table and the baby's underwear. Mrs. W. lives with a young laborer who earns just 600F a month, but she receives a pension. Two of her children have been placed with Public Assistance by the Minor's Brigade.*

The lives of the two women show many similarities. Mrs. W., a widow, and Mrs. G., a divorcee, each have a second spouse. Their financial situations are not so different because Mrs. W. has been receiving a pension since she became a widow, and Mr. G. changes jobs too often to have regular earnings. Neither of them finds enough security at home. They do not know how to knit or sew, and their education is far beneath their intelligence. Although Mrs. W.'s apartment is much more poorly furnished and her television set is not paid for, Mrs. G. has heavy debts that she tries in vain to pay off. While two children have had an authoritarian upbringing at Mrs. W.'s, Mrs. G. has often deposited her children with Public Assistance. Both women are incapable of arriving punctually at important appointments.

This brief description gives an idea of the metropolitan families, who all more or less conform to this model. And yet despite these similarities, or perhaps because of them, the group is not united. More than others, the metropolitans are unfaithful and play each other false. An infinitude of small subgroups are created, principally by the women, in an atmosphere of complicity expressed by using the familiar form of address or by the unbridled exchange of confidences. The men follow their wives in sharing these relationships but the friendships are short-lived. Individuals do not establish normal social relations within this group, which is formed only through rejection and not by choice. They have such need of communication and exchanges that a veritable levy of visits is estab-

---

*The Minor's Brigade is the enforcement agency that physically removes the child from the home on court orders. Public Assistance operates a variety of institutions for children (orphanages, homes for the retarded or disabled, etc.) and also makes foster-home placements. Where long-term care is involved, as seems likely in the present instance, the reference is probably to foster homes, whereas short-term care (e.g., while the mother is in the hospital having a baby) is probably given in an institution.—R.S.

lished between two couples until they get tired of it and quarrel. Feelings may become so exacerbated that the men and women come to blows; for example, we know of two instances when an abdominal knife wound required hospitalization.

In short, the metropolitans accept or reject each other according to affinities arising by chance from proximity. "Everyone looks out for himself here," trying to preserve family privacy, next door to others whom he helps to survive if necessary.

The Jews

The Jews came to France without really having chosen that fate, and they remain deracinated despite the time that has elapsed since their arrival ten to fifteen years ago. Although they are faithful to their religion, they cannot live according to it as they would like. They tried to join their coreligionists in the small pockets of Jews when they came to France, but they could only find one or two rooms there, and they have undergone a new uprooting with relocation. Whenever they can, they find bits of the community again and they draw new strength from the spiritual life dispensed by the synagogue. They purchase everything imposed by tradition in the Jewish sections of the city, the women taking turns going there because it is impossible to go every day. Replenishing their food supply thus poses a problem of conscience, and they get along on vegetables when they lack kosher provisions.

The Jews of La Halle maintain very close relations with all members of the family scattered around the city and take part in all the ceremonies concerning their relatives. They do not try to assimilate, as indicated by what one woman said on the telephone to a mover: "Not Saturday; we don't move on Saturday, it's a sin. We're Jews, you see!"

Despite certain outward appearances, they live as they did in Africa. The overweight women stretch out nonchalantly, lulling the youngest child to sleep against them. To see them, one would not suspect that they sleep half-dressed even at night, with three children around them in the same bed. We know three women who persist in going to the Turkish baths and spend the day there.

All the Jews live the same way despite slight differences in rituals, perceptible only to them, between the Algerians and Tunisians. Apéritifs are served at every table on Sabbath eve, and Passover puts everyone in an effervescent mood. For two weeks before the holiday, their apartments undergo a major housecleaning. The furniture being dragged and pushed around grates on the ceilings of the downstairs neighbors until late at night, and the apartments are repainted even if there is no money.

The Jewish group is certainly the most unified and solidary, but this does not prevent discord. Women insult each other in Arabic, fall out for several days and even bite each other, and then apologize. The children take part in the quarrels. The arguments between son-in-law and mother-in-law are prodigious, but that is part of Mediterranean theatricality. The members of a single family are really always leagued together, grouped around the mother; but the children, who have been raised outside the synagogue, more and more refuse to be different from their comrades in the project.

The Moslems

This is the most important group, not because of its numbers but because the others see it as the dominant group. The Moslems would not form a unified group in another context because, in addition to differing according to whether they come from the city or "upcountry" in Tunisia or Algeria, they are in different stages of deculturation. Both cause and effect, the choice of a French wife itself produces an acceleration in deculturation. The subgroup of mixed households represents half of the total group.

What unites the Moslems of La Halle above all is their solidarity in facing others. In the project they are considered like the others by the public authorities, and they mean to keep that prerogative, whereas in the street or at work they are exposed to latent racism. Their inner attitude is different from that of the other groups. The fact that they have obtained housing is considered an advancement, especially by the men, although we know two women who would prefer to live in a Moslem enclave. The yearning for a traditional way of life crystallizes around the M——shantytown: "It's like home. You can find everything for the holidays. You can go there when you want and stay over at someone's house. My wife would like to live there, but not me. My daughter is in the sixth grade; we're not savages any more."*

Some go to M——, some to S—— or V——, but all of them pay visits to relatives or friends in the Moslem pockets in other, sometimes distant places, either to find members of the same group or to establish relations on the political level. Several have support in diplomatic circles, and one of them is a collector of contributions for an Algerian mutual-aid society.

Acculturation, job status, and type of marriage are among the many factors that cause the Moslem group to break up into subgroups. The subgroup of men who work regularly achieves a standard of living that is among the best in the project; its way of life becomes more and more European, and it is taken as a model by the others. The subgroup of laborers who stop working from time to time and disabled men with modest incomes lives in a more traditional way.

The mixed group is less homogeneous. The women, who are all metropolitans except for one Spaniard from North Africa, lived through the most pitiful childhoods. Completely deracinated and defenseless, they accept the guardianship of their Moslem husbands, for whom the family still has meaning. They adhere to the Moslem group; they admire its solidarity, and it offers them a remnant of tradition. They are happy to visit the Moslem women often and to become like Arabs; "I feel like an Algerian," says one of them. In exchange, they are adopted by the whole Moslem group. The fate of the household thus depends principally on the man, his work, and what he

*Sixth grade is the first year of secondary school, which a child can enter only after passing the required examinations.—R.S.

has preserved of his moral code. It is among the mixed households that one finds the extremes: in one house the husband
cured his wife of alcoholism, while in another the husband
sent his wife out to become a prostitute. The mixed household
breaks down if the man does not assume the role of guardian
of the traditions, whereas in the traditional household it is
the wife who represents secure values.

The Kabyles insist that they be distinguished from the other
Algerians, and in fact there is a difference. Coming from moun-
tainous regions, they are very industrious and have kept their
moral code because they mastered the system of values of
their original ethnic group. Although married to Frenchwomen, they occupy leadership positions at La Halle and
advise the others in acquiring the European way of life. Other
Arab leaders take charge of settling internal disputes.

Cultural differences are abolished quite rapidly because of
these advisers. One family from the laborers' group was still
sitting on the floor and eating from a common plate two years
ago. Then they bought a table that went back to the kitchen
after the meal and some chairs that they lined up against the
wall, and they have just bought a dining set. But it would
be tiresome to multiply the examples of conforming to European furniture, and this would be a very elementary way of
quantifying deculturation. The analysis of one particularly suitable example will demonstrate that those who outwardly seem
the least traditional have an inner attitude and behavior that
would justify thorough study in another work of the phenomenon of transculturation.

A Kabyle garbage collector definitely rejected any outward
manifestation of tradition. He married a metropolitan whose
daughter he raised. He has six children whom he tries his
best to raise by seeking a balance between Kabyle ethics and
a European way of life. He threw out the oldest girl after
she had run away for a few days with a boy and though he
knows that the girl is on her own from now on, he cannot
go back on his decision. He feels guilty but will not admit
that he acted like all strict Moslem fathers, like the head of
the family who in Berber law is the arbiter in affairs of honor,

especially sexual matters. He tries to be a modern man and likes to acquire new gadgets so his sons will not consider him "backward." He bought a tape recorder in order, he says, to pick up Arab music and play it back, but he found a different use for the instrument. Since he leaves for work at 5:00 A.M., he can never be home when the children are getting up. So at night, when they have gone to sleep, he talks to them at length through the microphone, and the next day the mother has only to start the machine on the buffet. The father's voice then pours out his advice and reprimands all during breakfast: "Hurry up, don't spill your coffee, try to work hard," etc.

Paternal authority represents a power beyond question in Algeria. This man, who has no one to back him up because his wife is French, has had the astute idea of using an invention peculiar to technological civilization to ensure this authority, which is in danger of being mutilated, through the incantatory power of speech detached from the speaker. When he was ill, his wife brought back from the hospital a new Word from him every day.

His children do poorly in school, as he knows. He cannot find a way of raising them that combines the traditional and the European; he is looking for a moral and cultural norm but cannot find it. He says, "It's like talking to myself or to the wall. I don't get anywhere."

The effects of this transculturation are shown in the Moslems' feeling that they must provide themselves with openings into other groups in the project. The Moslem group, which exercises coercive force on its members, elsewhere evinces a vivacious sociability that serves its desire to learn and makes it the pivot of intergroup relations in the project.

But the aggressiveness of the metropolitans crystalizes around the Moslems. This is especially due to the fact that some Arabs irritate their neighbors by making the landing stink of broiling beef ears, by drying a butchered sheep's skin in the window, or by killing chickens in the bathroom. The metropolitans greatly dislike Arab music, which is always played at full volume and goes right through the walls. Still, the underlying racism disappears as soon as sympathy arises, and besides, the Moslems do not complain. There may or may not be some segregation in the various stairwells, depending on the chance arrangement of neighbors.

The Moslems and Jews no longer form what a psychiatrist would call a pathological couple, as they did on African soil. They can live side by side in the project without hostility. Facing a third group that does not know them and does not always understand them, they have drawn closer together and solid ties have even been created among some of them. A Jewish family in trouble may turn to an Arab family. Long outwardly adapted to the European way of life, the Jews provide models for the Arabs and serve as something of a transition between two worlds. The Moslems display much vital energy, and one sees a phenomenon of mutual contamination between them, the Jews, and the metropolitans.

From this chapter we can perhaps draw the conclusion that there is relative independence between common economic conditions (discussed in the preceding chapter), and attitudes and behavior resulting from different "ideologies" among the five ethnic groups. We should also note the beginning of interpersonal and interethnic relations that may thus already characterize the "subculture" of La Halle.

NOTES

[1]Menie Grégoire, "Le camp de Noisy-le-Grand," *Esprit* November 1964, pp. 858–868.

[2]One French family, consisting of a couple and five children, was evicted in 1965 and left the project to move into a shantytown.

Part II

THE INDIVIDUAL, THE FAMILY, AND THE PROJECT

We have seen that the transitional housing projects were created to shelter families and not individuals. The smallest apartments are offered to families with only one or two children; unlike the studio apartments in apartment complexes, they were never meant for single people. We have a heterogeneous agglomerate in La Halle composed of cells based on children. A couple is present in almost every case, whether or not it is durable or stable. Therefore, we shall first study family structures and sexual life through the various modalities of union and the different forms of the family, and then family life properly so-called, with its economic organization and methods of child-rearing.

6

Family Structures and Sexual Life

In La Halle, as in all underprivileged milieus, there is no bachelorhood as a solitary mode of life for men or women. All the women in the project have children, and they practically never live without a man even if they are listed as single. We note the man's relatively frequent abandonment of his wife and children, and the correlated tightening of family ties around the mother.

The compulsion to join together is found in all the groups. Among the Mediterraneans, it comes from the tendency derived from Jewish and Moslem societies for the family to be the model for all groupings. Among the metropolitans, it is due to the fact that neither the women nor the men can bear to be alone. Emotional ties are indispensable to them. Moreover, they are both incapable of providing for their material needs. It is impossible for the woman to assume responsibility for her own subsistence and, a fortiori, for her children, while a wife is absolutely necessary for the man to take his mother's place in looking after his food and clothing.

This common state of both mind and fact gives rise to different or successive modalities of union and to family forms varying from the single-family household to the more or less extended family.

Finally, sexuality plays an important role in relationships. Some households are distorted by outside liaisons but adultery principally takes the form of sexual games (in the Polynesian sense of the term) and the initiation of adolescents performed by certain women.

Modalities of Union

The family cell is based on the couple on one hand and children on the other. The couple may be joined in marriage or may abide by an oral promise, or even a tacit agreement, and live in concubinage or free union. We shall see what the differences are between these three modes.

Marriage

Legal marriage, whether civil or religious, is very often the mode used for the first union or, rather, for the creation of the first home. French couples are always married under the communal system, in which everything belonging to each spouse before marriage now belongs to both, but those in the project generally had no property at the time of their marriage.

Here we should distinguish among the three ethnocultural groups. The Arabs very often return to their own country to take a wife. Their fathers spare them any difficulty in choosing by having them marry a cousin, according to tradition. This preferential marriage is perpetuated in the Arab community in France, since each member of a family emigrated before or after some relatives. Some men who came to France when they were very young married a relative, with an uncle acting as go-between. The tradition of the dowry is still in effect.

The project's Arab households show great stability, even more so than in Algeria where new ways of life increase the number of separations and divorces.

The Jews came to France about ten years ago, so they had already lived part of their married lives in the French North African Jewish community. Traditions that are still strong protect the household and assure its stability, even though the husband and wife in several cases enjoy more freedom than Arab spouses. Not a single case of divorce is to be found among the Jews in the project.

The same does not hold true for the metropolitans even though only four cases of mutual separation have been recorded in four years. Among them, as we have seen, the absolute necessity of a shared life is not derived from the memory of a united family, and the ideal of the harmonious couple and family solidarity is rarely achieved. Emotional instability runs in both sexes but it is most often the men who go away, abandoning the children to their mother and not fulfilling their obligations. Separations are often de facto and not de jure because divorce means many difficult official complications.

Meanwhile, especially for the women, marriage represents an honor that should be attained at least once. It was put like this by one woman whose life had been an accumulation of dramatic experiences: "All the same, I haven't been a complete failure because I've been married."

The men and women generally married very young (sixteen to eighteen years old for the women), either because the girls were pregnant or the young couple thought its youthful love would last, or because the partners wanted to overcome solitude or escape the misery of their parents' home. One project resident explained: "When I found myself all alone in my roost, I was scared; I would have married a lamppost if it could talk to me." Later, the husband becomes alcoholic, changes jobs too often, or cannot provide the comfort anticipated at home; pregnancies come one after another; and this first union, fed by all the couple's illusions, comes apart, sometimes after many years.

The women are on their guard from then on. But since they are incapable of envisaging life without a man and find it impossible to provide for their economic needs, they have no alternative to seeking a new companion. They admit it themselves in an expression that shows both their disarray and their defensive reaction to life. Indicating her companion with her chin, one of them said, "I *took* him with me because I couldn't manage alone." Mrs. W., a widow at twenty-seven, said in speaking of Michel, age eighteen, "I *kept* him with me because he was nice." Their choice of words is highly informative.

Quickly, almost at first glance, the women size up the man who comes within range. If he is a feasible companion, they *take* him, and then they *keep* him or *send* him away. One often hears this type of remark: "I'm going to see what comes of it; if it's no good, the heck with it," or, "If I had to choose between the kids and him, he'd be right out the door." The woman authorizes the man to move in with her, and the man, who is alone, enters a home already formed. The woman takes possession of the man, as their way of speaking tells us. The stock phrase used by men or women for saying that Mrs. X. and Mr. Y. live together is that "Mrs. X. *has* someone."

There are innumerable remarriages and successive unions at La Halle after death, abandonment, and mutual separation, mostly among the metropolitans and mixed population. The women keep the home during and after separation while the man goes away alone; he very rarely brings the children of a first bed to a new wife unless he is an Arab. A matriarchal tendency is taking shape.

These chance unions—difficult, ill-matched, fragile, often involving emotionally unstable people—cannot all be submitted to formal, sanctified marriage. Indeed, if marriage almost represents a dignity in its legality, in other respects it threatens to subject the couple to coercive laws and to take away its freedom. Quite often, therefore, establishing a union in mutual freedom with a preferred partner will be favored over marriage. But concubinage must be distinguished from free union properly so called.

Concubinage

Concubinage is becoming established as a second-class marriage as in Roman law in the Byzantine Empire, when concubinage became a legal union inferior to proper marriage. It was distinguished from temporary union or *Stuprum* because it was durable, legal, and often honorable. Precisely these characteristics are found in concubinage today. Concubines receive a document signed by the mayor, showing that they live together as in marriage. The father recognizes his children, who bear his name, and they are beneficiaries of his Social Security; only the wife does not have her medical expenses covered.* Concubines consider themselves joined in the same way as married people and their union can be stable and lasting. One thinks of Goethe's proposal in "Elective Affinities" of trial marriage with renewable contract, or the formula of Antoine Loisel, the sixteenth-century jurist:

> To eat, drink and sleep together be
> Marriage, so it seems to me.

The project residents use the verb "to be married" followed by an adjective used as an adverb; they say, "to be married legitimate" or "to be married illegitimate."

There are sixteen concubinages at La Halle officially recognized by the government, with the records mentioning that these are concubines, as well as giving their names, but this is less than the actual number because others that have come into being are not yet sanctioned by usage. The oldest has lasted for twenty-eight years; the others vary from one to fifteen years. Concubinage occurs frequently in mixed households (Arab–French) and among those in which at least one of the two partners is not divorced from a previous union.

Free Union

Free union often precedes concubinage or marriage. It is not declared; some widows or unattached women in the project

*Social Security is national medical insurance and not old-age insurance as in the United States—R.S.

put the apartment in their name and hide the existence of a companion from the public authorities.[1] In this type of union, the man is a guest, and he has no legal existence. He cannot recognize his children and those born after he came are never legitimatized. This does not prevent the liaison from being permanent, but since the mother officially bears responsibility, one is again inclined to think in terms of a matriarchal tendency and even a matrilineal mode of filiation. In concubinage on the other hand, where legal union is perpetuated, family line proceeds from the man with the passing on of his patronymic.

Free union may be temporary and may then change into concubinage or marriage; in that case, it plays the role of trying out life together. It may be durable and follow a matriarchal tendency, and then it makes up a third type of union by itself. Or it may be used for successive, short-lived unions.

These informal unions are much more stable than marriage in most cases. Each of the partners can put pressure on the other since they can disappear without formalities, and each of them has a real feeling of freedom. Moreover, it often happens that after the concubines have "regularized" their situation under social pressure, the bonds loosen and the union deteriorates even though nothing foreshadowed that breakdown.

The marriage may also be legalized after what is thought to be a conclusive number of years or because one of the partners has become free through widowhood. It may even be legalized when one of them is near death, not for religious reasons but so that the partner can collect the deceased's pension if there is one.

In short, free or legal unions appear in the form of mutual economic and emotional aid and are relatively stable on the whole, considering the metropolitans' emotional deterioration. These unions are stable over time in the tradition-bound Mediterranean groups.

Exogamy[2] is the rule at present, but the project is only four years old and we cannot presume what will happen to the adolescents. However, the parish priest asserts that he has married only two young people from the project to each other, and the few who have gotten married have chosen a mate from outside. The family nucleus is patrilineal in most cases, especially among the Mediterraneans, but a matrilineal tendency seems to be taking shape among the others.

Forms of the Family

Given the intended purpose that the project has by definition, we would expect to find only single-family households limited to just the parents and their children, because these same families were previously crowded into tiny quarters. We would also expect the invasion by relatives among the Arabs. However, we seem to find several types of family not necessarily classified according to the laws of their group. Although it is true that at first glance the single-family household looks like the most frequent case, we find upon further observation that it appears with variants tending toward different degrees of disintegration. This disintegration is both the cause and effect of the division of authority between the parents. The father quite often gives up his role, as we shall see. Extended families are also found: a grandmother, a collateral line, or the second generation's children may be given shelter for very long periods.

We shall first try to analyze the "normal" or "harmonious" single-family households, then the families that have deteriorated in various ways, and finally the extended families.

The Arabs, Italians, and Pied-Noirs best represent the single-family household.

The extended family has been disintegrating in Algeria for a long time. Proletarization of the rural populations precariously settled in cities has disintegrated social structures. Family unity has been undermined by new economic imperatives, parental responsibility has been challenged by abandoning children in the streets, and the conflict between generations has sharpened under European influence. Family dispersion has favored the existence of single-family households.[3]

The Arab families conformed to the norm of society when they came to France and then to the project. Although we must not underrate the strength of the small Arab group in

La Halle or the extended Arab group in France, this does not prevent the Arab couple from being isolated from its original family. For economic and practical reasons, it is impossible for the couple to make frequent visits to family members scattered throughout the area. The couple can depend only on itself in this alien society into which it must integrate, and this is why family unity is not precarious and even shows much stability. Married mostly to cousins, the husband and wife are conscious of providing a twofold solidity to the family.

The wife tries to keep up the traditions and is strongly attached to dietary laws that her husband no longer observes. She is industrious and is not "afraid of work"; she reigns over her house with the youngest babies clinging to her skirts. Freer than on African soil, she is happy to "go up to town" to attend to her business.

The man provides his family's subsistence, monopolizes management of the budget, and makes many purchases himself, especially of food and clothing. He likes to stay home and entertain friends. He adulates his infants, taking them for walks and covering them with caresses. As he grows older, he is reluctant to work and demands that his sons replace him and give him all their wages. The adolescents put a check on parental authority by refusing to work or to have a marriage imposed on them. Nevertheless, the father still exercises some authority despite these tensions.

The mixed Arab–French household is more fragile, and its precarious balance depends on the partners' personalities. The father displays great authority, and the household is stable to the extent that the wife gives in. That is why she often seems mentally defective: the man takes his wife's lack of will or personality for obedience. The father must continually reaffirm a dominion that does not have the force of law that it does in French North Africa, and he sometimes becomes frantically dictatorial. The children's discipline suffers as a result, because the wife thwarts her husband's authority when she is alone with them.

Nevertheless, more than half of the mixed households are stable; in most cases, the father is attached to his home and

children. He still finds patrilineal filiation absolutely necessary, and when a divorce occurs in a mixed household the
father tries every means, including illegal ones if necessary,
to keep the children. That is why he is somewhat reluctant
to marry a French woman; he prefers to live with her in concubinage because the national laws do not adequately ensure
the man's supremacy. It should be noted that in mixed households of proven solidity, the men help the women in household
tasks and in caring for the children.

The purest case of the single-family household organized
around the parents and parental authority, and fixed in a time
when tasks were clearly divided according to sex, is the Pied-
Noir family.

For Father Carlo, nothing is more sacred than the family.
He has seven children. He almost seems to hold court at the
family table, with his oldest son, age twenty, on his left. The
son echoes the father's words and adheres to his philosophy.
They enthusiastically discuss the merits of their "old moral
code." The father is the sire and master, and his benevolent
authority is unanimously accepted. It is his task to "make a
home," shelter his family, and provide it with food. He must
ensure that his family line will be continued by transmitting
to the children the ancestral values of love of work well done
and a sense of responsibility. The mother, with her apron at
her waist, appears at the kitchen door to acquiesce to such
self-assurance. No danger threatens on the horizon of a life
which has yet undergone many vicissitudes. What but death
could undermine the hermetic bastion of a family so welded
together?

The oldest girl works in an office, and on Saturday she helps
her mother in the house. When she glides between the buffet
and her father's chair with a pail of water in her hand, saying,
"Sorry to bother you, Dad," she incarnates the image of peace
in a united family. Would you believe it could happen in La
Halle, where so many daily dramas are played out?

The mother tells the story of the grandfather's emigration
to Tunisia. The son knows all the family history, and in a
few years he in his turn will tell about Tunisia and the return

to France. He is not in a hurry to find a wife. He must have one who stays at home like his mother and who considers her universe, restricted to household tasks, as her kingdom and not as slavery. The men do nothing at home; they are waited on. The mother thinks this is natural because they have enough to do outside to provide for the immediate future. It is she who sees to it that the framed photos of the smiling grandparents survive moving day, and she raises the children to respect their father. Once they are grown, they cannot bring home ordinary companions. No visitor can get in without official warrant, and the young people to whom the house is open will be those promised in marriage. Carlo's family is an inseparable cell whose growth must be regulated.

This example of a harmonious family organized around paternal authority and maternal love is far from frequent in La Halle, where the district social worker estimates that only twenty families live in relatively normal equilibrium. This seems like a strict estimate, because the Arabs and Jews on the whole form a compact family nucleus around a mother who is the picture of domesticity and a father who holds onto his authority. But by rejecting the traditions, the second generation creates conflicts injurious to family harmony.

Most of the metropolitan families show some deterioration, and we shall see that certain others are not exempt from it. The principal cause is almost always a deficiency on the part of the father who is either absent frequently or completely, is replaced by a concubine, or has given up his role even though he still lives with the family.

The family climate in the project is rarely peaceful. Alcoholism is prevalent among half the adult population, and the clamor of arguments between husband and wife often breaks out on Saturday evenings. The man strikes his wife violently and she counters the blow. The children try to separate the belligerents to prevent the neighbors from intervening, or they flee outside to avoid being hit. The neighbors gather and try to reconcile the husband and wife, but their intervention sometimes degenerates into a general brawl and, out of vengeance or fear, they call the police. The arrival of the patrol wagon was once an almost daily phenomenon but it seems to have become rarer now.

One woman tells how her husband, throwing a chair at the ceiling, broke a light bulb and struck the grandmother by mistake in the dark. They repaired the damage the next day when the tempest had calmed, sending the grandmother to have her dislocated shoulder cared for at the hospital, and buying a new television set because the other one was smashed to pieces in the struggle.

The furniture often bears the brunt of the husband's angry outbursts. Bruises sometimes turn the women's faces and eyes blue, and one woman who was knifed in the buttocks exhibited her wound almost everywhere so they would believe her. In La Halle a knife is quick to flash in a man's hand, and the women know how to fight, but the consequences can reach unforseen dimensions; for example, the social services can take the children away and place them with Public Assistance, temporarily or permanently. There is a continual shifting in the number of children in the project; they leave and come back after absences ranging from a few months to two years or more.

In the calmer and apparently more orderly families, one perceives that the father unloads his child-rearing role on his wife and gives up all authority. He works far off, often for ten hours a day, to improve the family's daily life; at home, he rests and scarcely pays any attention to the children. If he is a weak man, he lets himself gradually be overrun by his wife's personality and finds his authority waning; he does not react to this situation and gets completely ousted. This happens relatively often in Jewish families, where appearances are nevertheless kept up. One sees the father seated at the center of the family table, and he is the one who opens the anisette on Friday evening. His wife serves him and offers him the best morsels, but it is she who makes the decisions and rules the family. The paternal role emptied of all substance is now just for show, and the father complains of having disrespectful children.

The father's absence is another cause of family transformation in La Halle. The father is replaced in every case, whether

this absence is permanent or temporary, or is caused by separation, death, imprisonment, or sometimes repeated stays in a
psychiatric hospital. If the father is gone permanently, the
mother re-forms the couple with a concubine or a second husband from outside. In case of temporary absence, the uncertainty of the situation makes the woman enter into a relationship within the project (we will deal with this further on in
the section on endogamy).

The father has thus been replaced by a stepfather. What
is the respective role of the spouses from then on? Among
the Arabs, Jews, and Mediterraneans in general, the children
belong to both parents. Among the metropolitans on the other
hand, one frequently sees the children of a single family
divided under three different names: the oldest children bear
the father's name, the middle children take the mother's, and
the youngest take that of the present concubine. Thirty-
year-old women are usually on their third union, not counting
passing unions that are ignored most of the time unless marked
by the birth of a child. Women who are left alone when they
reach their mature years frequently take a companion younger
than themselves. Here are some examples.

—The L.'s have each been married twice. It is she who
will decide whether their union will continue or the man will
have to leave when she gets back the four out of her five
children who were taken away from her.

—Mrs. Yolande N. is quite old but her youngest children
are still very small (seven and nine). She has seven children
at home, six of whom are entirely her responsibility. Meanwhile, her old concubine (age sixty-five) is slowly dying. They
have been living together for twenty years. The children are
split up under three patronymics.

—Madeleine S., age forty—abandoned by her husband, her
savings and furniture gone—set up house two years ago with
a young man of twenty-five. She then threw him out because
he was not sharing the expenses of the home, but he made
honorable amends and has been taken back.

—Mrs. W., a widow at twenty-seven, lives with a very young
man.

—Mrs. R., age forty, also has a very young spouse. She lived with him for some time and then "regularized" the union. She had had two unions before.

These families have a particular look. The oldest children are scarcely younger than their stepfather, whom they usually call by his first name and who is not invested with any paternal authority. These men generally have no children by this union and have not brought to the home any that they may have had by another.

The woman plays the role of mother for everyone. She is the pivot around which the whole family revolves. In matters concerning the children, she alone makes the decisions, sometimes consulting the oldest child.

The man willingly agrees to cohabit with the children of previous unions. His relations with them are fraternal, but if he decided to assert himself or take an interest in their upbringing, he would quickly be put in his place by the mother. The stepfather generally does not replace the father in this regard, whatever his age; the mother does not tolerate it and he does not insist. It is the mother alone who punishes, rewards, authorizes, and prohibits. "I don't want him to order my children around; I'm afraid he'll hit them; I won't let the kids call him 'Daddy,'" she says.

In short, the family is split in half after remarriage: the couple on one hand and, on the other hand, the children and the newcomer grouped under the mother's authority. The man provides for the whole family, and in exchange he finds a home. If children are born, he acts as a father to them, but in relation to the others he remains an affectionate brother who feels neither concerned nor responsible. One often hears, "If he were mine, I'd do something, but since he's not mine, I can't say anything." Now that she is rid of paternal authority and is secure in her economic and emotional needs, the mother reigns alone over her children. She has become the unquestioned head of the family.

These unions have always been successive exogamous monogamies. However, there are two open cases of polygamy, one Arab and the other Jewish.[4] The Arab had two wives and children of each of them at home. One wife died recently so the other is raising the ten children, but he talks about going to Algeria and choosing a new wife to replace the deceased one.

The Jew has maintained two households up to now: the one in the project with ten children and another in a small apartment in the city. He lived at the apartment from Monday to Friday with a young woman and two children, one of whom was born before this liaison, and he came back to the project for the Sabbath. The young woman died recently and her children were dispersed, but he continues his comings and goings and makes his three oldest daughters come with him. The family continues to gather together as a complete group just from Friday night to Monday morning.

Some forms of the extended family are also found in the project. The fact that they have decent housing prompts some families to give shelter to one or several persons or even a couple and children who are more or less related to them, for a temporary period which often becomes lasting. We will leave aside the invasions of relatives for four or five days seen among the Arabs on the occasion of a holiday and short-term lodging provided secretly, concerning ourselves only with relatives whose presence in the home is lasting or repeated.

It is not to the older generation that the family is extended: the project has just about ten old people, mostly widows. A grandmother who bears a large part of the household tasks, plays an important role with the children, and, in her ancient dress, represents the guardian of tradition is rarely seen outside of Arab and Jewish families.

On the other hand, one frequently encounters brothers and sisters of the father or mother in all ethnic groups. Among the Arabs, a younger brother or half-brother or nephew is often taken in for months at a time and is integrated into the family. Mustafa, age twelve, stayed in his uncle's home like this for two years. The metropolitan wife often takes one or several of her younger brothers under her roof in order to give them decent housing and to get them away from the parents' slums. Mrs. K.'s six children, ranging from a month to seven years, were partly raised by their maternal uncles, ages seventeen

and eighteen, who play with them and provide for some of
their needs. Maternal uncles seem to be present more often
than maternal aunts because the wife is afraid to bring a younger woman into her home. The relationship also seems to be
the wife's by preference, because after her marriage she continues the big sister's role she had in her parents' home.

Finally, an archaic form of the extended family is recreated
by some grown children who stay with their mother once they
are married, not because they want to but because of the housing shortage. Although it has the use of only one bedroom,
the young family is better off than the preceding generation.
It takes its time to find an apartment and does not have to
live in furnished rooms. The grandmother takes care of the
baby or babies while the young couple works, and both daughter and daughter-in-law let her raise the child her own way.
For instance, Mrs. F. houses both her oldest son, her daughter-
in-law, and their two-year-old daughter and her oldest daughter, her son-in-law, and their baby. One woman pushed her
ten children to the back of the apartment to make room for
her married son. However, the young uncles from eight to
fourteen show their jealousy. The older ones want a room
to themselves and are glad to turn out the young couple. The
younger ones must share their mother's affection with babies
who break their toys. The marriages of the second generation
living in the project seem to be solid but it is still too early
to assume this apparent stability.

Adolescents are not allowed to live with a girl friend at
their mother's; however, we may deem it an embryonic form
of the extended family when they impose their pseudo-fiancée
on the home. These girls show up daily for longer or shorter
periods and sometimes spend whole days at their sweetheart's
house even when the boys are not home. At Mrs. X.'s, for
instance, two girls chosen by the older sons keep company
with the daughters of the house. Jean considers his girl as
his fiancée even though he is just sixteen, while Robert, by
his own admission, has one just to "show off to [his] pals,"
but the girls are at the X.'s equally often. Even if the motive
behind these liaisons is semiplayful or the desire to show

off, this does not change the fact that the girls are accepted in the house. And no one in the family will be surprised if in a short time the favorites are renounced and replaced by new ones, who will also be admitted to the home.

In La Halle, then, family structures are essentially exogamous, and the forms of the family that can be found there range from the singe-family household, either harmonious or deteriorated, to the more or less extended family. One common factor is found among a very large number of families: the father gives up his role to varying degrees and the mother takes charge of almost all family responsibilities.

Endogamy[5]

But are there no unions of just a passing nature between men and women in the project? When endogamous sexual relations are established, it is first and always in the form of play. If these usually short-term relationships are prolonged into real liaisons, they become cases of polyandry or polygyny[6] because in principle every adult already has a mate. However, when a woman has no regular man, she is willing to play something of a courtesan's role; this is how one single woman, raising her children alone, took on the role of initiating young boys. Two or three women prefer freedom to concubinage, perhaps because they are getting old, but the women generally do not remain alone for very long, and these periods are a sort of vacation that make it easy for them to "play at" one role or the other.

Sexual Games

Sexuality is present everywhere and is commonly expressed by word and gesture. It did not seem to be taboo since the women were rather prolix about their personal experiences in this area, and sexual matters were usually treated lightly. But even though private life has fallen into the public domain, sexual acts had to be notorious to reach this observer's ears. In interviews, we ran into an unaccustomed wall of silence on this subject among our best informants: "Everybody sleeps with everybody here, but it's not up to me to tell you about it. Go down in the basement at 3:00 in the morning and you'll see for yourself." This answer shows that there is a taboo not on sexuality but on the damage to one's dignity that it entails. The informants who were willing to talk about themselves did not want to betray others by revealing necessarily adulterous behavior.

The gestures are evocative: right index finger stuck through a circle formed by the left index finger and thumb, stiff middle finger directed toward the open palm of the opposite hand and pointed at the enemy, or right palm brought down on the aperture of the closed left fist. But these gestures remain symbolic, and one hardly ever sees actual contact in public. Words and gestures can be threats or jokes. The words are most often used as expressions of anger in the form of sexual insults uttered by people of all ages.

In other respects, everything concerning sexual life is approached with great simplicity. A man asks advice on curing his wife's "coldness" or a woman complains that her husband does not satisfy her. Another man relates his wife's misconduct and insists on telling us that he is not the father of his youngest child. The women simply agree to the requested rendezvous or arrange them themselves. Men and women see each other at the window or meet in the courtyard; they pass over to the act in fun.

It is impossible to hide liaisons in a place so dense with curiosity and gossip. Cellars and apartments screen these clandestine "games" but automobiles are even better because they let the couple get away from the project.

As long as the family is not destroyed, great sexual freedom is tolerated at La Halle; amused criticism is as far as one goes. On the other hand, the prohibitions against incest seem to be strong.

Intergroup adultery seems to show up only on group fringes. In fact, it is important to point out that the Moslems who married according to the traditional laws do not commit adultery inside the project, and they have established a unanimous reputation on this point. Among the Moslens from mixed households, where there is greater freedom, we know of just a few individuals who court other women; they are always the same men, and the women they pursue are always Europeans. More exchanges come into play among the Jews; some of the men get into the good graces of metropolitan women, and the younger Jewish women have some popularity with the metropolitan men.

Polyandry and Polygyny

Outside of these kinds of games or sometimes following them, real liaisons are established without destroying the established order. They often arise during the husband's absence, especially if he is in jail or confined in a mental institution, and they continue after his return. This implies a rearrangement of the participants' lives. If none of the husbands is away, we have polygyny together with polyandry. There are three well-known cases of this type; the first two are three-sided, organized according to the personalities involved in each, and the third is four-sided.

In the first case, there is a mixed couple and a metropolitan woman whose companion has disappeared. She has become the second (illegitimate) wife of the Moslem man. The second wife has started to work, and, while she is away, the first wife takes care of all eleven children. The first wife acts as maid-of-all-work but in return the favorite, who is better organized, is willing to run back and forth between the two apartments to help her "co-wife." These three partners are known for their alcoholism. The first wife is by no means ousted from the orgies that bring all three together; she is just beaten often when she has not worked for the group or made a good enough dinner.

The second case constitutes a continuing drama. When a man who is subject to fits of depression went to a psychiatric hospital for treatment for the first time, his wife established relations with the neighbor upstairs. Each time the husband returns, the new couple arranges to throw him into a paroxysm of anger and then has him confined again on the grounds of his violent behavior. They have been going through the same process for many months, each time the husband returns. The neighbor's wife tolerates this situation, which gives her a certain freedom of action; however, each of them lives in his own home and raises his own children.

The third case arose from a playful sexual relationship. It involves two households living across the courtyard from each other, whom we shall call AxB and CxD. A. and C. are the men. We shall let B. tell her own story:

> At first, I couldn't stand him because he'd bawled out my children in the courtyard. Then I noticed he was watching me all the time from his window. I stuck out my tongue and made faces at him, but that made him laugh and he threw me kisses. I complained to my husband, but he answered, "If you don't look out the window, you won't see him." I couldn't shake out a rag or do anything without seeing that smile at the window across the way. Then I stuck out my behind at him, but he motioned, "Okay." I said to myself, "That's too much," and called him over just to see what would happen. That's how it happened; since then, we're always together. At first people stopped saying "hello" to me, but now that's over, now that they know my husband and his wife know all about it and have agreed.

The two couples have twelve children between them. C. is "on disability" and does not work so all his time is free. He drives A.'s old car during the day and takes B. out for a drive or to take care of official business for both homes. He is the one who repairs the car because he is handier.

Since AxB's household is better organized, it is B. who takes the initiative and considers it her duty to help D. in her household tasks. If the two men go fishing, the two women make dinner together at one house. CxD's daughters are learning to cook at B.'s, and AxB's children play and sing at D.'s. Either B. or D. picks up all the children at school; it makes no difference.

They keep their finances separate, and if C. "gets B. out of a jam" on the day he receives his pension, she always pays him back what she borrowed. They spend their free time together on Sunday, and holidays always bring the two families together at AxB's, whose apartment is more stylish. A. and D., who are weaker, accept this solution while the couple BC, who are more intelligent and authoritative, run the two homes by common agreement and together make every decision concerning them.

There is certainly geographic endogamy but it is found in a minor, play form that generally does not break up unions previously established by exogamic ties.

Special Cases

The presence of nubile young people in the project, where sexuality is intense, impels us to raise the question of prostitution. Is it practiced, and in what way?

There are no prostitutes in La Halle, properly speaking, and no woman admits to practicing that profession. However, there have been two cases of prostitution. While his French wife was in a psychiatric hospital, an Arab brought a minor into his home, ostensibly to take care of his children, and then turned her to prostitution in a red-light district. The girl lived in the project when she was not streetwalking. When the wife came back, she threw her husband out and he was sent to jail for pandering. Then, left on her own with no income, the wife in turn became a prostitute for two years. If a woman becomes a prostitute she practices her trade outside the project, in the districts of the city set aside for that.

Public report has it that two men are panderers but if so, their activity is not visible in the project and can only be carried on outside.

We know of at least two women who are easygoing about "letting men come up." Nothing distinguishes them from the other women, and we do not know whether they are paid for their services; nonetheless, they represent an embryonic form of prostitution. But four or five women are known to be what we shall call initiaters, and they behave differently. One of them who is married and has five children is especially fond of young adolescents. Her husband comes home from

work very late, so she has much free time. She is frequently
seen with a few boys and not only initiates them but showers
them with cigarettes and small gifts. When they are out of
work too long, she looks for work for them and presents them
at the factory, passing herself off as their mother. The adolescents are very fond of these women with whom they always
find refuge, food, and understanding.

While certain married women serve as initiators, a few older
girls represent another kind of special case. We have said that
women in the project live without a man only temporarily,
except for two or three widows who are already old, but this
does not hold true for the girls of the second generation when
they are of age and unattached and continue to live with their
parents. These girls give themselves to the young men for
pleasure, generously and without remuneration, and we know
of two who have accepted the consequences. Certainly a child
is often born out of wedlock but in most cases he is recognized
in a later union. However O., age twenty-five, and S., age
twenty-two, each have several children but live in the homes
of their respective parents. The fathers are young men from
the project; one of them is one of those younger brothers living
with a sister. All the children bear their mother's name, and
the fathers do not provide for their maintenance or education.
Not only do these two cases illustrate once more the existence
of extended families, but they provide two effective examples
of a matrilineal arrangement. The young women do not seem
to want to establish a home. O. answers this question with
an evasive gesture, and her mother says she is much happier
like this since she "only sees the good side" of men. She
is pampered a lot and taken out by one boy or another. Although
the mothers of the two young women are married themselves,
they are both motherly and capable and they bear all the
responsibilities of the home. Her three "sons-in-law" are very
fond of O.'s mother but when they come to the house she
requires certain services of them: one takes her shopping in
the car and another paints the apartment with good grace.
The tendency toward matriarchy that we have already analyzed
in the first generation is explicit in these two cases.

There is no sexual abstinence in La Halle. Moreover, one ascertains a degree of license in this area which comes partly from the fact that life in a confined environment hardly allows for privacy. The acts and gestures of the two partners are open to public appraisal and comments spread through the stairwells, but then those involved are quickly forgotten. The project laughs at its own vaudeville show, and today's spectators will be tomorrow's actors. If the vaudeville turns into a drama, that just makes the show better. But the actors do not always get off lightly from this complicated game of libertinage in which hazy complicity and brusk betrayal sometimes exacerbate passions. A Pied-Noir, for whom family solidarity is unquestionable, expresses it like this: "We're living in the midst of chaos here."

Actually, behind the apparent disorder or disorganization of the family, we are dealing with a real system created by an economic substructure. The man is needed to bring in the whole family's subsistence, whether he is the natural father of the children or not. In exchange, he unloads a large part of the responsibility on the mother. He does not have the preponderant role at home, either in matters pertaining to finances or (except for the traditional Moslems) in relation to the children, but he enjoys a certain amount of freedom.

Whether or not the situation is institutionalized—and, ultimately, free union is relatively infrequent—the family nucleus remains. Changes have little effect on it; it is just a matter of substitution, most often of the father. Co-spouses rarely occur, but where they exist and are tolerated, it is in a context of mutual help and division of duties. For economic reasons, the single-family household has a tendency to pass over into the extended family by giving shelter to collateral members or descendants. There is practically no prostitution, and it is not institutionalized. As for sexual play, it goes on outside the system and plays the same role as elsewhere, with the difference that here it is necessarily in public view.

So this really seems to be a classic, coherent system with a solid family nucleus in which the place of the couple is strongly protected. The majority of households are stable, and

68 The Individual, the Family, and the Project

those that break up are re-formed. A tendency toward matriarchy seems to follow from this system, which is characterized among other things by the reinforcment of maternal authority and the interchangeability of the men.

NOTES

[1]When the manager learns of it, he simply records the name of the man, preceded by a plus sign (+).

[2]This term is used in its geographic sense and not in the usual lineal sense.

[3]P. Bourdieu, *Sociologie de l'Algerie* (Que sais-je series); P. Bourdieu and A. Sayad, *Le Déracinement* (Editions de Minuit, 1964).

[4]When an ethnic group other than the Moslems is involved, the term "polygamy" is used in the physical and not the institutional sense.

[5]The term is used here in the geographic and not the lineal sense.

[6]Here these terms are taken in the etymological sense and do not designate institutions.

7

Family Life

The way of life of La Halle's residents cannot be understood without studying their income and expenditures, but there is something even more revealing than the budget itself. The way they manage their budget, their choice of purchases, and the motivations to which they respond—as expressed in their interests, privations, hopes, and joys—will reveal their notion of money and their perception of the world. Also, a certain form of relations and division of activities between husband and wife follows from their economic organization.

The Budget

Sources and Management

The budget is obviously one of consumption alone. The man's wages are the source of part of the income, but only a part. In fact, the family allowances and the housing allowance play

Table 8 Income (by month)

Sources of Income	A French Couple 5 Children	B Mixed Couple 6 Children	C Mixed Couple 6 Children	D French Couple Children in Foster Homes	E French Couple 1 Child, Others in Foster Homes
	Skilled Laborer	Garbage Collector (Public)	Factory Worker	Stock Clerk	Garbage Collector (Private)
EARNINGS					
Man					
Wages	900F	1,137F	800F	600F	600F
Pensions	0	0	0	430	0
Woman	0	0	0	520	300
FAMILY ALLOWANCES[1]	650	764	820	0	0
SOCIAL SECURITY	0	0	300	300	0
OTHER[2]	0	0	0	100	0
Monthly total	1,550F	1,901F	1,920F	1,950F	900F
Rent	-170	-250	-170	-150	-200
Total disposable income	1,380	1,651	1,750	1,800	700
Average daily disposable income per person	6.6F	6.9F	7.3F	30F	7.8F

Sources of Income	F	G	H	I	J
	French Couple, 4 Children, 2 Sons-in-Law, 2 Grandchildren	French Couple, 8 Children	French Couple, 4 Children at Home	Jewish Couple, 8 Children, 3 Grandchildren	Jewish Couple, 9 Children
	Truckdriver	Disabled	Plumber	Road Repairman (Ill)	Road Repairman
EARNINGS					
Man					
Wages	940F	0	1,300F	0	650F
Pensions	0	460F	0	0	0
Woman	0	0	0	0	0
FAMILY ALLOWANCES[1]	150	1,120	600	1,010	612
SOCIAL SECURITY		450	200		
OTHER[2]	800	0		520	1,480
Monthly total	1,890F	2,030F	2,100F	1,530F	2,742F
Rent	– 120	– 260	– 170	– 170	– 200
Total disposable income	1,770	1,770	1,930	1,360	2,542
Average daily disposable income per person	5.9F	5.9F	10.7F	3.5F	7.7F

NOTE: 4.94F = $1.00 (1F = nearly 20c).

[1] Family allowances include housing allowances (40–60F).

[2] "Other" includes pensions paid by working children (couples F, I, and J), alimony paid by former spouse (couple D), and a quarterly supplement in benefits (couple D).

a large part, sometimes exceeding total wages. In addition, private or military pensions and Social Security benefits sometimes replace wages or are added to them. Not only does disposable income come from several sources, but it is fragmented over time: pensions are paid quarterly, wages by the month, half-month, or week, and daily Social Security benefits by the month (although these benefits may also be received in installments).

In order to make a table of comparison between several families we have calculated their monthly incomes. The figures are true but do not indicate real distribution over time, and this particular aspect of the budget is important in La Halle for the distribution of expenditures.

As we shall see, the figures provide no understanding of the economic life of these families, although figures would be meaningful for other social classes. We know the cost of living, and if we ascertain, for example, that a civil servant with three children earns 2,000F per month, we know roughly his way of life. This is not the case in the project where earnings depend on unsteady employment and where liabilities, often heavy and concealed, allow the negligent observer to be fooled by the mathematical data on income. The raw data correspond but little to reality. In addition, the art of organizing the budget to make the best use of it varies from one family to another.

Since the analysis of budgets requires that some very precise questions be asked of those concerned, these examples have been taken from those who agreed to answer without fear; so it was not a matter of real choice but of chance. This is why Table 8 shows a gap: it omits Moslem couples who would not consent to this type of investigation. Some Moslems have savings, but they would never admit to them and no one knows where they hide their money.

Some explanations concerning the situation of each sample case will clarify this table, which shows only a certain constancy in total income and the daily average. In fact, the average daily disposable income per person in the project is between 6 and 7F.

Couple A., worn down by alcoholism, lives from day to day. It has 6.6F per day to spend. This amount is not far from that of couple B., which, judging from its home and way of life, appears to be among the most well off in the project. But B. is a municipal employee. He is paid monthly by a check issued by the district tax collector, and he withdraws money from his account by means of a municipal passbook, which functions like a postal checking account. It is easy for him to organize his expenditures.

Mixed couple C. presents a situation parallel to that of B., yet the two households are not comparable. C.'s furniture has been repossessed; the couple possesses nothing at the moment and must meet large debts. The wife is a bad manager and the husband spends a lot on his amusements; he is inclined to distribute money to certain women.

Couple D. stands out in the table because of its high economic average but this amount, although true the day the questions were asked, is completely misleading. The D.'s have been living together for barely a year, and they were each trying to free themselves by divorce from their previous unions. Their past has been a series of failures. When D. came into the household, repossession had left just one bed, two chairs, and a dresser; the gas and electricity had been shut off; arrears in rent amounted to 2,800F; and the household had neither linens nor clothing. Mrs. D. was not working, and at that time her companion had only a private disability pension of 1,290F quarterly on which to live. The children have been living in foster homes for two years since the court decreed forfeiture of parental authority, so no family allowance is collected. In order to regain custody of her children, Mrs. D. has again taken a factory job. D. did not want to remain idle either, so despite his precarious health he has become a stock clerk in the same factory. In so doing he has put himself in an illegal position because his pension prohibits his working. Mrs. D. has done the same thing by continuing to collect Social Security benefits. They live in fear that the fraud will be discovered, for then D.'s pension would be terminated, and since he cannot count on his health, he might one day have nothing to live on. This situation has gone on for six months. None of their earnings have been regular. She has worked periodically; he has changed jobs. They have restored the electricity and begun to pay the arrears in rent in small monthly installments. They bought a portable gas stove temporarily equipped with butane, some pans, some clothing, a mattress and two bicycles to save the cost of transportation. In addition, they repainted the apartment.

The D.'s situation is thus utterly precarious and is not consistent with the stated budget. They have never enjoyed this amount in reality, and it was just theoretical since the pension is only collected every three months and their jobs are very unstable.

The E.'s are waiting for their children to be returned. They have not claimed the part of the allowances due them for the little girl entrusted to them again for the past year. Although rarely unemployed, he does not have a steady job, and she works at home in order to balance the budget. A month after they were interviewed, Mr. E. lost his job and was unemployed for more than a month, so their average income fluctuates.

The F.'s balance their budget in spite of a rather low average. On the other hand the G.'s, who also enjoy 5.9F per day, have taken advantage several times of "aid" (800F,300F,500F) granted by the municipality so they could meet their obligations. Several months' rent remains unpaid. Wounded in Indochina and an invalid, G. receives a quarterly private pension of 690F and a yearly military pension of 2,800F. Everyday living expenses are provided for by the family allowances. The G.'s owe 450F in taxes, and some installment bills encumber the budget. Their income is regular but various parts of it come in on different dates.

The H.'s 10.7F per day is also illusory. H. had tried to improve his situation by "setting up in business with a pal," but he went bankrupt. Repossession having emptied the house, the H.'s lost no time in refurnishing and could not honor the numerous bills. Presently they are in tutelage.* The tutor is

*See *n.* 5 for an explanation of tutelage.—R.S.

slowly paying off 8,000F in debts with the allowances, so Mrs. H. does not have access to them.

The financial situation of the I.'s is catastrophic. The father has been ill for six months. He is presently in a rest home and has not yet collected Social Security benefits. The household has asked to be put into tutelage in order to repay more than 10,000F in various debts. But since Mrs. I. no longer collects family allowances, and since her two eldest refuse to work and she has ten mouths to feed, her income is so reduced that she lives off expedients, taking her family jewels to the municipal pawnshop and soliciting the generosity of her neighbors.

With 7.70F daily per person the J.'s live, if not in affluence, at least in relative comfort.

This disparity is not only due to differences in managing ability, which is a phenomenon encountered everywhere; it is also due to the fact that since income is collected in fragmentary sums, expenditures are provided for on a weekly basis in the majority of cases, while bills and installment payments are paid monthly. When a worker leaves a job where he has been paid by the half-month and begins to collect a disability pension at the end of a quarter, he must completely modify his system of apportionment. Thus, the project people generally have difficulty in setting up their system over a month or a year, since the calculations necessary to organize their lives are sometimes beyond their competence in arithmetic.

Workers are most often paid every two weeks, but in practice at the end of the first week they all ask for partial payment approximately equal to half of what they earn in the two weeks. The truncated wage is still called "pay." Often "we don't eat meat the day before payday," and the day that the "paymaster" distributes the family allowances, no wife goes out. Total wages vary slightly from one half-month to another depending on whether the worker put in overtime or worked more quickly than usual if he is on piecework. Though not very noticeable in an annual budget, these differences are welcomed joyfully the week that additional wages have been recorded because the people of La Halle have no way to find supplementary resources (such as raising chickens or growing a garden).

Wages and allowances just suffice to ensure their existence. Some of them live continually a month behind and use the allowances to pay the various debts of the preceding month. That is why they organize their expenditures easily and usually for a week, with difficulty for a month, and never for a year. The women we questioned spontaneously explain their daily and weekly expenditures as well as the cost of rent, but often forget to set forth all the bills (gas and electricity, as well as the annual expense of taxes).[1]

In order to examine the organization and amount of expenditures in detail, we thought it better to present the raw material of the answers to the question, "How do you organize your budget?" We preferred not to rewrite and thereby falsify the informants' comments or the unfolding of their thoughts, which follow the order of their preoccupations. The enumeration of their expenditures thus seems to become richer and less tedious, and setting up a table of expenditures not only proves impossible but would give a scientifically false result.

Mr. and Mrs. B. manage the budget together; Mr. B. answers first.

> I'm paid by the month and my municipal passbook is handy. It lets me put money aside sometimes. My last savings disappeared during my illness. From my pay we take out 1,000F for the rent (240F) and the installment bills: 420F in all for the washing machine, the "frigidaire," the radio, the couch, and the sewing machine. We've got a year more to pay. We also pay for the children's schooling, and we buy some little things for them, like a pair of sneakers. With the remaining 200F or 300F, we stock up on groceries and we eat the first week. The rest of the time we put aside 250F that we leave in the cupboard; that's for food. We do a big shopping together on Saturday and spend 150F. I've suffered too much to deprive my children of food; I don't ever want them to know hunger. On Saturday we buy a lot of meat, groceries, soup, vegetables, and drinks: apple juice, lemonade, Vichy water. We don't drink alcohol, that's a saving.

Mrs. B. continues:

> We don't spend anything on cleaning clothes; I do it all myself. Father does the Sunday morning "deluxe" shopping alone; he's

quick to spend 40F or 50F for cake, fruit, and a few nice things.
I do a little shopping every day, 10F or 15F for bread, milk, little
things. That's at the supermarket. He brings back steak from where
he works because he gets a discount, and at times he buys some
odds and ends like pillowcases when he sees a good bargain. With
what's left in the account we pay the gas and electricity by check.
Since he doesn't smoke, that's always a saving, but he has the
habit of having a bite every day at the bar. That costs 2.5F. He
always carries some money, a few 1,000F bills [old francs, equal
to 1/100 of new francs], for gas for his bike and in case he needs
it. We don't spend anything else, we don't have any amusements.
We can't go out even during the day. With all these kids we need
two taxis; one won't take all eight of us. It costs a lot, and to go
where? What Mohand does indulge in is betting on the races on
Sunday—he only plays for 3F—and a chance on the national lottery
in almost every drawing. Maybe he'll win some day! I never spend
any pocket money, I cut my own hair.

Eight hours a day, Mrs. D. fills bottles by machine, to the
rhythm of the production line in the factory where she has
been working for a short time to improve her income. She
would like to be able

...to put one pay aside for big purchases, rent, gas and electricity,
and keep the other for food and upkeep. That way, with his pension
we could fix up the house a bit and pay off the debts little by
little with the rest. For food, you have to count on 20F a day.
As it is, we spend 6F a day on lunch at work and 6F in the evening
on food. We buy canned vegetables, fruit, butter, cheese, Vichy
water to drink, and a lot of coffee. Saturday and Sunday we spend
twice that much. You can't stint yourself all the time, so sometimes
we have chicken or roast beef.

It is she who manages the whole budget, but she puts some
money in her husband's wallet. She cannot go to a single tradesman because of old debts that have dragged on since the
time "when things were so bad."

I owe at least 500F to the druggist up the street. There are certainly others—I don't know any more. My husband charges things
everywhere. I don't dare go to town any more and I do all my
shopping at the supermarket or the Monoprix. The open market
is too far away, and Saturday I'm dead tired; I sleep.

He doesn't spend anything, he doesn't even take pocket money. I buy his tobacco for him, three packs a week. On the other hand, since we never drink any more, either of us, and we don't spend on wine any more, every Friday night we buy a bottle of champagne that we drink with the people upstairs; we pay for it—one week them, one week us. And since we're all alone and we get bored, we go to the movies on Saturday for a change, or to the fair; we take the money from the kitty.

Mrs. E. says,

Here is how I go about it. With Georges' pay (600F) at the end of the month, first we get rid of the rent (200F) and some installment payments: 150F for the dining set, 75F for the washing machine, 100F for the vacuum cleaner, couch, and mattress. We've still got eighteen months to pay; that makes 370F. With my dressmaking at home, I draw 50F to 100F a week. That depends on what I have time to do. I have to get along on what I earn for food and incidentals. Fortunately I dress the kid myself. I go to the butcher on Rue de la Mairie because he has "specials" and gives credit . . . and the horse butcher too. We eat meat for lunch and supper. My meals are always carefully prepared with appetizer, meat, vegetable, cheese, and fruit. I spend 120F on paté in a month. I pay for it all at once. And in the evening there's soup, meat, vegetables, and cheese. We drink 1½ liters of wine a day. There's always mint drink for the little one; once in a while we buy an apéritif and I make liqueur myself. Only I run on butane; in spite of my two bottles a month with the water heater, it's cheaper than gas (24F). When I have some dough, I buy at the open market and stock up on groceries at the Monoprix; otherwise I live from day to day and I buy at the supermarket. No one will give credit here, except in town, if even there!

What else do we have in expenses? Taxes, 180F a year. Tax on the TV; we don't pay it because it's not declared; since we moved without leaving an address they haven't found us yet. And then we have fire insurance (120F a year)—that's rare here—and insurance on the cat.[2] Since we barely get by, we pull in our belts when that comes due; and then Georges manages to get good pickings from the garbage. He gives me his pay and takes a little pocket money from the cupboard for his cigarettes, but he would really like to have a good bit of money on him. We don't go out, we don't go on vacation, we do without everything so we can have a comfortable home.

Mrs. F. has to feed grown married children who work far from home, and she also has the two youngest to raise.

My husband is paid every two weeks. The first week he gets 180F on account; right away we take out the kids' bus passes and school lunches. Just for transportation it takes 10F for Fatou, 7F for Kilou, and 15F for Jojo. I give Fatou 5F a day for his lunch. We also have some minor expenses: the children's pocket money, the baby's milk.

Saturday and Sunday my husband and I do the shopping for three days, in the rotten old Dauphine that isn't insured any more. Then he leaves me 20F a day for food. He keeps the money; he gives me some as I need it. I use eight loaves of bread a day, three liters of milk and a half a pound of butter every morning, half a pound of coffee every other day.

They are big and eat a lot, and they work. I see to it that my table is well provided. Every evening there's meat, 15F at least, especially beef and veal, rarely mutton, but some chicken and rabbit. Drinks are brought in every week: a case of Evian, a case of beer, a bottle of grenadine and one of citron, five red wine and ten white.

We don't make a special meal on Sunday because we eat well every day. But my husband's pay isn't enough; I have to draw on the pension the children pay me. I spend almost 50F a day on nothing but food, and I take food to Jojo, who is just starving at the barracks.

With what's left we pay for the gas, electricity and the cleaners'. I have to pay 13F a month for cloth, and then the installments: 124F for the washing machine, 50F for a set of linens, and 50F at the jeweler for the young couples' weddings and Fatou's watch.

I pay the rent when I receive the allowances. It's about the same thing. At the end of the month there's nothing left. We never go out; we don't dare go for a ride any more in that uninsured car we bought for 500F. We don't go to the movies, and for pocket money my husband just takes his cigarettes and 3F on Sunday for the races.

Mrs. H. insists on forewarning us right away that they are big eaters and she hates a poor table, so she needs 250F a week for food. She does a big shopping twice a week. Her husband gives her all his pay and takes 10F a day in pocket money (cigarettes and bar), and 3F to 5F for the races on

Sunday. His old car, perpetually broken down, costs a lot for gas and repairs. The H.'s go out in the car quite often on Sunday, although they do not have the means to pay for insurance renewal. They think "it doesn't pay to deny yourself everything, life is dull enough as it is," and they do not take their debts too hard.

The G.'s spend 300F a week for food for ten people, pay the rent (260F) and the installments on a suit for the father and their third washing machine (102F). The husband spends little pocket money (cigarettes and the races), but he himself manages the money from his pension which he keeps and does not hand over to his wife. For the children's clothes, "he goes and begs from the good Sisters, and tries to manage somehow for the rest."

Of these six cases, three men do not turn their wages over to their wives, but one is a Kabyle who cannot fill out the checks, and the couple manage the budget together. The second gives his wife a sum of money every day, but he keeps nothing for himself because his wages are totally absorbed by food. The third does not turn over his pension; this is not the fruit of his labor but, even more than wages, is a personal asset, the compensation for the moral injury of "no longer having your two hands to work with." In general, however, it is the wife who takes care of expenditures, except among the Moslems.

The accent is unanimously put on food. Almost all of the budget is devoted to it, and the word "meat" recurs insistently. Food in sufficient quantity insures survival. It is not out of gluttony that they eat a lot of meat or butter; it is from fear that one day they will not have any, as has happened to them in the past. All the cases cited here have known real starvation in their lives. In hard times at the end of the month, more than one woman gets along at midday (when the husband is away) on a bit of bread and an onion, more than one family dines on bread dipped in coffee. We should note this fact which is revealed only by direct observation, since not having enough to eat is considered a disgrace.

Thus food is the principal concern of all. That is why it absorbs almost all the budget, and why there is nothing left at the end of the month, whatever the income. Rent takes second place in their concerns because it contains the latent threat of eviction for nonpayment. What remains then? Finding the means to pay some bills for furniture, which also plays a prominent role; clothes have less importance; and nothing more remains for amusements, which are sacrificed (see the end of this chapter).

As to the monthly utility bills, they crop up as indications of a deficiency in earnings and standard of living, and are unconsciously omitted. For the people of the project, it is necessary to survive week by week, with the tenacious hope that "next month we can make out better" by trying desperately to augment income.

The traditional Moslems act in a slightly different way. The man manages the budget. Food has less importance in their eyes; they do not stake their honor on eating meat twice a day, and they get along on little. On the other hand, holiday feasts absorb all their savings. Meanwhile, two or three of them are reputed to be secretly amassing enough money to move back to North Africa. In general, they are slowly infected by that fever for fixing up the apartment, which we shall discuss again further on. But they are patient, and those who have regular wages gradually become "the middle class of the project." The Moslems pay the rent, the doctor, and the druggist scrupulously.

Among the Jews, the wife is responsible for apportioning expenditures concerning food and the house, but the man keeps part of his wages. As with the Arabs, food devoted to religious holidays takes precedence over balancing the budget. "The holidays are sacred. We buy all that is required in Saint-Georges even if we have to sell our jewels, even if we have nothing more until the end of the next week."[3] In hard times, they get along on fried potatoes, bread, homemade pancakes, and vegetables soaked in vinegar (of which the women always have a bottle). On the whole, they are considered worse at

paying bills than the Moslems, and they go into debt more
often. Furnishing their apartment assumes as much importance
in their eyes as in those of the metropolitans.

Thus it can be said that all the budgets are limited and
in precarious balance. They let people live from day to day.
If illness or some other unforeseen occurrence crops up, the
balance breaks down.[4] The most pressing things must be taken
care of first, so purchases are "put on the tab" at stores that
allow it. This is what happens most often in the old
neighborhoods, but this is impossible in La Halle because
they have to pay cash in the self-service supermarket, and
the town does not welcome this clientele. The only resort
is not to honor certain bills. Sometimes a grant from the municipality is enough to make up the deficit but often, when too
many arrears accumulate, the bailiffs appear and the debtor's
goods are repossessed. A truck comes and takes away the mov-
ables, and one has to start from the beginning again. The only
way of not reaching that extremity is to appeal to the Tutelage
of the Family Allowances[5] when the debts assume dangerous
proportions, but tutelage is ordered by the Children's Court,
and this measure is considered humiliating and proof of
incapacity.

Tutelages generally last two years. Since 1962, there have
been seven families in tutelage, of which six are presently
in progress, two having been renewed. Four are French, one
is Jewish, and the other Algerian. There are forty-nine tutelages
in the whole judicial district, which includes eight communes,
so those of the project represent 14 percent of the total in
the district.

Method of Purchase and Payment

On their arrival in La Halle, the residents possessed little
more than beds (in insufficient number, because of the
crowded condition of their former lodgings), a portable stove,
some kitchen utensils, and a television set. They were granted
an apartment and immediately felt the need of having a home.
Social and economic pressures are such that they are not free

to choose whether they will have certain articles of furniture, and it is impossible for them to wait. Furniture is an element of prestige to which they are subject. At moving time there was a race to furnish, which launched financial disorders that have since been somewhat straightened out.

Table 9 shows very clearly in what order people furnish their apartments, and this order is the same for all. Beds are always mentioned. It is a question of those children who formerly (and quite often still do, particularly among the Arabs and Jews) slept three, four or five in one big bed. Henceforth, bedrooms, and therefore beds, must be given to the children: one per child, if possible, is a general aspiration. The refrigerator, television, and dining set are of the same order of urgency and interest, but the refrigerator is the most important. The dining set is only an extension of it, so the owner may accept one that is unsatisfactory because it is of poor quality or was bought secondhand; this will be remedied later. But the refrigerator is a symbol of the larder that one takes pleasure in seeing full and, like food in the budget, it takes first place. Moreover, all the project families own one. It generally comes before improved cooking appliances, if the old portable stove can still last.

A television set appears as soon as places to sleep and eat are assured. The greater number owned a television set before moving to the project, and a few are on their third set. When the sets disappear in repossession, they spring up again almost immediately. There are as many television sets as refrigerators. Television has a symbolic power, for not only is it the link with the outside world and a source of amusement but, by giving its owner the title of television viewer, it makes him the equal of every other viewer of any other social class. It is unthinkable not to have a television set at La Halle.

People think they have successfully accomplished furnishing their home when they have beds, a refrigerator, a television set, and a dining set. Much later comes the washing machine, which has no symbolic value but only a practical one; it may add to prestige, but in a minor way. All desire a bedroom set, but it is an element in personal satisfaction rather than

Table 9
Purchases Made, Desired, and Planned (in order of importance)

B	D	E	F	G	H
		Purchases: First Necessity			
Vacuum cleaner	Children's beds	Sewing machine	Beds	Beds	Kitchen furnishings
Refrigerator	Dining set	Beds	Dining set	Table and chairs	Range
Children's beds	Four-burner stove	Gas range	Kitchen furnishings	Refrigerator (third)	Dining set
Television	Kitchen furnishings	Dining set	Water heater	Television (second)	Refrigerator (second)
Motorbike	Refrigerator	Refrigerator	Refrigerator	Radio (gift)	Television
Dining set	Television	Kitchen furnishings	Two-channel television*	Washing machine (third)	Two trundle beds
Bedroom set		Two-channel television*	Gas range		Washing machine
Gas range			Washing machine		Car (third)
Washing machine					
		Purchases: Second Necessity			
Sewing machine	Washing machine	Washing machine			
Couch	Dresser	Couch			
Armchair	Bedroom set	Arm chairs			
"Deluxe" radio					

Desires and Plans

Car	New water heater	Bedroom set	New refrigerator	New refrigerator	Bedroom set
Carpeting	Mirrored medicine chest	Household linens	New dining set	Two beds for oldest children	New car
Bedroom curtains	Linens	New washing machine	Curtains	Dining set	Apartment in city
Wallpaper for dining room	Pictures	New curtains	Fine linens	Secondhand car	
	Carpeting	Car	Car		
	Vacuum cleaner		To buy flowers very often		
	Chandeliers				
	House plants				
	Car				

*Older television sets were equipped to receive only one channel.—R.S.

prestige because the bedroom is not a room one exhibits. At La Halle, in fact, one outfits his house as much for others as for himself.

When they think they have acquired the essentials, the residents contemplate buying what they call luxuries, and from that moment their own personality emerges. That is why the second part of the table is more differentiated. It is interesting to note that radio appears as a luxury; in general, everyone has a small transistor set that is not mentioned and is considered negligible.

The vacuum cleaner is solely an instrument of prestige for the housewife, since the tiled floor is quickly cleaned with a damp rag, and no one has carpets except a few Jews.

The longing to own a car keeps watch deep in everyone. It seems rather like the last stage, the height of power, the symbol of those who have "arrived": "When you have everything and a car too, then you can finally stop and live."

For people who have just a very small amount of linens that are washed too often and always worn, these are a luxury and appear far at the end of their yearnings. They buy the "trousseaux" offered to them by textile salesmen. Batches of sheets, cloths, napkins, and blankets of inferior quality are set at the feet of the housewife, who lets herself be tempted.

The people of La Halle are the object of considerable soliciting by canvassers and door-to-door salesmen for whom they are easy prey. Stores are far away, temptation at home is constant, and example is contagious. At holiday time at year's end, each apartment is visited each day by three or four salesmen. During the rest of the year, the project is visited two to three times a week by various salesmen.

The residents are offered all the furniture an apartment can hold, bedding, every electrical appliance, watches and all the jewelry likely to tempt them, cases of bottled wines, carpets, knickknacks, pictures, doilies, and toilet soap. One woman admits she bought a vacuum cleaner because she had her "hand forced by the salesman." The only ones who never come by are the agents of the publishing houses. Only once a "sort of medical dictionary" was offered to Mrs. F., who paid a deposit but never received anything.

The residents are also the victims of swindling by water-heater repairmen who take away the apparatus and do not come back or disappear with the deposits demanded for the next day's repair work.

Not a day passes without the mailboxes being filled with advertising handbills and applications for loans and credit, all ready to be returned to the sender.

There seems to have been a slackening in the infatuation with buying from door-to-door salesmen: "The handkerchiefs and sheets come apart in shreds in the first washing." The residents have gradually learned to be on their guard, but they still remain credulous. If an unlicensed street hawker comes some Saturday and spreads all the linens in his van on the ground, men and women are seen to run up in large numbers and applaud his spiel with joy. They hesitate a moment. The Moslems, who believe in gifts and are tradition-ally accustomed to the game of bargaining, make up their minds first. The others imitate them, carrying off merchandise of the lowest quality for 200F paid in cash, thus imperiling every other project or simply the balance of the weekly budget.

One might think that as their needs are gradually satisfied their purchases would decrease. Nothing of the sort, first because their desires grow more rapidly than their disposable income, then because advertising and fashion make them change their desires, and finally because of a very important factor that must be taken into account, namely, wear and tear.

We have seen that the list of projects for each sample case contains several headings. Illustrated advertising of furniture has made La Halle aware of the comfort of couches and armchairs previously absent; we are now seeing the kind of furniture that goes in the living room carried into the first heading, and it will soon become as urgent to have this as a dining set.

Wear occurs extremely fast in the project. It has two sources: insufficient purchasing power and ignorance. Having too little money to spend, the people buy the cheapest articles, which quickly wear out. This is particularly true of furniture, linens, and bedding. On the other hand, electrical household appliances, which are of nearly equal quality and thus do not entail that danger, are worn out by ignorance of the mechanisms. If G. has to buy another refrigerator, it is because his wife defrosted the freezer with a hammer. More than one housewife is still a bit afraid of the washing machine mechanism, which the children put out of order by playing with the buttons. One woman who had bought one resold it because she "couldn't get used to it," and another admits that "although [she had] a machine, [she] can't keep from washing by hand." It should be noted that very few of the housewives have a pressure cooker. Certainly, if one considers that it is designed for busy women, those in the project hardly need it, but they say above all that they are "afraid of it because it explodes."

Thus, instead of becoming able to buy what they consider luxuries, the project people on the whole must renew the primary necessities several times.

The place of purchase depends essentially on the means of payment. We have seen that it is rarely possible to buy food on credit, so it is bought for cash at the supermarket, the open market, the Prisunic*, and a few stores in the town. But all other purchases are made on credit and regulated by installment contracts, including clothing (except hosiery). Each one strives, therefore, to find tradesmen who allow him easy terms and "give him a good price," and he is often forced to remain faithful to them because "I have an account over there" or "they have a file in our name there."

These regular, favorite stores are generally located outside the town in the adjacent, better patronized suburbs or in the city. Table 10 shows the spread of acquisitions over the six cases already observed.

Distant stores are found by chance during a drive or other outings, while those in the city are restricted to certain neighborhoods. No one goes to the finer department stores, and only one cheaper one receives some patronage. People do not seem to return to their old neighborhoods in the city for their shopping. Many of them have no favorite stores and change with each purchase. One merchant in the town has

*Prisunic and Monoprix are chain stores selling groceries, clothing, household goods, etc.—R.S.

had all the Arab customers for a long time because he lets
them bargain by allowing several successive price reductions
on the same article; when B. realized that this merchant raised
the prices before bargaining, he informed his compatriots who
withdrew their business.

Payments are most often made in cash and in person. Money
orders are rarely sent; they require the effort of going to the
post office and filling out the form. Although the rent can
be sent directly to the collector, it is left at the caretaker's
with a tip.

Defenses against Financial Limitations

Although they seem to enjoy some degree of comfort, the
people of La Halle live amid perpetual privations. They travel
little, they do not "go out," and they do not go to shows because
"you have to dress up and go to the hairdresser to go out."
They desire "luxuries" that they cannot acquire, or simply
want to buy fresh flowers. If they earned more, they would
spend more on food because they would like "to invite and
be invited by friends, to make holiday meals more often,"
which they cannot indulge in now. They are in the midst
of a rich consumer's society and are subjected to the solicita-
tions of the market, and they feel a severe sense of deprivation.
Exacerbated by the emulation born of proximity in a
closed-off environment, their needs grow and always exceed
their available funds. They buy and spend as much as possible.
Their whole will is strained toward the maximum in acquisition, and their imagination toward the means of acquisition.

If the tradesmen abuse their ignorance and good faith, they
take revenge by acting like tough customers. When television
sets were furnished with coinboxes and ran for an hour for
1F, clever boys used to alter the controls and the machine
would run endlessly. When the salesman came to collect the
money, he found the door shut; finally, tired of the silent
neighbors' ironic glances, he stopped coming and abandoned
the machine to its triumphant owners.

Those who know with certainty that they will not be able
to pay nevertheless let the salesman leave the item he is selling.

Table 10
Favorite Places of Purchase

	B	D	E
Hosiery Shoes (1 pair) Cheap clothing Accessories	Prisunic Store in town Sales	Prisunic	Prisunic Homemade Material recovered from garbage cans
Shoes (in large number) Major clothing (suits, coats) Good clothing	Regular stores on street of cheap shops in city (credit)	Wholesale odd-lot store	Regular store in town (credit) Homemade
Children's outfits at beginning of each season		Municipal pawnshop Salvation Army	
Furniture Bedding	Town Annual fair Door-to-door salesmen	Wholesale odd-lot store	City (unspecified)
Household appliances	Town Door-to-door salesmen	Fellow workers	No regular store
Radio, television	Town or city	Fellow workers	Door-to-door salesmen (credit)
Household linens ("trousseaux")	Door-to-door salesmen (credit)	Door-to-door salesmen (credit)	Door-to-door salesmen (credit)

	F	G	H
Hosiery Shoes (1 pair) Cheap clothing Accessories	Prisunic	Prisunic Flea market Parish (charity)	Prisunic Store in town
Shoes (in large number) Major clothing (suits, coats) Good clothing Children's outfits at beginning of each season	Neighborhood of street vendors and surplus stores in city (credit)	Neighborhood of surplus stores in city (credit) Semeuse vouchers* Gifts of the parish Salvation Army	Town Big bazaar and street of cheap shops in city (credit)
Furniture Bedding	Neighboring commune City (street of furniture stores)	Municipal pawnshop	Regular store in distant suburb (credit)
Household appliances	Door-to-door salesmen	Regular store in city (credit)	Regular store in city (credit)
Radio, television	Door-to-door salesmen	Regular store	Regular store
Household linens ("trousseaux")	Door-to-door salesmen	Door-to-door salesmen	Door-to-door salesmen

*Credit coupons purchased for a fraction of their worth, used as cash and repaid with interest.—R.S.

Then they announce later that they are insolvent and call for someone to come and take back the item, which they have enjoyed "gratis" for two or three months. In fact, some salesmen only require a deposit at the time of purchase. Besides, "there's too much injustice in this world; it can't be wrong to take a little money from those who have too much," says one woman.

The development of the food business adjacent to the project is evidence of this concept. The first store went bankrupt because of the incredible number of thefts and the competition of the supermarket when it opened. The supermarket has just changed management and has been slightly modified for some time. It is better patronized, decorated, and lighted, but the supervisory personnel have been reinforced. The police were present when the store opened, children were no longer allowed to come alone, and the shopping baskets were searched at the exit. Here is what the women thought of it:

> In the old days we all stole—very little—but to steal a can of crabmeat or paté you had to shop and pay for the other merchandise. If you can't steal any more, we'll all go to the Prisunic, and too bad about the two kilometers. They think they're so smart? They'll go bankrupt and it will serve them right; they just shouldn't have brought in the cops.

They were right; the supermarket has given in, the shopping baskets are no longer searched, and the housewives have come back. Casually and without reflection, they risk going to jail for 5F worth of canned asparagus that they give to a favorite neighbor who does not dare to steal.

To the question, "What is your estimate of the percentage of people who steal?" eight out of fifteen answered 50 percent, four 60 percent, and three 90 percent. Thefts occur outside the project, but also inside it: "The basement, it's a pity, you can't put anything there. Motorbike wheels are taken off, tools disappear. I had plugged in an electric circuit that gave a shock to anyone who touched the padlock, but the caretaker made me take it off."

But there are other, less onerous means of acquisition. Flea markets are very common. The Arabs prefer the one at the west entrance to the city; the others tend to go to the north and east entrances. It is there that they buy old secondhand cars and spare parts so they can make one that runs out of three old junks, but it is sometimes difficult to obtain a license for it. There they also buy all sorts of odd objects and secondhand clothes that are resold if need be. The municipal pawnshop is also a place of great resort; they buy clothes and furniture there for moderate sums.

Scavenging is a highly prized means of acquiring objects or supplementary income. The garbage collectors are spoiled: they find much in very good condition in the garbage from rich houses. All the E.'s curtains and bedspreads come from garbage cans, and B. once brought home a pile of plates from this source. The project garbage cans are also examined, even by the caretaker. And when a man finds himself suddenly out of work, he goes to the dump and gathers bottles and nonferrous metals, piles them up in the basement, and then resells them. We know there is an underground circuit of secondhand buying and selling that has ramifications on the outside, but our informants are silent on that subject.

The amount of trading solely within the project is very hard to estimate because the informants are reluctant to admit that they have bought "something that comes from someone else in the project." One woman said, "It's better to give it away, because there's no way to get paid." Yet we know that secondhand sales take place from one apartment to another, but the deals go on between close friends and by word of mouth. Only baby buggies are advertised in notices at the caretaker's; just that which comes from children is not degrading. As a rule, they would rather buy from the flea market than from a neighbor. On the other hand, gifts are numerous, notably children's clothing.

But these purchases are not satisfying, and one discerns a sharp, constant desire to find supplementary income. The people of La Halle "pull every string" and traffic in everything. They declare themselves in ill health, collect benefits, and get hired elsewhere. They work fraudulently if they are "on disability." They ask for aid and get free school lunches. They demand and obtain free medical assistance with which they

trade by reselling medicine at a reduced price to those for
whom it is intended. When the doctor and druggist refuse
to play this game, they change practitioners. One doctor we
questioned does not think this traffic goes on, but the people
admit it themselves. The most common traffic is in fuel oil.
The meter is put out of order, and oil is pumped from the
central tank and sold to neighbors in the Le Pas project, which
is equipped only with individual heaters. Those who find these
means repugnant are reduced to working overtime. In order
to earn 950F a month, F. leaves for work at 5:00 A.M. and
comes home at 9:00 P.M.

Finally, solidarity comes into play at the level of survival.
A couple that is too badly off borrows from neighbors and
always finds a lender who not only does not deduct interest
in advance but who knows that he runs a high risk of not
being reimbursed. The amounts vary from 5F to 500F. These
loans are made within small groups bound for some time by
friendships that disregard ethnic lines. The women help each
other and join forces, unbeknown to their husbands, when
their unsound management keeps them from "making ends
meet" that week. They also loan each other sweaters that they
often do not see again.

Gifts from one family to another are frequent but presents
(i.e., new items bought to be given away) are infinitely rarer.
A peculiarity of the women, gift-giving occurs only among
"close friends."

Conclusion

The economic mode of life of the project's adults can be defined
as a continual series of privations together with a desire for
both a balanced budget and consumer satisfaction.

The internal and external soliciting directed at them prevents them from keeping regularly to a severe budget restricted
in favor of a future that is better but too far off. They free
themselves from these heavy limitations by enjoying ostentatious or unanticipated expenditures in a budget designed solely for the short term, and they live from day to day. If a

financial catastrophe comes along, it will be borne fatalistically, and they will call on the social services. This fatalism and a certain form of magical thinking cause them never to envisage that a catastrophe could happen, and to hope unflaggingly that one day they will have enough money to answer their needs and desires. That is why they believe in luck. They pursue it by using conjuring rites when they bet on the races every Sunday, and by not going twice in succession to the same ticket window to buy tickets for the national lottery. Besides, what can happen to them? The worst would be to return to the slums from which they came, and a situation already experienced, even if painful, does not cause the same anxiety as the unknown.

Pecuniary difficulties are never viewed as a complete tragedy or rather, since tragedy is often an almost daily occurrence, it has lost its sharpness. They know how to "bear hardship," and the will to live makes them find many wiles and expedients to procure income. It matters little if the future is ruined by the expenditures of one day. Besides, what future? They are completely aware of their dead-end situation, and the future is not even considered.

If money has a quality of power for them that they express by dropping large tips in the hands of gas-station attendants and caretakers, they treat it like free men conscious of its intrinsic nonvalue. Less submissive to it than one might think, they quickly forget the lost wallet, the loan not repaid, the salesman's cheating. If the fruit of long hours of work is spent in an instant or drunk up in champagne, we might bear in mind that this is due to a will to be free of constraints.

To summarize, then, consumption is generally restricted at La Halle because of a lack of pecuniary means; it is always short-term and without plans for the future actually leading to a determined number of purchases. It engenders dissatisfaction in the residents, who try to acquire as much as possible and remedy the economic deficiency by a variety of expedients. It is interesting to note that what the project people define as luxuries would perhaps be considered necessities elsewhere. Both cause and effect, money itself is not constantly sought as such, and there is even awareness of its nonvalue. Finally, the future is not considered. It is the past as a negative situation that is to be avoided as a future. The latter remains just a continuation of the present, as survival "from day to day."

Husband–Wife Relations

We have seen that in general the husband produces part of the income and the wife manages it. This situation can engender a harmonious complementarity between man and wife or be a source of conflict. This is why, before considering the sources of conflict, we should study the division of duties between husband and wife, differentiating the special cases according to ethnic group.

Division of Duties

It seems that there is no decision taken by common agreement between husband and wife. Division is a fact. It varies according to temperament, time, and circumstances.

The ideal husband for the women of La Halle is the man who "earns a good living, hands over his pay, and doesn't run after women." The ideal wife is one who "is clean, and knows how to keep house and raise the children." These two definitions indeed correspond to a real primary division, which is most observable and which conforms to the working-class way of life in general: household and family duties fall to the wife, and the husband is responsible for bringing in the money. Going into detail beyond that only leads to a nondifferentiation of duties. The father's role in particular is not specified outside of his function as breadwinner. This is so even when his earnings are in competition with the family allowances, which the wife appropriates as her own (one always hears the women say "my allowances").

Household duties, although traditionally the specialty of the women, are often too heavy for them when the babies arrive one after another. Then the husbands prepare the bottles, take the baby for walks, bathe the older children, and wash the floor and the dishes. In most cases the spouses complement each other as best they can, each using his own skills. It is not always on his wife's orders that the husband spends time on household tasks, but rather on his own initiative and because he likes them: "About that I can't complain; he makes the beds, does the dishes and doesn't think anything of sweeping up. If I could earn as much as he does working out, he'd be glad to stay and do the whole house; he's a homebody."

Although the men often volunteer for the mechanized tasks and like to do the cooking and shopping, they must often carry out their wives' orders in the domestic area, and those who are reluctant to do so are publicly accused of shirking. They justify themselves by arguing that they take on the heavy jobs or that they put in a lot of overtime, but none of them retorts that it is not a man's job.

Conversely, odd jobs are not reserved for the man. It is common to see the wife repainting or recarpeting the apartment, because she likes to or because she takes the initiative on these jobs or has not been able to get her husband to do them.

Only the Mediterranean men usually are waited on and do not help in the house. The wife assumes all the household duties among the Pied-Noirs and Jews, and once the husband is seated at the table, he never gets up. Among the Moslems, a tendency toward nondifferentiation of duties is developing if one judges by Houria's complaint about her father: "He won't do anything in the house, yet here almost all the Arabs do their best to help their wives."

Official procedures, even those concerning adult offspring, devolve upon the wife as a rule, except in case of her obvious incapacity or among the traditional Moslems. In general, the men would rather explain at length how to proceed than do it themselves, and in exchange they may take on the dishes during the wife's absence.

The husband would like to be freed of all obligations by the act of laying down his pay at the end of the week. He is still willing to sweep and carry the shopping basket but

he declines all responsibility, especially concerning the upbringing of the children, an area in which he is hardly
privileged as an instructor. Although he exercises his authority
and issues sanctions, he is inclined to shift onto his wife every
decision that has to be made, even though he may openly
criticize her later.

Each of them chooses a different disciplinary system, and
this disharmony, which makes any discipline of the child
impossible, is a perpetual source of conflict. Among the Jews
and Arabs, it is most often the mother who tries to transmit
a crumbling tradition from which the men are the first to escape.
The training of the children, which has become difficult in
the midst of an alien society, provokes arguments between
the parents who cannot agree on what should be allowed.

Sources of Conflict

We have already spoken at length about the spectacular, noisy
forms arguments can take, and we shall not return to them.
Occurring especially after drinking, they are only the exacerbated expression of a latent aggressiveness that broods continually within the family since it is not expressed outwardly among
people for whom independence is impossible.

The causes of unhappiness and family discord are many.
We shall analyze here only the most visible, which are also
the most superficial; their deep roots go back in the history
of the individuals and are nourished by frustrations they have
suffered and still suffer. The economic and social structure,
which crushes the project people and prevents them from actually surmounting difficulties, must be kept in mind.

Lack of money, insufficient wages, the constant waiting for
the arrival of fragmented subsidies—these constitute some of
the principal reasons for quarreling. There is no conflict concerning possessions since there is no inheritance, and in the
best of cases the couple had only a little bedding at the beginning of their union.

If the husband's wages are insufficient, the wife breaks out
in complaints: "You should just get a new boss; you don't

know how to manage," or "What am I supposed to do with the pay he brings me?" The oldest son's wages, often equivalent to the father's, stir up discord and aggravate the concealed contempt surrounding the head of a family incapable of providing it with a comfortable life.

The women's complaints about the men's pocket money are frequently heard. Although mothers consider it normal for their sons to demand money for their diversions, they implicitly reject their husband's right to draw on the common funds for his solitary amusements. "You can't blame him. He's sober and all. But he can't keep from having a snack at the bar every morning instead of taking a piece of bread from the house. That's 3F a day, for nothing." "He earns good money; that's why I forgive him for not doing anything in the house. But Mister Big-Shot takes 10F in pocket money every day to pay for his pals at the bar. Don't you think that's overdoing it?"

If a man is much too intemperate, his wife does not hesitate to threaten intervening with the boss and "having his pay stopped." Usually the threat is enough, for this line of action is equivalent to cutting off part of the man's virility. Those who show reluctance to turn over their whole pay are vehemently criticized at regular intervals.

Not turning over wages provokes lasting conflict in the mixed households. The Moslems are used to managing the budget themselves and turn over just small daily or weekly supplies to their wives, who are considerably frustrated by this procedure: "The men who don't turn over their pay—don't even talk to me about them." As they grow old, the men end by yielding to this custom of French households, though not without difficulty.

The second great theme of the arguments is the discipline of the children. A punishment coming from the father is never respected by the wife who spoils the child when his back is turned. This is due to the fact that the man generally interferes only when the children have done something foolish; then the wife thinks the punishment is too strong and the argument breaks out in front of the children: "You didn't have

to hit him; you're just a bully." The wife who has assumed
responsibility for the children does not like the man to meddle
in distributing sanctions unless she asks him. Conversely,
when the children grow up and escape her authority, she asks
for the father's help but he has his revenge by taking care
not to interfere: "If your kids are hoodlums, it's your fault;
you didn't know how to raise them; now you can shift for
yourself with them." This lack of division of responsibilities
creates a constant climate of discord.

One might think that the arguments are settled sexually,
but refusing the conjugal duty is the women's secret
weapon: "When we've had an argument, I don't speak to him
for three days. He can even come and coax me in bed, but
nothing doing. With men, that's the only thing that keeps them
in line." That weapon cuts both ways in La Halle. It is easy
to revenge a refusal: a man has only to run openly after a
neighbor to launch an outburst of rage from his wife.

In regard to adultery, pretended or real, blackmail is used
between spouses. The men are rarely complaisant, and more
than one woman takes a beating on a simple suspicion. The
children witness these arguments as well as the others: "Tell
the lady that there's a gentleman who comes when I'm not
there; tell the lady that your mother is a slut," says a father
to a five-year-old child. Therefore, the wife must be sure of
herself to refuse her husband "his pleasure."

If discord about raising the children festers and breaks out
in shouting, the violence usually remains verbal. But if conjugal love is at stake, aggressiveness is expressed in actions.
The man strikes heedlessly, first with his bare hands, then
with various blunt or cutting instruments when the wife rebels
and feeds the argument with insults and deadly remarks: "We
were getting along, but he hit me three days ago; now it's
over, and I know he'll make a fresh start." "He often hits
me, especially, I think, because he's afraid I'll go away."

Spouses are often afraid of each other. The wife is afraid
she will not be able to fend off or return the blows fast enough.
Thus one woman would rather sleep in the basement farthest
from her home than share her husband's bed the nights when

he is angry. But the men dread the unexpected reactions of their wives, who may suddenly disappear some night, leaving all the children. When they reappear two days later as though nothing had happened, the husbands are so relieved that they "start with a clean slate" and life starts all over, inaugurating a period of peace. The peaceful time may last so long between some of them that it fools the observer who listens, astonished, as the extent of a quarrel increases in the "quiet stairwell" that had not been the scene of any dispute for six months.

Another, but infinitely milder, source of discord is furnished by the superiority of one over the other, conferred by level of education. Actually, the lack of education of one partner is usually a subject for joking, which can obviously degenerate into an argument. However, tension arising from the wife's superiority in literacy is particularly noticeable in the mixed households. The man suffers from the difficulty of expressing himself and his powerlessness to communicate in writing. The wife, who otherwise bows before the authority of her husband, does not miss a chance to make him suffer for his inferiority in front of witnesses. "Luckily, I'm here; if he was alone, poor man, . . . " or, with somewhat perfidious intent, "He doesn't do too bad for someone who can't read or write, huh?" This advantage of the literate over the unlettered plays the part of detonator when the conjugal atmosphere is charged with electricity.

Leisure Activities

Leisure activities are never evoked as motives for discord, even if the wife complains that the husband does not like to go out. There are three reasons for this, in our opinion: La Halle's residents play practically no games; leisure activities in the generally accepted sense of the term are rare; and they are pursued, not separately, but by the two members of the couple together.

In fact, one never sees people playing boule* in the courtyard

*A kind of lawn billiards or bowling.—R.S.

although the terrain is suitable for it, and cards are not very popular either.[6] Even the Arabs do not play any more. This is because neither the town nor the project, unlike certain old streets in their former suburbs, has the familiar setting of the Moorish café to offer them. Stripped of the context in which they were developed, the games have practically been abandoned. The rarity of games thus prevents any dispute that might arise from one of the spouses prohibiting the other from joining a group of players.

This absence of games can be interpreted in two ways. The residents may be too desocialized, too deracinated and bereft of traditions to recreate leisure activities in the form of collective games. Or perhaps play forms an integral part of a life and daily actions not taken seriously, so that it is not necessary to divide time in two and label one part worktime and one playtime. Or it may be both simultaneously.

The project people complain about the lack of leisure activities, but first this term must be defined in relation to them. For them, leisure activities mean leaving the project, going somewhere and, preferably, paying to be entertained. In other words, it is going for an outing or to a show. Amusements at home among friends do not enter into this definition but are included in the notion of celebrations.

To what kind of show can they hope to go? They do not go to the theater, opera, or concerts, they do not frequent the music halls or supper clubs, and they know nothing of museums and art galleries. There remain the movies and the traveling fair. Some women admit that they would like to see an operetta, and some young women would be happy to go to a dance, but they consider these wishes unrealizable. The men would rather attend an international athletic match, "but since we see it on TV ..."

Where do they really go? Not even to the movies, because the one theater in the town offers little of interest, and nocturnal outings to the city require leaving the children alone and coming home late in a taxi. On the other hand, all the project couples visit the annual fair at least once during its stay, some as many as seven or eight times. They are attracted by the shooting galleries, lotteries, and candy stands more than the rides. The women, as well as the men, like to try the games of skill.

In addition to popular entertainments, "taking a ride in the car" is a leisure activity, as well as walks and picnics, which all love. Those who own a car are privileged. In winter they stop at a country "tavern". Some make do with bicycles and pedal along the river until they find a spot to stop. A very few go on an exceptional outing by spending the afternoon in a bowling alley, for instance. Those going out on foot take a walk on the city boulevards, and this walk, intended during the week for doing some shopping, is highly prized: "Our only pleasure is to go for a walk in the city, both of us, while the children are in school."

Leisure activities are pursued in pairs, as a couple. The children are not altogether included in this notion; if they can be dispensed with, there is true relaxation. Therefore, those who are too loaded down with children never go out while those whose children are grown regain the freedom for diversions reserved for husband and wife, alone or in company with another couple.

For instance, two men may decide to "go up to the Café de la Paix to play pool"; they are followed by their wives who knit or gossip while watching the players. Even fishing is not necessarily just a man's amusement: "If he leaves at 5:00 in the morning, I don't go, but if he goes fishing Saturday afternoon, I go with him. I sleep on the grass or read till we go home."

Betting on the races, which is considered not as a game but as a persistent obligation to try one's luck, is an undertaking of the couple, indeed, of the family. Although the men visit the betting parlor alone, the wives have helped choose the horses and often make up their own list.

Vacations are considered the supreme leisure activity, but for many they remain a dream. It is estimated that 15 percent to 18 percent of the couples, or twenty-seven to thirty families, go on vacation. They are always the same ones: those who have sufficient economic means or relatives "back home" in the country to take them in. Four or five families go camping. Hardly any family can indulge in renting a cottage near a beach or even in the country. The unprivileged never vacation.

Because they are exceptional, leisure activities are linked with the notion of festivity, as expressed by one woman ("For me, the biggest celebration is to go away on vacation") who actually materializes this superimposition of the two ideas by giving a farewell dinner for her friends the day before departure. (The notion of celebration will be dealt with in the last chapter.)

There can be no dispute about leisure activities between the husbands and wives of the project, on the one hand because of their rarity due to financial limitations, and on the other because it is easy for the couples to agree on amusements. In case tastes are not similar, this is an area in which there are mutual concessions because leisure activities are always pursued together. Even the Moslems, who like to go out alone, conform to the local fashion by going on outings with their wives, especially if they have a car to protect conjugal privacy. As to the Jewish couples, their leisure activities are associated with religious holidays, which are spent with the family.

It might be thought that conjugal relations are continually marked by the quarrels we have discussed, except during recreation. Financial difficulties, multiple infidelities, and uncertain methods of child-rearing give birth to conflicts whose real extent is sometimes exaggerated by the violence of their expression. But in fact, despite these sources of conflict, life is gradually stabilized between compromise and submission between a man who works for the family group and a wife overwhelmed by responsibilities who both begs and rejects her husband's help.

To summarize, the division of duties in La Halle is not really different from the rest of society, but we must note the very important magnification of the wife's responsibilities due to modest income and material difficulties and perhaps a man's role that is more unobtrusive than elsewhere. The sources of conflict are also not specific to the project. They are polarized around child-rearing and adultery, but the arguments about money seem more violent because of the scarcity of pecuniary resources. It is these violent arguments that we must study. Perhaps they take different forms than elsewhere because of the shortage of money and the impossibility of really envisaging a future.

This chapter on family life is organized around the budget and relations between husband and wife. This connection becomes meaningful if one considers that conjugal life is conditioned by family economic life, with its particular modalities all centered on the problem of income and material survival. The close phases of conjugal relations are those of a mutual tolerance, and the aloof phases seem very marked. Mixed or ambivalent relations appear only toward the end of life after reciprocal compromises and submissions. Perhaps a hypothesis could be constructed on the importance of the conditions of life in the structuring of these relations. In many households, for instance, the problem of whether the man's wages are turned over to the wife or whether he is denied pocket money provokes apparently regular (often weekly) periods of tension shown outwardly in aloof relations. On the other hand, the couple's common preferences in leisure activities and financial restrictions on amusements are experienced in the close mode.

The development of this hypothesis would lead to the question whether close, aloof, and mixed relations are not of a different type than those of other social classes, since the economic conditioning is not the same. In the households in more favored classes, would there not be a predominance of mixed or ambivalent relations linked more to difficulties of a psychological or moral order than to poor material conditions? In the project, compromises are made from day to day through the temporary adjustment of practically insoluble financial difficulties, and ambivalent relations do not occur continuously until old age, when the problem of survival is posed less sharply.

NOTES

[1] The residents of the project are for the most part completely exempt from taxes, paying only the furniture tax, which varies from 120F to 150F. The furniture tax is paid yearly by the person who occupies or has furniture in a house or apartment, whether he is the owner or tenant, based on the rental value of the residence and the size of his family.—R.S.

[2] Their cat is insured by the Animal Protective Association.

[3] Saint-Georges is the Jewish section of the city.

[4] Even with Social Security, the shortage in earnings is enough to unbalance the budget.

[5] A semipublic organization. The tutor receives the total family allowances, with which he pays off the debts.

[6] Still, some women play a game of belote [a card game] or petits chevaux [a table game] in the afternoon.

8

Children and Adolescents

Child-rearing

The number of children in the project varies around 750. Living proof of their parents' different cultural backgrounds, these children all play together in the courtyard. Are they brought up differently from each other? We shall look at how they are raised as babies and then as they grow up, and at what their relations are with the family, the school, and the outside world, and we shall try to understand what becomes of them as they go through adolescence. But before doing this, we should take up the problems relative to birth by returning briefly to the adult world.

Birth

One may wonder if there is any birth control at La Halle, if a certain number of children is commonly desired, or if people rather let nature take its course. Everyone thinks it is normal for a couple to have children. All the same, it should be noted that the young men living in concubinage with older women do not seem to want any. Among residents, three or four children seems to be an optimum number, but this figure is most often given by mothers of large families who admit that they did not pose the question beforehand. "If I had known, I wouldn't have had any," they say. The young people would like to have small families in order to "get the most out of life." But no one considers the only child desirable because "you have nothing left if you lose it."

Actually, children are born without really being wanted. This is true even of the first child, who is conceived immediately after marriage if not before. Sometimes the natural children may even attend their mother's wedding. These questions are approached without any shame, and the child is not made to bear "its mother's blame" as in other milieus. It is not dishonorable to be recognized after marriage.

The number of children per household is proportional to the persistence of traditions in the family and to its economic underdevelopment. In addition, it is a function of almost absolute ignorance of anatomy and physiology among men as well as women. In fact, simple observation shows that the greatest number of children is found among the Moslems, Jews, and the poorest metropolitans.

The Moslems are traditionally happy to have many children, and the submissive women accept each new pregnancy without complaint. The wives in mixed households complain more of their husband's selfishness in this repect. Ignorance of the physiological functioning of the sexes is carried to its height among the Moslems. One woman claims that her husband is still ignorant of the relationship between cause and effect after having seven children. This is corroborated by the confession of another Moslem: "If I'd known that you could not have children, I wouldn't have had so many, but I thought it was my wife's fault because they all have a lot in her family. It was a doctor who explained that it came from me."

Even if they know what causes pregnancy, the metropolitans are scarcely less ignorant and are happy to throw responsibility for pregnancy on the women. According to the wives, the men "don't want to take any precautions." If necessary, some of them use contraceptives that can be seen in the morning where they were tossed from the windows, and on the whole, no other contraceptive method is tried. Some women do not even know they have to douche, and they are incapable of telling the length and rhythm of their menstrual cycle.

Children are the normal price of the sex act. But if the metropolitan women do not hold it against the children for having been born by chance of different fathers, they unconsciously make them bear the responsibility for their painful delivery. In almost all the metropolitan families we know, one of the children is loved less—the one who made his mother suffer most. One hears this kind of reflection voiced in front of the child: "What I went through for that stinker—the forceps, oxygen, the works. I nearly croaked because of him." One woman prefers her second son "because he's the only one who came out like a letter in a mailbox."

For the exhausted women haunted by the idea of a new pregnancy, two means are left: abortion and ovariotomy. The Moslem and Jewish women wait for their "wombs to stop all by themselves" or for the doctor to decide to tie up their tubes. Among the other women, the possibility of an abortion, as well as comparison of different abortion techniques, is approached very simply in conversation. This does not mean that all the women abort themselves or that there is an abortionist in the project, but a certain amount of mutual aid among the women certainly comes into play in small subgroups in this connection. Some prefer the possibility of a fatal accident to a new baby, and once they have successfully aborted they will do it again, using their imaginations to find the instruments. So it is that they substitute an aquarium air tube for the probe no longer carried by the drugstore. Others praise the success of "ivy tails." They attend to their usual occupations for a week until the ivy stem, worn continually, sets off a hemorrhage. They decide for themselves whether they have to go to the hospital for a curettage. One of them has already gone through this procedure eight times, another six times. Aborting drugs are sneaked out by those who work in pharmaceutical packaging and are swallowed indiscriminately and without medical supervision, but mechanical means are generally preferred.

The greatest liberation comes from surgery. The women who have had a "complete" (hysterectomy) like to tell everyone that they "aren't afraid of anything any more." Those women who have had their tubes tied off must continually have "the knot" felt through the stomach wall, and the doctors are often begged to do this.

Pregnancy is generally declared in time, and its progress is followed by the clinic. The woman's life scarcely changes during pregnancy. She attends to her occupations without paying any attention to her fatigue or the approaching birth. The women do not follow any special diet or pay any attention to "cravings" for food, which they simply satisfy if the occasion arises. We have not discovered any rites or superstitions concerning the presumed sex of the unborn child.

Those women who are not covered by Social Security hide their early pregnancy and take any kind of job in order to "get the Security opened" and be entitled to benefits and prenatal leave.

Except among the "richest" people, no one prepares a layette any more than the Moslems, who think it brings bad luck (though this belief is beginning to disappear). In fact, mothers count on help in kind from the municipality and possible gifts, and they can always complete the baby's layette later with the addition at birth to the allocation. Let us remember that children's clothes are given away and not sold in the project.

All the project women give birth at the hospital. There are two reasons for this: they prefer to avoid the material difficulties of delivery at home, and it is impossible to find a midwife or doctor who will attend them. The mother's absence, however, poses the problem of what to do with the other children. Generally they are left with Public Assistance while the mother is hospitalized, and the father picks them up when she returns. This is why she is reluctant to stay the normal length of time (five days or more) and goes home at the end of the third or fourth day. Sometimes, some women refuse to leave their older children with Public Assistance; they are driven to the hospital at the last minute by the husband, and stay there just twenty-four hours. But these are exceptional cases.

After the birth of the first child, the men become indifferent rather quickly on the whole. They are never present at the delivery and do not feel part of it. The Moslems in mixed households do not give the help their wives expect since they are used to the delivery being exclusively the women's affair. On the other hand, the Moslems in traditional households replace the missing communal support by accompanying their wife to the hospital and watching effectively over the home.

The project women are generally attentive to every new birth, and neighbors and friends visit each mother at the hospital.

Care of the Infant

It is quite striking to see that project babies are raised almost in the same manner, whatever their ethnic background.

Swaddling is hardly continued any more by the Arab women, who wrap the arms and shoulders of the newborn with a scarf. They stretch their legs out together and lay the child on them in order to diaper it, not neglecting to fasten the little gold fish or the bit of coral on the swaddling for protection. But all the babies have their limbs freed very quickly.

The Arab and Jewish babies are held much longer and more often, rocking to sleep on their mother's bosom as she walks slowly up and down the apartment. If they continue crying, they are passed from hand to hand until someone manages to calm them. Even five- or six-year-old brothers and sisters are scolded if they do lift the crying infant quickly enough. The archaic custom of masturbating the baby has been observed in two Jewish families; the babies were female and the older little girls were given that task. No question was raised about it.

The metropolitans keep a sharp guard against rocking the children ("No coddling, it spoils them"), and we have not often noticed pacifiers being used. However, "you can't let him cry, that makes his father mad," and this is where differences between groups disappear because the best means of preventing babies from crying is to give them the bottle.

Babies in all the project families are fed when they cry. When asked, "Do you set feedings every three hours?" the metropolitans answered, "No, I give him a drink whenever he's hungry," thus going along with North African customs. According to two doctors we interviewed, the babies are overfed and grow very well.

Breast feeding is little used on the whole. The Arab women breast feed the first children for a few months, then bottle feed the later ones. The metropolitans frequently nurse the two oldest. They say, "It gives them a better start," but one of the doctors advises them against it in order, he says, "to protect the children from alcoholism and not to deform the young women's bosoms."

The children are sometimes fed cooked cereal starting at one month and at three months they eat pureed food from a spoon or are introduced to chopped raw horsemeat. The amount of condensed milk put in the bottle is often whimsical, and some women say they do not trust the measures marked on the glass. Despite early weaning, a bottle is given at night until eighteen months to two years.

Toilet training is done early, according to the women. In reality, they actually present the pot to the child at six months but they are incapable of sticking to a strict schedule and continue washing diapers for a long time. There is no strict rule about it.

The infants are healthy except for rare cases of rickets, their progress is followed relatively closely on the medical level, and they are vaccinated regularly. The PMI sees about twenty children up to two years old every two weeks. The nurses estimate that more than half their clientele is Arab. Moreover, they find that the Arab mothers pay attention to the advice they receive and follow it as best they can. In contrast, the metropolitans come irregularly and must often be summoned by letter. The French women are reluctant to come to the clinic ("There's a line; you have to wait with everybody") and prefer to take the baby to their regular practitioner. They reject the obligation to come regularly for consultation as they do other constraints. Weighings are irregular ("You can see for yourself if the child is growing").

The women take fright quickly if the baby is sick. They do not call the doctor but prefer to take the child to the hospital. They admit being "afraid of not knowing how to take care of him," and they would rather "they keep him till he's over it."

The child crawls on the floor on hands and knees for a long time before learning to walk. He usually has no playpen and hangs onto chairs. He is allowed to crawl at leisure and when he can walk steadily, he is permitted to go in the courtyard (for which he clamors) where he joins the troop of the smallest children.

The babies go out little. They sleep in the sun in their buggies or are walked by their mothers while they are very small. When they grow bigger, they are too heavy to carry to the bus, so they most often stay at home until they are strong enough to go and play with the other children.

Baptism and Choice of Name

The word "circumcision" is always translated as "baptism" by the Jews and Arabs out of a kind of shame on their part in front of the ignorance of the ethnic majority. For economic reasons, baptism takes place in the same way in the three groups. They generally wait until they are through having children to baptize all of them, large and small, at one time or at two times in the large families, first the older children and then the young ones. This lets the Moslem father give just one celebration for his scattered relatives in honor of the occasion. Even the Jews, for whom circumcision of the male child is prescribed on the seventh day, sometimes delay until the second is born because problems of finance and distance prevent them from looking for a rabbi within the required time. Despite economic difficulties, there could not be a baptism without the traditional cones of sugared almonds.

A social hindrance is added to the financial one among the metropolitans. The child is very often baptized privately at the hospital by the priest who visits the sick, but formal baptism is put off until later for lack of godparents. In fact, most of the metropolitans are so solitary and so bereft of family that they do not know anyone to ask to be godparents of their children. Godparenthood has great significance for them and they are reluctant to ask this service of just neighbors. When someone talks of a true friend he has met in the course of his life, he adds, "besides, he's the children's godfather."

The Jewish ceremony brings all the relatives together and unfolds absolutely according to the traditional rites. The Moslems, on the other hand, make do with the hospital for circumcisions, especially in mixed households. Some people are sometimes disappointed with the result after the operation [perhaps because the foreskin was not entirely removed, or grew back later]. Others go to the M—— enclave to look for a specialist whom they pay according to a certain scale.

The choice of first names, which are mostly quite common ones, follows certain fashions and influences. The traditional Moslems follow modern North African ways coming from Cairo. While the older children are named Ali or Fatima, those born later bear names like Kerim, Mondher, or Souraya. In the mixed households, it is often the French wife who chooses the first names, which are still Moslem, either from a list given to her by her husband or out of friendship for some acquaintance from a Moorish café. The Jews have abandoned the custom of giving Hebrew-sounding Christian names, such as Maurice for Moses or Albert for Abraham, and one finds only fashionable French names among the newborn, like Veronique, Isabelle, or Patrice. The metropolitans give their children the names of popular singers, like Eddy (Eddy Mitchell) or "chic" names like Hervé or Nadia. Either the father

or mother chooses the name and only rarely is the father's
or grandfather's name passed on to the child.

The Child in His Family

Parents commonly complain that it is impossible to raise the
children properly; the children become lazy, disobedient,
unbearable, dirty, and rude after moving into the project.

The children of La Halle are raised out-of-doors, almost as
a group. Their universe is made up of the project and its surroundings. They run away from any supervision, attracted by
the space in the vacant lots and the large number of playmates.
"The kids disappear in the wink of an eye as soon as you
stop watching them from the window."

On the other hand, the parents have a rather vague concept
of discipline. They are aware of the goal to be attained but
do not perceive the relationship between ends and means.
Besides, no matter how hard they try, their children's lack
of discipline is always blamed on them. Stereotypes have been
created according to which the children of La Halle are "badly
raised and uninteresting."

What then are the relations between parents and children?

1. SANCTIONS

Sanctions are the same in all families. Punishment is most
often corporal, distributed with bare hands and with the aid
of various instruments (straps, chairs, broomsticks), and preceded by shouts and insults (for example, "foul-mouthed" or
"rotten"). Punishment by the father is exceptional and is given
for a transgression whose gravity is determined by his mood
at the moment. The blows have little effect; the children are
used to them and they are not treated brutally, relatively speaking. "Our parents give us a beating if we do what we're not
supposed to; but it doesn't matter, we do it anyhow because
we'll get a beating anyway," says an eleven-year-old. The girls
are hit somewhat less, especially after age twelve.

Other punishments involve depriving the child of something. The most widespread, varying in length of time, is

"taking away TV." The most efficacious is not permitting him to go outdoors, but the parents seldom use this method because "we're the first to be punished; there's no more peace in the house," and the child who slips off adroitly is not called back. A child is never deprived of food or dessert; this is not considered "a smart punishment," and the parents claim "it's bad for the health."

Blackmail and bargaining go on continually between parent and child. All day long one hears, "If you do this, you'll get that," or "Come back home, it's late," and when the child does not move, "Come on, I'll give you a penny." The children demand a reward for every effort. For instance, they will not go on an errand if it interrupts them in their games unless their mother lets them buy a franc's worth of candy. If she offers half a franc, they refuse. If they sense resistance on the mother's part, they use blackmail to make her give in. They set their conditions authoritatively: "If you don't give me some money for my marbles, I won't do the shopping tonight." One of the rare good students put it in a more refined way: "If you don't let me play in the field until dark, I won't do anything more at school."

When resistance does not give way on either side, mother and son argue like two adults and the insults fly. "He's getting tough, I'm not the boss any more; he calls me 'slut' and 'whore,' and when I ask him to do something, he says I make him puke."

Rewards have no more effect than punishment. They are often spontaneous and do not really sanction effort. They most often consist of pieces of change. Some mothers, especially the Jewish ones, keep a constant supply of change in their apron pockets and distribute it all day long. From the age of three or four, children go by themselves to buy caramels. "Going out" is a reward granted by the father, and it is made twice as much fun by goodies because it cannot take place without being accompanied by peanuts, ice cream cones, and soft drinks. Toys are not considered a reward by either parent or child but as a due. They are given out once a year at Christmas, and during the rest of the year the children are bought "the little trinkets they need," such as marbles, jacks, and jump ropes.

Parents are willing to resort to threats, especially "putting them with Public Assistance," but they never appeal to reason to get the child to admit he was wrong.

2. FAMILY DISCIPLINE

The teaching of elementary good manners is done by the mother. The father comes home late and tired and is not interested in the rituals of "please" and "thank you." The women attach great importance to "politeness and all that." They are sincere when they talk about it, but do not know how to teach it and show themselves incapable of demanding it consistently. They rarely thank the child and never say "please" to him.

Table manners are very flexible. The children often serve themselves, and they are not always required to sit at the table. It is difficult to feed them, and the mother gives in to their whims in food. More than one would rather take a snack—a big piece of bread split and filled with tuna, meat, or cheese—and go back to play. Others eat before the adults if they are too hungry to wait. All of them eat rather clumsily, scattering the contents of the glass or spoon and helping themselves with their fingers in preference to a knife.

Bedtime is no more regulated than meals. Among the Jews and Arabs, the children go to sleep anywhere—on the living-room couch, in the mother's arms, or on the father's knee—and are carried to bed later. Most of the time the children go to bed without saying "good night." No one shows them any tenderness at bedtime, no one leans over their bed, no one tells them stories. They do not know any fables or fantastic adventure stories except the ones they see on television, and their parents are as interested as they are in these stories, discovering an unknown world in them.

There is no loving ritual, then, and no coddling during the day. They are reserved for calming tears, even if these tears are due to a justified scolding. (A big child is not left to cry any more than a small one.) That is how affection is mostly shown, usually concretized by sweets.

Washing does not escape the irregularity of the other routines except among a minority of very clean families. The water heater is often broken, and there is a lack of towels. The men seem to change underwear more regularly than the women, and it is quite often they who supervise the children's Sunday washing. The children come home from the vacant lot black with dirt and coal, they are completely free to play in water or mud, and they do not get scolded inordinately for soiling their clothes. They hardly ever wash unless ordered to do so, and the parents confine themselves to stating that such-and-such of their sons is a clean or dirty person.

The problem of enuresis arises quite often. It is resolved as follows in two well-known families. In one, the "pissers" are given a smack every morning. No disapproval is shown in the other because the mother remembers that in her child-hood she had to kneel and contemplate her wet mattress every morning.

It is the mother who directs family discipline most. The father plays a minor role but he is generally feared, especially by the Moslem children: "When the father is there, they don't move." His authority is sporadic rather than constant, and the children may reject it or get around it. Uninterested in the principles of discipline, the fathers simply require that the children be present when they are and that the children be almost silent and leave them in peace; thus comes the much-envied luck of some children whose fathers come home very late.

On the other hand, the parents are at one in laughing together over the "silliness" of the children, "who are little imps and there's no one who can play tricks like them." These include such things as bringing field mice, tiny insects, and rubbish into the bedroom, cutting the kitten in two with the bread knife, exchanging their mother's watch for a plastic toy, or bringing home a ten-franc bill and everything that sharp eyes enable them to find in the street.

The parents do not have a precise idea of the role of the older children in relation to the younger. The older children are by no means invested with the right to punish the little ones—quite the contrary—but they must watch over them during the mother's short absences. When the younger children get bigger, the older children teach them how to behave among their peers without the parents' okay, as is done everywhere else. The parents tend rather to use the little ones as spies and tale-bearers of the bigger ones' doings when the latter begin to escape their authority.

3. SEX EDUCATION

When questioned about this, the parents answer that they will give or have given the children sex education. In reality, the children do not receive any information. The parents admit they are embarrassed and do not know how to go about it. Still, they think this education is necessary and wish the school would take complete charge of it. They add that they have nothing much to teach the children anyway since the children teach each other.

Birth is not a mystery, and the girls speak freely to their mother about her pregnancy. There is more of a shadow around conception even though the children soon become aware because the adolescents practice great sexual license. Moreover, the children are not kept out of the adults' lives; they share their love problems, listen to their dirty stories, and observe their revels. They always know all about their parents' liaisons, by the latter's own admission.

The only instruction the mothers think they owe their daughters is to warn them about the possibility of a child's being born. The mothers' answers are consistent and all of a type: "As soon as the girls have their first period, you have to put them on guard against the silly things they may do; you must tell them, 'Now, that's the end of playing with boys, spreading your knees and putting your legs in the air. If you play with boys, you'll have a baby.' That's how my mother did with me." When a girl complains about her mother not letting her go out at night, the latter answers, "It's all the same to me if you go out, but I don't want you to bring back a balloon." The Moslems give exactly the same answer: "Your father will kill you if you bring back a big stomach." The fathers say they take charge of putting their boys "on guard," but certainly with less conviction. As we have already said, a baby is the price of the sex act, so sex education consists only in the interdiction of that consequence without any explanation.

This extremely simplified sex education, viewed solely from the point of view of the danger involved, is like all other education given by the project parents. It is an education composed above all of a certain number of prohibitions, which are not always fixed, and not of examples. It is thus triply limited: by this fact, by the lack of parental tradition and instruction, and by the lack of influence of any other milieu.

The Child Outside

It is commonly thought that when the child starts school, his circle of social relations will grow and he will undergo a normal enculturation. But this is not the case here. We shall see that the child's universe remains limited to the project and the games within it, that school is just an obligatory outside activity with no real link to the project in either the children's or the parents' minds, and that the scholastic results, which are poor on the whole, are both the consequence of this state of affairs and the cause of an almost general lack of ambition.

At School

Until third grade, the project children go to a school also attended by children from neighboring buildings, while students in higher grades are distributed in other schools in the commune.

According to the primary-school superintendent, the school is not suited to the people who have devolved on it. The teachers are young and inexperienced, and none of them asked to be assigned to this place; there are always two or three unfilled posts when school starts in October. There have been four principals in four years. Like the teachers, they ask to be transferred when they are assigned here, and living quarters customarily put at their disposal remain vacant.

This school does not resemble a village or neighborhood school at all; it is not implanted but stuck on. The instructors, refusing any permanent assignment here, have no influence over the people, who are quite hard to win over. In addition, some teachers more or less unconsciously conform to society's judgment of these people. Without admitting it, the school personnel secretly practice racism, contemplating unenthusiastically these heterogeneous classes on a low cultural level who are hard to teach. Although this dismissal is barely noticeable, it is forcefully perceived, exaggerated, and envenomed by the people of La Halle. It is in this context that the project children start school, undisciplined, ignorant of constraint, silence, and elementary good manners, and perfectly devoid of any knowledge.

The opposition between parents and teachers will quickly show up, but one must know what the concept of school is in order to understand it. In the project people's minds, the principal goal of the school is to teach the child to read and write. They are absolutely unaware of its disciplinary role, and at the furthest extreme one might even say they deny that it is entitled to this role. "They would do better to teach the kids how to read instead of worrying about things that are none of their business." The school is a bastion where the teachers are all-powerful, and their compulsory procedures are sometimes considered a blow to freedom: "I kept my daughter home yesterday afternoon just to buy her some shoes, and last night they already sent word. They overdo it!" The parents cannot conceive that a half-day's absence could be harmful. Regular effort is unknown to them.

The teacher has no prestige, perhaps because he does not play any role with respect to the adults of the commune. It would never occur to the project residents to seek advice from him. He is conceded only the right to teach.

Yet he must teach without being severe. The people tolerate

a child's being punished for poorly done homework, and the punishment is to consist of additional homework. But they absolutely will not stand for the child's being penalized for a lack of discipline in class or, still less, during recess.* If the teacher slaps a child for some brutality during recess, for instance, the family rebels. The child complains to the parents; they console him; and then everyone bursts out at once, making comments in front of him about the misconduct of the teacher who "has no right over him." They promise to avenge the child by "going and telling that bully what we think of him." They recall the incident with the neighbor's son that was settled by getting rid of the teacher.

There was a sizable incident following the breaking of a lunchroom window. An Italian mother went to school to take up her son's defense and, embarrassed by her difficulty in expressing herself, slapped the principal. More women invaded the principal's office; their anger made them raise their voices until they were shouting, and, after they had copiously insulted him, the principal threw them out. They meditated on their revenge and the most audacious wrote to the Minister of Education to lodge a complaint: "If they punish him once more, we're going to go up and make a stink." "And besides, they don't do a good job of teaching our kids; they're stinkers."

School is a place where you must send your children but where you also get rid of them during the day: "I won't hide from you that I send the kids to school just to get rid of them." Failing the CEP† has no importance if the children know how to read. If they have learned nothing, it is because the teachers do not like them. The parents have absolutely no confidence in the teachers, whose role is viewed as coercive only.

As a corollary, school for the child represents a place he has to go for no well-defined reason. For the reasons previously cited, and because the parents are too ignorant to judge the

---

*Recess activities are supervised by the teachers.—R.S.

†This elementary school diploma is given only to the child who is not going on to secondary school.—R.S.

child's progress, there is no communication between the school and the family. Children are left free to play outside until late at night "so we can have some peace," but the parents hit them if they get a zero on a lesson or laugh when a little girl announces triumphantly on coming home from school that she was last.[1]

The teachers are sorry that they have only strained and aggressive relations with the parents. Parents rarely come when they are summoned to a school meeting ("we have better things to do"), and in 1966 only five mothers bothered to attend the celebration at the end of the year, although this is a peaceful diversion. The teachers can practically never talk to the parents about their children's behavior or progress.

The project children do not take part in any extracurricular or after-school activities, and very few stay for after-school study period because they have to pay for it. Only one-fourth of those asked go on the winter vacation ski trip, and the influence the teachers may have during this month of living with their students is abolished upon return to the project.

Only 25 percent of the children attend summer camps, and two-thirds of these go with the "club" from the project, led by three coaches whom they know well, so they do not enlarge their circle of friends.

Thus, the absence of any bond between the school, reduced to its simplest expression, and the family is an important phenomenon at La Halle. It prevents the child, left on his own in a limited milieu, from developing anywhere but in the project, and it makes him impenetrable to the secondary milieu. What he is taught at school does not cause him to make comparisons with his own condition in life, for instance, as it does among young peasants. At La Halle, the parents' example takes precedence; the teacher is wrong and his teaching is null and void.

The best proof of this is the behavior of children from traditional Moslem homes. The illiterate Moslem parents want their children to be eligible for social advancement and they know that education is the sine qua non of that advancement; in this, they heed the propaganda spread by the three countries

of French North Africa. Their children's schooling does not
pose any special problem. If they are incapable of supervising
the children's studies, at least they come when summoned
by the principal and follow his guidance counseling.

Moslem girls are a special case. For them, much more than
for their brothers, education represents an escape from tradition, liberation from parental guardianship, and refusal of an
imposed marriage. Moslem girls try to pursue their studies
as long as possible despite difficulties.

The scholastic results are mediocre, and it can be said that
the children as a whole hardly ever go beyond the fourth-grade
level. Their adjustment problems begin in the first grade. During the 1964/1965 school year there were five first-grade classes
at the boys' school. Each had twenty-eight students, and the
project children were evenly divided among them. They were
all in the bottom half of their class, so the best students from
the project reached only fifteenth place. Half of these boys
had to repeat the class.

Fifteen out of the seventeen students in the girls' and boys'
catch-up class live in the project. Yet on the whole, their backwardness in school cannot be imputed to their intelligence,
which is normal and sufficient for primary grades, but to a
generalized lack of interest in school activities.

They need instruction that is not traditional but concrete
and individual. They realize that they are poor students, and
they compensate for this failure by discovering other criteria
of worth in the vacant lots. They make it a point of honor
to succeed in gymnastics and to test their young strength.
School, where they are relegated to the rear benches, is gradually abandoned at all levels. About twenty children entered
the first year of high school* but there was only one girl in
ninth grade. They quit in the second year to go to technical
school, then get tired of it after a year and look for work.
The boys refuse to study much more than the girls, who are
generally more conscientious.

*This is a secondary school offering academic and vocational subjects, but
it is terminal and is not for those who are preparing to enter college.—R.S.

Absenteeism from school is less prevalent than one might expect, however; it shows up in three ways. First, the children run off to the vacant lots on sunny June days; the parents say, "You can't send them to school any more . . . and since it's almost over anyhow . . ." Second, the mothers keep the older children home from time to time during the year so they can help out. Finally, those who have had a slight illness take advantage of a few days' convalescence granted by the parents and spend this time outdoors.

Of an enrollment of 562 at the girls' school, the average number absent daily is around 43. The lowest was 29 and the highest 120, but only on one day. The principal thinks this number is fairly normal and comparable to other suburban neighborhoods.

The irreducible absences are special cases and are always boys. The following case is cited. The principal sent for two brothers who had been absent for several months. They hid in the bathtub during this visit from the school official who was told that they were now being raised at their grandmother's. They finished up the year in the vacant lots.

On the whole, therefore, the children's low scholastic level is due to neither their intelligence nor absenteeism, of which there is relatively little, but to the total lack of communication and continuity between the family and the school. The school's role is solely to teach reading, as five little eleven- and twelve-year-old girls expressed it in answering the question, "Do you read at home?" "Oh, no," they said, "it's not worth the trouble because we know how to read!" The children seem very ignorant, lost in space and time, and without ambition.

We were struck by the embarrassed silence at first to the question, "What would you like to do later on?" and then the girls and boys answer, "work." We have to be insistent for the boys to name a few jobs; these are always the same, and mechanic is a very popular one. At age ten, if their imagination is stimulated, they want to be a veterinarian or an industrial designer, and one would like to be a science teacher. The girls will be hairdressers or salesgirls, and sometimes typists. One admits blushingly that she has thought of being a steward-

ess. But these responses are in the nature of a dream not
admitted to the parents. They dimly know that neither they
nor their parents will have the perseverance necessary to
obtain these envied positions, which they tend to think are
reserved for a privileged class. At fourteen they will look for
work and think no more about these inclinations. At ten, while
there is still time, no one arouses their curiosity or inspires
them with the necessary energy.

The parents are completely unaware of the role they should
have in this connection. Certainly they do not want to see
their children become laborers, but they have no idea of what
the children's future could be and they leave them with the
entire responsibility for building it. When the adults are asked,
"What do you want your children to do later on?" they give
absolutely identical replies:

"To get their hands on something."

"To earn a good living."

"To have a good job."

"To go as far as they have the brains for. It depends on what
they like; you can't force them."

Here again the answers are not precise. What is a good job—a
technical specialty? Something requiring a high level of education? They do not know and, having no notion of the required
scholastic level, they ingenuously think "it would be nice if
[their] son were a doctor." Meanwhile the child is still vegetat-
ing at ten in the elementary grades. If one points out that
he seems to have gotten off to a bad start on secondary school,
they reply, "The child is young; he still has time." It is therefore impossible for them to promote a desire in the child to
really change his condition.

The project children meet other children at school. Do
friendships arise that might have a determining influence?
This does not seem to be the case. The teachers have not
noticed any real segregation in class or during recess, but the
departure from school and return to the project is an interesting

phenomenon. No child tarries on the way to accompany a friend who might live elsewhere. All the children from La Halle go home together as though in a hurry to leave one world and come back to the other, their own. It is mutually true that no outside child comes to play in the project.

There are two worlds and two times: the school world that provides playmates for the time granted to it and the project world where one is at home and play is mingled with living. Games at school follow the fashions and rhythms of all schools. The La Halle boys are feared for their brutality in games of speed and for their skill in marbles, where they always win their opponent's marbles. The girls play circle games and jump rope. Between twelve and fourteen, they would be more inclined than the boys to make friends with outside girls but, like the boys, they save these friendships for schooltime, which they prolong a bit by leaving early and not hurrying home as fast as their brothers. It seems that the project is a haven for everyone and outside relationships count very little.

Outside of School

It is useless to dwell on the banal, regimented school games; they are much less important to the children than those carried on in the project with always renewed passion. Outdoors constantly, the children extract all sorts of materials from the extraordinary mine of rubbish in the vacant lots. They learn about technical skills, bartering, and economy from the older children and are initiated into defeat and victory, love and hate, obeying and commanding. They find out about deception, betrayal, and pain. They are tough and do not come home to complain but settle their conflicts physically themselves. The project with its group games is their real school of manhood.

The important games are divided between several poles of attraction: the fire, the shacks, the garbage dump, the stagnant pools and "lake" in the vacant lots, and expeditions through the overgrown gardens. The deep puddles teach them prudence, and there is practically never a deplorable accident. The basements are welcome in cold weather. There are also individual, dangerous games in league with the adolescents, i.e., organized theft or real sexual stimulation.

These games have no connection with the adult world. The children never ask their mothers for any play materials, such as string, and they never tell what they have been doing.

Each of the two projects has its own gang, and the two gangs are rivals. La Halle's, which is younger and larger, is afraid of Le Pas', which is better organized. The Le Pas gang is led by two fourteen-year-old "bosses" with five or six completely devoted "drudges," while the La Halle gang is led by three Moslems about twelve years old, whose bellicose and destructive activities provoke fights. At the leaders' signal, the two gangs wage war in battle array. The prize is very often the shacks, each gang staking its honor on destroying the other's shack. "You get pretty beaten up."

Although they are rivals, the two gangs live side by side quite peaceably during long lulls separating the armed assaults, and they immediately ally against any outside invasion. Two or three times a year, some poor nomads settle at the end of the road for a few days. The two united gangs declare war on them. They lay siege to their wagons from some distance, look the others over, and shout at them: "Your wagons aren't as strong as our houses. Tonight there won't be anything left of them, and you'll have our arrows in your behinds. Besides, the cops will come and clear you out." The children assert loudly indeed that they belong to the project.

From early spring on, each gang has its shacks, which reveal their authors' personalities to some extent. Built from old box springs, bottomless garbage cans, stolen tools, and scrap iron of all kinds, they look like the shantytown shacks the Moslem children have seen. There is always a door, and some improvised but evocative furniture lines the inside with pseudo-beds. The more elaborate ones with posts and tarpaulins, sometimes replaced by a sheet they have sneaked out or an old bedspread, look more like tents and are used by the older children (ages twelve to fourteen). Quickly built, they spring up and disappear fast despite the fact that the boys are there almost constantly.

Last year we made a big, four-room house, but a boy who's in reform school now burned it down on us. Now we make tents, it goes faster. When we're building, we come early in the morning and leave late at night so we can have some peace. We take turns eating or else we get a snack at home. The construction boss has a better bow and he mounts guard. Anyone who comes near gets an arrow.

Each gang has favorite spots for its shacks. They are sometimes pulled down to avoid destruction by the enemy, who prefer to attack when their opponents are away.

The boys are almost always armed with slingshots, clubs, or bows but, despite the care with which they make their weapons, they are not attached to them and break them easily. The group sees to it that everyone is equipped and looks for materials for everyone. Flexible wood for bows is torn from the hospital's bushes. "Last year we found some iron wire in the cars; it was very good. This year we didn't find anything in the cars, but there was some fishline in a garbage can that we divided up." The arrows are of hollow wood, called "pipe-wood." They stick a small piece of iron in the wood and splice them together. The arrows are armed and dangerous, and their aim is true with or against the wind.

The boys also go hunting. They shoot at birds or have contests to improve their technique with slingshots or bows. They do not realize it but they like to kill animals. Field mice stimulate their imagination: armed with old pans, ten of them lie in wait at the mousehole and whoever catches one is the owner of it. He may take it home and try to tame it or open its stomach with a rusty can "to see its heart and show it to [his] pals." "We don't kill earthworms because they're sacred; if you cut them in two, children die." "It's bad to kill cats. We like animals; we only kill grasshoppers and rats."[2]

The fire is not a game but a job. Two fires burn almost continually, one in the field near the rear wall, the other near the entrance to the project. They are fed with various combustible materials, from old tires to boxes scrounged from around the hospital kitchens. The children work on the fire in shifts despite the caretaker's prohibitions, and though the fires are scattered or extinguished at night by boys urinating in a circle, they unfailingly spring up again.

They scrounge through the gardens and learn to glean materials that are useful for play or trade from the garbage dump. They apply their skills for profit with the children of the neighboring "domain," where they are already conscious of the class difference: "We play marbles to get soldiers; that's the only thing we go to the 'Domain' for, because they're richer and have lots of soldiers."

Like the adolescents, they make their first trades within the project: "I tried to swap five soldiers for a hundred marbles Claude earned washing a car, but he wouldn't"; "I sold my old bike for two hundred marbles. I'd rather have nothing; it didn't go fast enough."

Although still turned toward the world of childhood with their games on themes inspired by television (such as Robin Hood or Belphégor, where their rivalry for the hero's role turns the game into a fight anyway), they are very attracted by the adolescents to whom they already feel very close. A few privileged children slip into the older groups where they have gained acceptance. "Those little guys" (ages twelve to fourteen) serve as slaves, so they are entitled to be initiated into theft and sex. One of them confesses ingenuously, "I know how to ride a motorbike; soon I'll be able to steal them." "He has a brother who's a thief. He's a little hotshot with the bow." When the adolescents tease each other in the basement, the "little guys" act as lookouts and demand the right to watch in return.

In cold weather, their domain is the basement, where they play hide-and-seek and appropriate whatever they find. The caretakers chase them out but they come back in through another door.

They have little respect for adults in general: "Since the cops had the basements cleaned out, if the caretaker hears us scooting around in there he kicks us out. Then we razz him and his old lady too; that makes them mad"; "the other caretaker died; it doesn't matter because he was old."

The girls play with the boys and are sometimes invited to go hunting, but they do not take part in the wars except in subordinate roles, such as bringing food to the sentinels. On the other hand, they are allowed in the completed shacks, where they mimic the game of love, and they borrow bikes or are given rides on strange vehicles built by the boys (for example, a garbage can mounted on an old baby buggy chassis). Up to age seven or eight, they have some areas reserved next to the buildings where they erect houses for their dolls with old cardboard boxes they have retrieved. When they are bigger, around twelve to thirteen, they stay at home more—singing or listening to records, trying their hand at knitting or crocheting, or learning how to set their hair from their older sisters—while waiting for the tomboys of their generation (who are still busy waging war around the shacks) to get a little older.

At fourteen, the boys give up their games in the "field" for men's activities, work, and recreation. They change their age group and are accepted among the adolescents. Meanwhile they grow up in freedom without ever really running up against parental authority, showered with sweets and small change, ignorant about what is taught in school, unconcerned about their future, and happy to be living together under the instruction of the older children in a separate world of their own bounded by the project.

Choice of Vocation

Leaving school is an important stage in the child's life. It does not make much difference whether he has obtained the CEP. His parents have quite an appreciation of this elementary-school degree, which brings back memories and to which they still accord all its worth. But while they show some pleasure if their son receives it, they have no more reaction to his failure to do so than to an act of fate. They are ignorant of the CEP's actual unimportance in relation to success in entrance competitions for trade schools (they say, "If he has his diploma, I'll find him a good place") so they cannot inform their children, who do not know what possibilities are available. The teachers talk about these possibilities in school, but they especially stress the necessity of going into a vocational school, mentioning those in the area. The parents do not always fill out the registration forms, and the children understand just one thing: they will not be out of school for three years, which seems much too long to them. They take a vocational guidance examination, but the overworked counselors have just a brief interview with them, and the results are imprecise or unknown.

The old hopes, desires, or wishes have already been abandoned. Yet the child would still like to learn a trade, without knowing too well which one, because he knows that a skilled worker "earns a better living." At the same time, he is torn by the desire to earn money immediately, to be able to have a different relationship with his parents because of that economic semi-independence than he had as a student, and to change his age bracket by entering the almost-adult world of the young men.

His inclination to become an apprentice disappears when difficulties arise in working out a contract with a master. The documents must be filled out and sent to the crafts guild, and the contract may not be broken. As soon as the future apprentice realizes that he or she will receive just twenty centimes [about 4c] an hour and will be tied down to evening classes, he gives up any idea of apprenticeship. He is aided in this decision by the example of the older youths who earn 1.5F or 2F per hour as laborers, which seems enough to him for the moment. Another contributing factor is the parents who leave the choice up to him, as incapable as he is of looking beyond the immediate future and liable to be hoping for the earnings the child will bring back. The choice is made: armed with the CEP or not, the fourteen-year-old goes to work, leaving the protected world of school to enter abruptly into that of the adult laborers.

In which factory, and how? They go to work in any factory in neighboring localities and are hired by cooptation ("Pierre

Untel is going to get me into his factory"). Very often it is the older ones who undertake to get the "kids" hired. Failing that, the father will ask a "pal" to get the "kid" in or the mother herself will knock at the door of some shop. The boys generally do not apply for a job themselves the first time; they are afraid to.

Things are a bit more circumspect for girls. Distance and bad company are feared. The mothers get their daughters into the small electrical assembly, pharmaceutical packaging, and yogurt factories in the town by the same system of cooptation. The youngest girls most often start work as stock clerks.

The youngsters no longer have the protection of the school world and its rhythms, from which they wished to be released at any price, they are different from those still enslaved to school, and they are conscious of living through a transitory period of life. In order to bear their emancipation and sudden loneliness, they can only draw closer to each other, no longer just for long play periods but to share their adult amusements, their uncertainties, and their experiences. They enter La Halle's large community of youths, which is tucked around its members and is impenetrable to adults, and from which they will not emerge until marriage or military service.

In short, we can state that the children's group is free of the constraints usually exercised in society by parents and teachers. This freedom is greater than elsewhere because their parents have not really settled on any system of discipline.

At first glance, socialization seems to proceed as in the rest of society, but the importance of two special factors should be noted. On one hand, school is not viewed in the same way as in other milieus; the children, and the parents, see it as a constraint and accept it only to learn to read. On the other hand, the children's neighborhood groups are those of the project, which causes reinforcing of an enculturation specific to the project.

The freedom won by the children corresponds in some way to a freedom the parents desire for themselves. Two attitudes give evidence of this: before birth, mothers seem to have an easier choice than elsewhere as to whether to keep the child, and after birth, as soon as the baby is really walking, he is free to go out.

Adolescence

The project youths are more difficult to study than the adults or children, for their territory is unlimited and their vast range lets them escape from view. There are many of them because they have stopped all childish rivalry and joined with the boys from Le Pas, and they are visited daily by former young residents who have moved away. Temporary or permanent departures (due to placement in an institution, prison terms, military service, or moving elsewhere) make the physiognomy of the group changeable. In 1966, La Halle alone had about 115 adolescents, of which there were 61 girls to 54 boys and about 74 Europeans to 23 Jews and 17 Moslems.

Before studying their activities and way of life in the project, we should differentiate them by work, family, sex, and ethnic group.

Starting to Work

The young boy goes into some kind of factory, bravely, intoxicated by the money offered (1.5F to 2F per hour). But he will realize very quickly that his work is uninteresting and that it is difficult to make a place for himself among the others, who make fun of him, do not see to it that he learns the technical operations, send him several times a day to buy wine, and leave him to sweep up the shop. He will also realize very quickly how low his pay is, helped to do so by his mother, who complains about his wages. "I don't draw any allocations for him any more, and when I've paid for his commuter's ticket, his meals and his pocket money, what have I got left?" In addition he must be dressed more casually than at school, and sometimes special work clothes must be bought for him. Yet the young boy will persevere for some time even though he does not even know what he is useful for. When asked, "What do you do in your factory?" the adolescents always answer, "A little bit of everything." Too young to run the machines, they are not steady workmen and will not be so until they are eighteen.

Sometimes the employer holds out the promise of a raise, a promotion, or a share in the profits. They generally get a raise of a few centimes an hour within two months after they are hired, and then their salary stagnates. Also, the employer often takes them on trial for two weeks, claims it is not long enough, and prolongs it until the end of the first month; he then fires them after having paid them the minimum wage.

The boy suffers his first shock, loses self-confidence, is afraid of being scolded and hastens to find work again with the help of a "pal." He may keep the second job longer than the first, but he may also be fired for the same reason. After he has wandered around like this for several months, not only has he earned hardly anything and lost his right to paid leave, but he has also begun a series of failures that will be matched by an acquired habit of not being a steady worker.

In general, it can be said that the fourteen-year-old boys work regularly for a year and then because of weariness, lack of interest, and the exploitation to which they let themselves be subjected, they become discouraged and gradually give up the effort. Sixteen-year-olds work least; this is the "bad age" from the vocational standpoint. Too old to accept the drudgery kept for the youngest employees or to begin an apprenticeship they regret not having taken and too young to be eligible for the machines, they go to work only under parental pressure.

The length of each new period of employment varies from one morning to a year; in the latter case, this time is broken up by long periods of idleness. The better-organized boys "go on Security." One hears a boy announce, "I'm going to get put on the sick list; my wrist hurts from lugging crates around. I've been working three months." Others just give up. If they quit a job after two or three days, they often do not even go to pick up the wages due them.

The number of boys working regularly is hard to determine. They are the ones whose parents absolutely need their wages to live on or who have found "something that doesn't pay bad." They are considered to be working regularly if their idle periods between two jobs are very brief. One can count up to twenty-five boys (almost half of those at La Halle) out of work at a time.

Their eagerness for work depends on the season and on what the rest of the group is doing. Before the year-end holidays and summer vacation, the boys rush to find jobs in order to have money to spend. If almost all the adolescents are working, the last three out of work are caught up in a veritable frenzy. Working also depends on the family structure; the two oldest Pied-Noir boys evidently have regular jobs.

Some constants can be defined in the behavior of the project's adolescents. Not having had any constraints during childhood, they cannot bear the authority of the employer or the foreman, so they resign from a job they find interesting because of a justified remark by the foreman. They are frequently the instigators of violent arguments in the shop. They have no occupational interests. Work is just a synonym for money in their minds, and it has no relation to any skill. Gaining a skill does not tempt them between sixteen and eighteen, and they would rather be idle than work for low wages. It is impossible to get them to sign up for an FPA course[3] and they are incapable of taking the smallest step themselves. We shall give some concrete examples.

Example 1. Maurice, age eighteen, has an Apprentice's Certificate as a machinist. He holds some sort of job six to eight months a year and is now washing cars. He refused to join the metal workers' union although he says he would rather practice his own trade.

Example 2. Vincent, age eighteen, no CEP, has done almost no work between fifteen and eighteen. He has had all kinds of sporadic jobs, for example, delivering oysters for a fishmonger. He ran away from a Supervised Training Public Institute*

---

*Supervised Training is an agency of the Ministry of Justice responsible for children under court supervision (juvenile delinquents and children in need of protection). It operates both Public Institutes, where the children live and learn a trade, and local offices providing educational and medical supervision to children remaining in their own homes—R.S.

where he refused to go to the shop. He has been working for six months for a large moving company where he is well paid (2,000F a month if he does moving out of the country).

Example 3. François, age eighteen, CEP, would have liked to have been an automotive worker. He enrolled in an FPA course, went on probation, earned good grades for three months, and then suddenly gave it up. He remained idle for a while, then became a bus conductor and gave that up after eight days. He has done nothing since then.

Example 4. Paul, age seventeen, CEP, had worked in various factories at fifteen. He started at a bank as a junior clerk and worked there regularly for two years. He bought an old luxury car for 500F but he was unable to maintain it. He gave up his job and has done nothing for three months.

Example 5. Robert, age eighteen, no CEP, little education, practically never works. He is employed sporadically for a week around the holidays. He refused an offer, made on his request, to teach him to cut leather in a shop.

These examples are not special cases but could be multiplied to infinity. The adolescents find any vocational training repugnant and are attracted only by the wages they receive at the moment. They refuse to come to grips with the adult world by taking responsibility for bothersome procedures, so none of those who are out of work is registered on the unemployment rolls. They always say they are going to work the next day, and probably they end up believing it.

This pattern does not vary by ethnic group. Young Jews, Arabs, and metropolitans all feel they are in a transitory period, and they know they will find a job when they want to work. The job market affirms their view. What is the good of working for a miserable wage for years if they can get better jobs at age twenty when they are released from military obligations and are the required age for the machines, without the need for previous training? They feel rather like men on vacation with the responsibilities and duties of adulthood (for which the boys of fourteen want so much to be eligible) put off for the moment and "as long as we can take advantage of it."

The girls' problem is slightly different. They begin working a bit later, either because they try to continue their studies for a year or two or because their mothers decide to keep them home a while to help with the housework. At fifteen or sixteen, the girl will have a keen desire to work in order to gain some independence but her choice of occupations is very limited. Like her brothers, she can only be an unskilled worker; even to sell perfume or shoes she will have to be satisfied with an apprentice's wages.

Girls, therefore, have the same difficulties as boys, but they show less occupational instability in time and space: in time, because their need for independence and money sustains them in their effort, and they would have to do housework if they stayed home; in space because, tiring more quickly than their brothers and being reluctant to go far away, they must make do with the local or nearby job market. There are certainly some adolescent girls who run away from work or change jobs often, but they are proportionately fewer than the boys. Moreover, many of them know they will not work beyond the birth of a second child so that even boring work, whether short- or long-term, will be only temporary.

The Moslem girls are the only ones who really make a future for themselves. Unlike the others, they show much courage and tenacity, and occupational skills have some meaning for them alone. They are not anxious to work in a factory and they know how to wait. We have already said that they count on their studies in order to acquire some superiority.over their parents and hence a certain independence from the family and to put off a possible marriage, which is an incentive the Moslem boys do not have. They do not find manual labor repugnant, and they acquire good technical specializations. One of them has just received her Apprentice's Certificate in dressmaking but she is going to continue training until she receives a supervisor's certificate in order to become a shop foreman. Another has completed her back schooling (due to not having gone to school in Algeria) and is studying for an Apprentice's Certificate in corset-making. She herself took steps to find a technical institution and her school is located in the city, which implies a great strain in going back and forth. Two girls are in seventh and eighth grades of the high school; another is in the commercial section.

The Moslem girls from traditional homes form a separate category in the adolescent group. The other adolescents generally have no occupational skills and no other ambition than earning a little money from time to time until those decisive stages on the road to adulthood: military service for the boys and marriage for the girls.

Relations with Parents

While innately few things have changed in the life of the young man who continues to live with his parents, transformations are in fact being carried out in the parent–child relationship. The adolescent immediately adopts the specific behavior of the working son toward his parents, and the daughter follows the same path. This consists of demands upon the mother, who has kept her authority up to now. The attitude is summed up in this oft-heard question: "I work, I give you my pay, what more do you want?" In exchange for his pay, the boy demands not only complete freedom but also enough of the clothes he likes, a watch, pocket money, and impeccably ironed shirts. He quickly turns into a domestic tyrant. The mothers are weak with their sons. They still try to maintain their authority a bit while the boys are young, but they soon respond to their logic like this: "What am I supposed to tell him? It's true he works, he doesn't earn a bad living for his age; he really ought to have fun."

Parents are generally quite happy that the children are working; they are in a hurry to "see them fly with their own wings." They very soon consider them to be adults. At fifteen, the son is almost "a man" and the daughter is a young woman; at eighteen "they're old enough to know what they're doing." Paradoxically, both father and mother defend them against society and cover up their faults, and the mother continues to take care of their laundry and to keep the foods they like in the refrigerator, to eat after some nocturnal outing.

The parents are interested in their children's physical development and gaze on them proudly if they are strong. If a girl is pretty, they worry whether "she's already running after boys," but the father stands aside for the mother in regard to reprimands or advice to be given to his daughter. On the other hand, he grows closer to his son, whom he allows complete freedom. Does this mean that the boy is free and the girl supervised? Not exactly. They are both free, but the girl must account for what she does, not be seen too much with boys in the project, and not come home later than the agreed hour except on Saturday. Sometimes the mothers worry if the girls do not go out enough and advise them to go "have a little fun, or else it's no kind of life." Some teach that "the boys are supposed to pay; you have to order them around and take advantage of them." The mothers are especially afraid for the very young girls, but they are marriageable around seventeen and the risks are smaller. Marriage is a guarantee and an end to the mother's responsibility.

The working girls, like the boys, require their mother to have dinner ready when they come home. Some no longer make their own beds, and all of them stop helping with the housework except on Saturday and then only if they like to do it. They do not always take care of their own laundry.

Of course, these remarks do not apply to the Moslem girls. They go out just with the family, talk only among themselves on summer evenings in the courtyard, or are asked to go farther off, out of sight, so as not to set tongues wagging in the Moslem community. Moslem fathers watch very closely (but not always successfully) over their daughters.

The adolescents do not exercise an educational influence on their younger brothers and are not interested in the youngsters' progress or future. "He'll do what he likes; it's up to him to make out." The girls pay more attention to their juniors, and the Moslem girls are veritable second mothers to the youngest. It is the older girls who advise the mother and who go and see the teacher about the youngsters.

The relationship between adolescents and their parents is most often established around the pole of money, or rather pay. After age sixteen they are often far from freely consenting to contributing their wages, and the mother prides herself on her authority if the boy hands over his pay. The girls are generally more docile. A better-accepted formula is to pay the mother a pension for food every week or two weeks, with the remainder and any overtime pay to be freely disposed of by the children. The children often determine the size of the pension themselves.

Refusal of spending money gives rise to all kinds of blackmail and pressure on the parents. The Moslem fathers are grasping and stingy with pocket money. Ahmed took revenge for his father's having always taken everything by staying out of work for a year. After this hiatus, he gave his father a gift of a month's wages and, under threat of getting himself arrested immediately, obtained an arrangement whereby he paid just a pension. Mohammed was unemployed for a year and a half; then his father agreed to let him buy his own clothes and pay his mother an amount determined by how generous he felt that day. Many adolescents do not work because they do not really have the reward for their effort at their disposal. They tend to think it is part of the parents' duty to feed them along with the rest of the family.

If the father earns low wages, there is also competition in regard to earnings that often gives rise to stormy discussions. The son often earns as much as the father, and the mother is inclined to take the son's side. These fathers had better not limit the son's freedom or oppose his demands. The adolescents who earn their own living feel equal to their parents.

Pocket money is also a factor in arguments. If the young man turns over all his wages to his mother she gives him 15F to 50F every Saturday, which is not enough, given boys' appetites. They then use emotional blackmail, beg some subsidies during the week, demand a motorbike, get installments on their pay from their employer on the sly, or (in the rarest case) sneak some small change from their mother's change purse.

Money is also a cause of competition and quarreling between brothers and sisters, either because one earns more than the other and does not pay a larger pension or because the girl who wants to continue her studies is begrudged being fed by her brothers for doing nothing.

All the young people, except the Moslem girls, adopt the

same attitude toward work and the relationship with parents. Nothing distinguishes Vincent (a Frenchman) from Robert (a Jew) or Ahmed (a Moslem). They work sporadically, enjoy the same freedom, and have the same tendency to reject parental authority and remaining family traditions, the same need for money, and the same requirements of their mother (to whom they give some subsidies when she complains too much). They conform to the single model of La Halle adolescents, who are subdivided more by age bracket than by ethnic group because all cultural differences are voluntarily abolished.

The age groups can be schematized as follows. Until age sixteen they still submit somewhat to parental authority, turn over their wages to their mother, have less money to spend, and work more regularly. It is especially between sixteen and eighteen that the boys as a group exploit their freedom and their leisure time, flee from the adults out of preference for the "pals' world," spend a great deal of money, and earn some now and then. After eighteen work becomes more regular, military service is lying in wait, and they feel "old." When they return from service at age twenty, many things will have changed, and they leave the young people's group as they entered it—quietly.

Among the girls, however, age brackets are less important than ethnic differences. Maturing early, they are already women at age fourteen and are destined for marriage, official or not. They are turned toward the boys but just expect to have individual relationships with them and do not really form a part of their group.

They do not form a girls' group either and do not group together except in two's and three's of those who like each other. Despite some apparent supervision until age sixteen, they are free very young but they stay home more after work, which is a real entrée to independence for them. They are more tractable and work more regularly than the boys, but are demanding in matters of dress. They are flirtatious and feminine even in pants, and they receive a lot of understanding from their mothers.

The Jewish girls' behavior is scarcely different except that they like family life more and inherit from their mother a residue of tradition that they respect somewhat more than their brothers. They learn to make the traditional cakes and are busier around the house. They represent the middle ground between the very free metropolitans and the more-supervised Moslems.

The Moslem girls enjoy the least freedom at present, but they are carrying on a silent struggle to win it. They are few in number and they depend on each other and group together when they can. They obey their fathers on the surface and hardly ever approach boys, but they fully intend to choose their own husbands. They recreate the society of women that has always existed in Moslem countries.

The Gang

We shall try to define it and narrow down its form before describing the gang activities that partly determine the boys' system of values.

DEFINITION

All the boys have a strong feeling of belonging to the project, but within the total group changeable and informal gangs arise around one or several leaders. These gangs form and dissolve as members leave or form affinities for one another.

The group manifests itself as such only if some particular event occurs but its existence is incontestable. When Ahmed refers to "the kids in our gang," we should realize he means his "micro-gang" or "Vincent's gang" although he does not mention this name, but when he says "the kids from the project" he means the whole group of adolescents. The gangs in the project are not secret but they are difficult for the observer to discern.

No racial segregation is practiced among the adolescents; there are other criteria of selection. They are united by the same social status: their temporary age bracket and the fact that they belong to the project, of which they have taken possession much more than the adults. They are perfectly aware of the social distance separating them from the adults and the outside world, and this distance is a factor in the forming of groups.

The La Halle adolescents' group suffers doubly from the hostility of the preceding generation, in the town and in the project. Six boys all claim that "the cafés in town don't want us because we live here." They tell of the trouble they had getting into La Perle, the only bar that stays open until 2:00 A.M., because "the owner thought we were going to mess up his café!" The police often have an eye on them, and they complain of being stopped more often by the police than the town boys "who make more noise and act worse." They also complain that they have trouble finding work because when they give their address the employer answers, "We'll write you."

They are no more secure vis-à-vis the project adults. When they stand talking in small groups beneath the windows in summer, "they bawl us out all the time; we don't know where to go." As a matter of fact, they get not only insults but also pails of water thrown at them. Once in summer 1965, a sixteen-year-old boy was wounded in the thigh by a rifle fired from one of the windows. The police were alerted but could not find the guilty party. The boys are well aware that the police, who are called too often, are not interested in the people from what they call "the souses' project," and still less in what happens to the young people.

The parents who allow their son to go out on his own do not let him bring his "pals" home. The adolescents as a group are driven out by the adults, and they are not allowed to take shelter in the apartments. This social distance in the project as well as in the town partly determines their choice of territory.

THE TERRITORY

What is striking at La Halle is the adolescent's selective and differential way of occupying a space belonging just as much to the adults. Since almost nothing was anticipated for their

use except the club, which is much too tiny, they have reserved
the few, uncomfortable corners that are a bit sheltered from
sight and are not frequented by the adults. They bundle
together against the wall of the former store; this wall has
a projection on which they can climb to sunbathe, cut off from
the street outside. They line up in the passageway joining
the buildings—a gloomy, cold, drafty place where they
nevertheless feel sheltered. They stand still and speak little.
They pile up in the stairways, as many as ten sitting one on
top of another. Their special domain is the basement, where
they repair their motorbikes, sleep when they are temporarily
on the outs with their parents, and hide escapees from detention centers. The cellars are normally locked but they break
in the doors to appropriate these spaces that are also a favorite
place for stealing.

With the complicity of a few adults, they enjoy refuge in
some apartments. They come at night to play poker, listen
to records, or dance. Sometimes they do nothing but drink
coffee and talk. The evening goes on so late that the boys
no longer have the energy to leave. We will let Cecile (age
seventeen) tell about it herself:

> There were always a bunch of guys from the gang at A.'s. At 4:00
> A.M., since a lot of them didn't feel like going, they all went to
> sleep on the floor. There were sometimes as many as ten under
> the table and everywhere. Those who were cold hung onto the
> animals [three dogs and three cats]. Micky and Dede, who had
> a much better place of their own, slept with Franck in an old
> bed. They had put in some seats from stolen cars; during the day
> they were put up against the wall like a couch, and at night they
> put them together to make a bed. I slept there with Franck. When
> Franck left, I slept on a board swiped from the basement, laid
> on four chairs. We covered ourselves with coats and fought the
> cats for the fur jacket.

We know of three of these apartments that we purposely call
refuges. The young people feel comfortable and at home there,
and can tell stories about sex all night long without anyone
criticizing them: "We can do whatever we want; they understand us."

The gangs' world is vast. In the first place, the adolescents escape the project and meet the boys of the two other transitional housing projects. They always meet outside, and they have assembly points that go in and out of fashion. To the parents who sometimes ask where they are going, they reply, "To take a walk." They have a curious way of disappearing: there they are, motionless, and then you cannot see them any more. They do not leave together or go and pick up the others. They have a semisecret way of communicating: they know where to meet, and messages circulate by word of mouth. They are well acquainted with neighboring communes where they frequent this or that bar. They adopt one and meet there almost every night without prearrangement, and then the gang headquarters is moved. Last year they used to go to Barbiche "because they had cards and dice." Right now they are going to La Perle "because we've started playing pool." For how long? They know all the "chic" taverns and outdoor restaurants in the vicinity, and the night spots where they dance "bop." They go to the city where their favorite haunts are the dance halls in the student neighborhoods, the movies, and the attractions of downtown and the big boulevards, the "Luna Park" of the place. They do not know about places like St.-Germain-des-Prés. They leave the project without a precise destination at first, then an idea comes up at the café, and they leave for an hour, sometimes coming back the following morning.

SELECTION AND HIERARCHY

Taking into account society's barriers against them and the difficulty of self-realization, in their occupations for instance, the tendency to form groups may be considered a defense mechanism of young people denied complete participation in the adult world. It is with their contemporaries that they feel secure and can symbolically play adult roles.

Leaders emerge through a process of selection and become apparent in the hierarchy arising within the group. The selection process takes place by itself, taking into account the personality of each person but operating according to precise and immutable criteria, of which the three principal ones are personal prestige, wealth, and the faculty for rebellion and opposition to adults. Of course, only the boys' personal qualities matter, and no account is taken of the more or less privileged situation of the parents. It is a society with no heritage.

Prestige is conferred by physical bearing, manner, attractiveness, and popularity with girls. Moreover, one must not only be a good dancer but must also dance "bop," that is, be fond of avant-garde rhythms. It is better if you look older than you are.

There are real prestige contests in which hair and clothing are important factors. The leaders set the style, which follows society's models from a distance but not slavishly. The handsome boys wear business suits, white collars, and ties to advantage even during the day. In order to economize on their one suit, they often wear, with affected nonchalance, a heavy pullover, an open checked shirt, or a turtleneck collar to hide the missing shirt. It was they who started the style of buying pea coats at the flea market and wearing them in winter with the collar turned up.

Many Mediterraneans are among the leaders because their razor-cut black hair, their matte complexion or early beard, their natural elegance, and their innate sense of rhythm ensure popularity with the girls and enable them to win prestige. They are the ones who set the tone at present.

By *wealth* we must understand not possessions but the money one has to spend. The boys whose pocket money is not too limited are thus invested with great prestige compared to the others, from whom they are outwardly little different. They follow about the same fashions in clothes but often wear an ID bracelet on their wrists. It is important to be one of their followers because you can have a lot of fun with them. They spend money liberally at the bar or the fair—as much as 300F (or two weeks' pay) in one night. They have expensive amusements, go far out into the city, and may even "swing a car," but they do not always win the girls as easily as the others.

The *"warriors"* are mostly different. They have not given up wearing blue jeans, belts, boots, and jackets (called "fur jackets" if they are lined with sheepskin), and they started the style of affixing the eagle on the back of the jacket. They carry on a more overt opposition to society. They ride motorbikes, preferably stolen ones, and have weapons hidden in the basement or at home that they do not really use: rifles, switchblade knives, bicycle chains, carefully manufactured bludgeons, and brass knuckles. Their ring finger is sometimes adorned by a skull-head ring with two points soldered in the eye sockets. Their hair is uncombed. They prefer expeditions, hunting, and fighting to dances. They are the "toughs" and the group depends on them if there is danger of their territory being invaded. They have "girlfriends" with whom they sleep but they pride themselves on not being sentimental about them. All have some legal record and are acquainted with detention centers and jails (prison confers unprecedented prestige and high esteem). They almost never work or have "rotten jobs." When they dress like the others and even wear the others' clothes, it is with the aim of avoiding the police, who especially keep an eye on those who wear leather jackets. All the boys know this; as Robert put it, "We have to dress like snobs for them [the police] to let us alone; that's why we do it."

The different leaders are not separated according to how they have won prestige. If a boy has several of these required qualifications, he is esteemed all the more.

The other boys form a kind of lower class in relation to the leaders; they are neither rich nor handsome, and they work every day for very low wages, hand over their pay, and get along on a little pocket money for the movies. There are also the timorous and the thrifty and those who dance the tango to accordion music. And then there are the younger boys of fourteen or fifteen who represent the youngsters, those who "have not yet arrived" and whose qualifications are still just potential. Although they are different, the boys coexist in peace, and they all belong to the group.

COMPOSITION OF THE GANGS

Preferential relationships promote the formation of gangs within this adolescent group we have described. These do

not divide the group horizontally into social classes, but vertically into gangs including several age brackets and several
kinds of individuals. When a few faithful followers group
around three or four leaders of the same type, the gang is
formed. Other boys will adhere to it, depending on its
activities. This mass—now smaller, now larger, wavering from
one gang to another— is composed of many younger boys
and gives them a chance to prove themselves so they can
then join the ranks of the faithful. They replace their elders.
The leaders are always seventeen to eighteen and a half, the
faithful between sixteen and eighteen. Those age fourteen
to fifteen serve as "drudges" and are invited to follow their
elders. If they have special leadership qualities, they can
gather together the enfranchised members of their own age
group and form a separate gang instead of being integrated
with the older boys.

The gangs may dissolve, divide, or be absorbed for a time,
with the oldest members leaving secretly without warning
the younger ones, for example. This is what gives them that
informal, blurred aspect that puts the observer off the track.

Most of the time the activities the gang decides on determine
the number, kind, and age of the participants. The constant,
optimum age of the gang is between fifteen and a half and
eighteen and a half. Beyond that age the older boys usually
go out together. Their games change, they become "old," and
their greatest incentives are cars and the girlfriends with whom
they aspire toward more individualized and durable relations.
Then the gang is limited to four or five "pals," but these boys
are still part of the whole group, and they are the first to make
a stand with all the others and even take over the leadership
if danger threatens.

Disputes are rare within the gangs, which are united despite
outward appearances, but treason is not forgiven and results
in exclusion. Here is an example of treason. One of the boys
took an adult's wallet from his jacket at the café. In order
not to get caught, he slipped it into the pocket of Robert, who
left. Robert should have waited for explanations and orders
upon returning to their territory, but without warning his peers,
he gave back the wallet, thus undoing the others. Some men

from the café came down to the project to "give the boys
a lesson." The incident was three months ago. Robert was
excluded and has not yet been taken back in as a leader, and
the others go out without him. He has committed the most
serious offense: betraying his own society in favor of adult
society.

The girls are almost never part of the gang. Cecile is our
only informant about this. She is a special case: her parents
threw her out, and she is completely free and belongs to Henri's
warrior gang. It should be noted that she underwent trial by
fire at her own instigation in order to be accepted by the boys.
She bears three round scars from cigarette burns in a triangle
on her left wrist. She is definite in her opinion: "There are
very few girls in the gangs. They bug the boys and they're
snitchers. The boys always have problems with them."

The gang is a male group from which the girls are excluded
unless they show exceptional qualifications. They are sometimes allies but are hardly ever used as anything but sexual
partners. According to Robert, Ahmed, and Jacques, the project
girls are either "yokels, too serious, or whores." They are
nonetheless invited to ride on the back of the motorbikes to
admire the boys' prowess, and to dance or play with them
in the club at night. On their side, the girls do all they can
to ingratiate themselves with the boys. They pay for the whis-
key and give the boys small gifts in cash or in kind.

These gangs are not organized; they form fortuitously around
a leader who has reached the required age and has the required
characteristics (prestige and the ability to oppose others). The
semidissolution of old gangs and the recasting into new ones
goes in cycles of about two years. They are more of an agglom-
eration than a solid group, and there is solidarity but it is
not absolute. One helps only those in trouble and mutual aid
must be paid back. Moreover, they cheat among themselves.
Physical competition creates superiorities that are harshly
exercised. Finally, group discipline is not really coercive and
is used totally only in case of treason; the rest of the time
it is lax. Everybody's freedom is thus respected by all; for
instance, the boys are not subject to strict appointments, and
the girls never belong to the group.

RELATIONS WITH OTHER GANGS

The gangs of La Halle feel strong on their own terrain. The leaders contract alliances with other gangs, especially those of neighboring projects. These alliances come into play between gangs for a given activity and take in the whole group for a "rumble" against an outside or distant gang. When they think a gang is going to attack, they take refuge on their own territory and the "toughs" gather the "lower classes" together. They claim they can easily bring together two hundred boys, allied warriors who will come and lend them a strong hand. The attackers generally retreat in the face of this mobilized force, and the fight does not take place.

One fact should be noted: in order to exclude Robert, Vincent sought the alliance of a gang at the opposite end of the city from La Halle, which is a considerable distance away. He gathered fifteen boys who came at midnight to make an enormous racket and inflict a punishment on Robert that left him bruised and kept him in bed for two days. Robert betrayed the adolescent society; he was punished by outside adolescents, in short, by a special tribunal.

Fights often occur among small groups, for example, when leaving the movies. There are also real duels, as Jacques testifies: "I had a fight yesterday at the movies with some bum who insulted me. We didn't keep it up because we didn't want to collect a crowd, but I have to fight him. I have a date for tomorrow; I'll take along some pals as witnesses."

Language

The whole La Halle group uses the same language, larded with current slang and purposely coarse. It has no secret language, properly speaking, but rather certain codes or key words that all the boys call loudly, at any time, as a kind of rallying cry. They address sexual insults to each other affectionately, by way of greeting. When they run out of these, they make up some and the game ends when they get on each other's nerves and begin hitting each other.

It is not necessary to speak in order to express themselves, and they often substitute pantomime for verbal expression. Thus, a hearty thump on the back replaces "hello," which they never say. When they do not like a passerby, they hold their noses, and when they talk about motorcycles they jerk their fists sideways. A word may lose its precision and take on several meanings. For example, "rotten" is used to modify that which is ugly, dirty, broken, ill, bad, or unpleasant, whether it is a basement or a face, but this usage is not special to the project. The coarse words are preferably pornographic, and they often use references to eating, for example, "You're going to get a fist shoved down your throat."

They give each other nicknames that may be diminutives, made-up words, or derived from a physical defect. Distinction as sexually worthy or worthless gets them names like "Missy Josette," "Micky the Smoocher," or "Captain Big-Ass."

Activities

These are principally play activities and often delinquent ones too, because there is hardly any borderline between the two. When the boys stroll up and down in search of inspiration, the results of their expedition cannot be anticipated.

PLAY

Those who are not working get up each day at noon and keep busy with something while waiting for the others to come back from work. They go to the project club every evening. Some go to bed at 10:00 and others go to town to end the evening with a game of pool, join up with bits of other gangs, go around to a few cafés, or ride their motorbikes on the highway where, because there is less traffic, they can race and do acrobatics with their legs stuck straight out. Night protects the boys and hides all sorts of secret activities, especially with the girls.

The periodic activities are those of Saturday night. Everyone is outdoors and they meet all their "pals," go to the movies first (it does not matter which one) and then to dance in one of the "chic, student, bop" dance halls where only young people go. On Saturday night they travel much farther away than during the week, spend more money, and come home in the wee hours. These same activities are repeated on Sunday.

These activities utilize the amusements offered by society but the young people have other games they decide on at the moment and do not continue. "We get caught up as though by impulse and afterwards we don't think about it any more; we almost never do the same thing twice." Here are three examples of unusual activities reported by Cecile:

> We decided to go fishing for crayfish in the river. There were about ten of us splashing around. Bernard was the only one who knew how to catch them in his hands. We brought them back in a fur jacket. He had them cooked at his house and we ate them on the stairs with bread. After that it was winter and we didn't go back any more.

> We've gone hunting sparrows sometimes in the plain with rifles, but the boys never kill anything. Then they shoot near each other's feet to scare each other. Your feet shake; it's fun! [Later, two boys sawed off the barrels of their rifles to make revolvers. No longer able to aim, they riddled the gutter with bullet holes, but the caretaker's anger prevented them from starting this game again.]

> One night a fellow said, "Come on, I've got an idea," and he took us to break into a grocery store run by a little old man. We wanted cigarettes, candy, and drinks. We waited until the street lights went out and then went over the grille. We found a courtyard but the door was bolted. We were afraid of making noise breaking the window. We left without anything, but we had a good laugh just the same.

Their aggressiveness toward the society of which they would like to become a part often underlies these sporadic activities, and their hatred is directed especially at the "homos" and "snobs" they would like to be. When the warriors do not know what else to do, they indulge in "chasing homos" in the woods: "When we find one, we throw him on the ground and beat him up good." They also go after old women's bags.

But the extraordinary outings are those in a car. If the motorbike is the symbol of the sixteen-year-old boys who talk fervently about their "machine" and call it "my jewel," the automobile exerts still greater attraction on those still under eighteen. A true symbol of manhood, it provides escape, speed, comfort, and the dream of being someone else, but it is very difficult to get one. They sometimes steal cars, or else they have to beg "the big guys," the young adults of twenty-one, to take them. The owner's prestige reflects somewhat on the passengers. Taking a ride in a car is one of the project children's greatest pleasures. "The big guys don't want to take us to the city. What they like to do Sunday afternoon is to keep driving in the country without stopping. On the way we tell stories. We don't even look where we're going and sometimes, coming back, we get lost," says Jean-Claude, age seventeen.

SEXUAL ACTIVITIES

The adolescents make too strong an assertion of their virility for us to assume completely that it is true. Their sexual games for men only, the exclusion of the girls from their male groups, their way of dancing with each other and often cheek-to-cheek, and yet the absolute necessity of being seen with a girl tend to show a certain ambivalence. It is to combat the fear of not being virile that they marshal their attacks on homosexuals.

They like to compare genitals, putting them on a plate in order to measure them. They also expose them in the "photomats," and the pictures give rise to great outbursts of laughter.

They do not fool the girls: "They think they're he-men, but they're afraid to be seen in their shorts by a married woman." The girls are not afflicted by this ambivalence; they are feminine and flirtatious.

It is hard to unravel the boys' attitude toward the project girls because several phenomena overlap. There is a dichotomy between love and sex in the boys' minds or in their unconscious behavior. "To have a girlfriend" is to go out with her and share her amusements openly in front of your "pals"; it is to like her for a while without taking on responsibility for her.

According to Robert's brutal but rather fair sketch, the project girls are "yokels, too serious, or whores." If they are "yokels," that is, plebians busy with the factory and the house, you cannot take them out because they will have no prestige with your "pals." If they are "serious," you cannot sleep with them for they will insist on marriage. If they are "whores," you cannot make much of having them.

The solution is to change girlfriends often or choose them from outside, and to consider the project girls as pseudo-sisters belonging to the group with whom they can share a mutual initiation or practice playing the game of devoted knight. In short, they can sleep with the project girls and like one from outside, or else have an independent sex life and show some chaste tenderness toward a project girl. The important thing is to have reserved rights to one girl and at the same time be able to boast of many sexual relationships. They do not want to live as a couple so they need two or several girls, and they make it a point of honor not to be attached. They say, "You don't have any women; if you had a girl, you'd be serious."

Sex is still in the realm of play or initiation. Besides, even though they mature earlier, the girls are willing to play the game for a while, and they would be as free as the boys were it not for fear of pregnancy.

So we see two kinds of behavior, neither of which excludes lying and inconstancy. Here is an example of the devoted knight's behavior:

Two brothers (Yves and Jean) like two sisters (Malika and Zohra) but the father, a rigid Moslem, decided to marry off his daughters himself and locked them in so they would not escape. Malika and Zohra watch at the window for the two brothers, who come and sit at the foot of the wall. They have sworn to their worried gang to "fight with knives against the father and the fiancés and to kill all of them." Malika and Zohra have promised that they will not let themselves be married off, and they have given earrings meant for their engagement as gifts to the brothers. But the time passes, the girls still do not come out, and the blond brothers seduce two

Jewish sisters from the opposite landing with the Arab girls' jewelry.

Here is an example of purely sexual behavior in which an outside girl is put at the clan's disposal by one member:

> One night Baba found a girl wandering around. He hid her in the basement and slept with her on the promise that he would keep her with him. When he came up, he passed the word to André who in turn used the girl, taking Baba's promise on himself. Micky then took his turn to go down, promising a safe shelter, and then came Henri. (Henri was the "bête noire" of the project girls, using force to make them give in; he acted as though he would strangle them or held an old saber against their stomachs.) He took the girl back to the street and left her. [Reported by Cecile.]

Cecile tells of another example:

> As long as I was Baba's "woman," no one else touched me. But one day when I criticized their expedition, he suggested taking a walk in the plain. I didn't suspect anything. In the field, he signaled the others. "You don't criticize anything any more; you obey or else I'll put them all on you." I was scared and I always obeyed after that.

What she says is corroborated by another girl, Patricia, age seventeen: "The boys from here, when they're in a bunch, they feel strong. They may take a girl to sleep in a pal's bed; his mother doesn't say anything. They share her if there's no little kid to give the whole thing away."[4] Using the girls in this way is rather typical of the warrior gang, who derive their boldness from the clan's strength and assume a droit de seigneur.

Meanwhile, another kind of group sexual behavior was related to us by a doctor who is now treating a ten-year-old boy involved in this strange rite. Late at night, five or six couples would meet in the basement and put on blindfolds. The little boy was assigned to look at and compare the boys' genitals and choose the partners, who then coupled without a word and without recognizing each other. What can one think of this rite, in which sex is taken out of any context and the partners are chosen by a child who probably represents both the innocent hand that draws lots and the eunuch?

It should be noted that the adolescents do not go to the professional prostitutes in the red-light districts, whom they call "sluts," because they have to pay.

So they change girlfriends frequently and do not become attached, and they think one seventeen-year-old is "ruined because he likes his girlfriend and doesn't change off. If he marries her, he won't have lived." Being virile thus enjoins "having" a girlfriend for an audience (this does not necessarily imply physical possession) and at the same time proving, sometimes publicly, one's sexual capabilities.

The boys' attitude toward illegal paternity is simple: they are ignorant of the consequences of their actions. Pregnancy just happens. The adults say of an adolescent, "He had a child in the project," and not with whom. If the girl is from the project, the boys are satisfied not to reveal themselves; if she comes from outside, she is driven away. In both cases she is abandoned during her pregnancy.

They refuse to admit any paternity because they have no official woman and do not live as couples. Two or three years later the same boys will marry the girls they have gotten pregnant. They will look "seriously" for girls at around twenty, when they shoulder their responsibilities more easily. The lower age group considers itself on reprieve and its relations with girls are still in the realm of play.

ECONOMIC ACTIVITIES WITHIN THE GANG

Possession and Trading

Possession may be conceived of as concerning things acquired, duly or unduly. Other people's belongings are not in the least respected, and they are freely appropriated. The boy's attitude toward struggle and his lack of consideration for the intrinsic value of property certainly plays an important part in his choice of misdemeanors.

Purchase and trading are other means the adolescent uses to build up a hoard. But before studying them we shall try to define what is important in the boy's eyes, to investigate whether the fact of living almost as a group results in a kind of pooling of possessions, and to find out what constitutes a gift.

The La Halle adolescent takes anything he finds without knowing what he will use it for. These are his reserves, his wealth. This is why he regularly rummages through the city dumps: "You find all kinds of little things there to save up and swap." The boys search especially for knives, forks, and the little cartons still full of jam from the Orly airport garbage cans. They collect the usual plunder of things that can be turned into cash, especially nonferrous metals and bits of electric wire, which they then get together and strip. They sell their little piles to secondhand dealers, but if someone's collection is much too small, he gives it to the others.

In looking at this patient rag-picking, account must be taken of the parents' mentality, their fear of running short, and their thirst for material goods. Scavenging is carried on by the adults, and some mothers show hardly any curiosity about the source of their sons' loot—that strange heap of things cluttering up the closet, the bathroom, and the space under the bed. On the other hand, some young adults are not averse to accompanying the boys on expeditions in order to put them to work and even steal the fruit of their pillaging, as Pierre (age eighteen) recounts:

> They'd dug up a big roll of cable and they went every night and cut off pieces to sell to the secondhand dealer. Mimi and Totor [adults] took their car to go and look for the rest of the roll, but the cops were there. Then they swiped the boys' stockpile. Totor was strong. If they hadn't been willing to give up their loot, they would've gotten a helluva beating.

The boys' belongings, however acquired, are divided into four groups:

(1) Those that remain entirely their own property;
(2) Those that circulate among the others;
(3) Those acquired for the group;
(4) Those that serve as a means of exchange.

(1) The first group involves goods of symbolic value, external signs of wealth and prestige according to the adolescents' code

of values. The motorbike comes first. It is carefully watched over and loaned stingily to friends and a few girls for short rides inside the project, but in any case, it is not put at the disposal of the group. The boy is the master of his "machine," which he wears out very quickly.

Then come tools. These boys, who have so much trouble becoming interested in a trade, all own tools that are jealously kept and put away: all kinds of keys, hammers, files, and screwdrivers designed for repairing and doctoring motors. They scrounge them from the cellars or from an employer but never buy them, on principle.

Portable phonographs are a rare mark of wealth. Everyone uses them but they are never moved without their owner, who plays the machine himself. Watches are an entirely personal belonging. Other things that arouse admiration and envy such as portable transistor radios, boxing gloves, or a revolver with a useless cylinder, are not loaned out though they are not always used; the essential thing is to own them. Finally, the adolescents have dogs and cats of whom they alone are the masters.

(2) Clothes are circulated even though they remain personal property. They are loaned in two ways: temporarily, for instance, as a favor to a "pal" who is going out with a girl, and for a long time, when they are essential to someone who has nothing. In the latter case, the borrower, boy or girl, must be in trouble, for example, running away from home or a penal institution. They know that clothing loaned for an indefinite length of time will be given back only when it is worn out, but this does not matter. They can refuse it when it comes back soiled.

Records are private property for group use and are stored at one boy's house: "We don't buy them. We all have a bunch of them. B. keeps them for us. When we have them, we bring them to his house."

(3) Things acquired especially for the group are usually articles of consumption. We have seen how the crayfish were eaten by all those on the expedition. It is the same with drinks: they always have drinks in the summer because they know

where the nearest brewery is, and two boys take charge of supplying the others from the parked trucks. They steal apples from the overgrown gardens for everyone to share. One woman tells how an urchin stole two cases of Camembert from a truck being loaded and brought them nimbly home on his bike: "We had a good laugh and we all divided up those cheeses on the landing between the neighbors and the gang of kids."

Small amounts of money are often pooled to acquire things that the gang could not otherwise get, for example, they take up a collection to pay for a movie ticket for someone who is insolvent. This is not out of generosity but because it is important for the "pals" to enjoy the fun of the moment together.

However, boys may be dishonest to the group, as is shown by the following example. Five or six boys planned to go hunting and pooled their money for cartridges, but the next day the two who owned the rifles left before the stated time and fired all the cartridges. The others could do nothing but think up some kind of revenge.

(4) Except for the goods described in (1) and (3), everything the adolescents amass is a means of exchange. An infinite number of things circulates among them, and we shall try to study how this is done further on.

A good is something endowed with purchasing power, that one can enjoy or disregard. The concept of gifts excludes giving something they are tired of or that has no more cash value. It always originates in the fondness of one adolescent for another, whether of the same sex or not, but the boys generally give things they own and are fond of (clothing, boots, knives, money) to either boys or girls, while the girls buy things for the boys (razors, cigarette lighters, underwear, socks, shaving brushes, mirrors, cigarette cases).

Underprivileged as they are, what the adolescents see of the world is the wealth to which they have no right. For them, the model of the man integrated into society is the one who has wealth at his disposal, receives gain and profit, and has what Proudhon calls "the right to windfalls."[5] They feel that their right to exist is impaired, and, as a defense against their perception of a painful reality, they act careless about the small belongings they have as though these were unimportant. This failure to attach value to things also comes from the difficulty they experience in placing themselves in time; only the moment is valid, so things have only momentary value.

Trading. Although the project represents an open milieu, it seems to us that it has many prisonlike aspects. Besides, the adolescents living there are more or less in contact with delinquents running away or returning from penal institutions. Their mentality is absolutely no different from what one finds in a boarding school. They have little money to spend or they refuse to use it for useful purposes, so they have very little access to outside commerce. An internal commerce springs up, as in boarding school, with diverse and mixed-up transactions. These are difficult to analyze because they do not take place in broad daylight, and the young people keep strangely silent about them even though they talk quite willingly about their thefts. It should be noted that those most devoted to trading of all kinds are the boys who have least—who are not working.

In order to understand the spirit of these trades, we must not forget that for most of the boys absolute value has no meaning, either for things or money. All that counts is satisfying a need. And finally, they are used to the fact that there is a market for secondhand goods.

It is almost impossible to distinguish goods of symbolic value from useful objects that are simply exchanged, since these values are unstable and vary with the individual. However, chrome, hubcaps, spare parts, and everything connected with motorbikes have a constant market value and are really used as money. The boy who has no money saves up chrome, knowing he will be able to sell it because the boys frequently damage their vehicles.

We have tried to deduce the laws of exchange from the adolescents' obscure explanations. When they meet in a café, for example, one boy asks another, "Would you have a rearview mirror? I'll trade you for a steering wheel." The other boy does not have one but promises to get one by tomorrow. He may offer the steering wheel to a third boy but more likely he will offer a little money or another object so he can keep the steering wheel, because each boy is trying to make up his own stockpile. Through this chain trading process, one can procure "comics," a set of shelves, clothing, boots, chain bracelets, belts, knives—and all kinds of things.

The prices are not regulated but are left to be freely decided by the interested parties. Certain items are reputed to have great purchasing power or a high market value, like a switchblade knife, which it is prohibited to carry. A knife worth 20F retail may be traded for an 80F jacket, and this is an honest and normal transaction.

The exchange value also depends on how difficult it is to convince the owner of the desired object to part with it and how long it takes to make him give in. Then there is bidding, and the prices rise in obedience to the law of supply and demand. The buyer must sometimes wait until the coveted item has passed through several hands. It takes patience, inventiveness, good memory, perseverance, and the ability to wait. It sometimes happens that hard trading drags on so long that the buyer no longer wants the desired object.

The exchange value, which is relative, irregular, and dependent on how much the object is coveted, also changes with the current fashions, for example, the vogue for imitation leather pants that were all the rage. "Henri bought some fake pants at the American surplus store* and stole three pairs because he could easily swap them," according to Cecile. When too many people have a fashionable thing, its price drops; conversely, when it is too hard to get (for example, eagles on the jacket back), the fashion is dropped.

Trades are made not only horizontally between two comparable items but also vertically between dissimilar things; this is how they trade for money. This is not completely a sale because it does not take account of the real value of the item.

*Stores selling surplus goods from American post exchanges in the area.—R.S.

Besides, the word "bought" is meant only for new things. In the exchange of one good for another, the word "buy" is replaced by "have": someone *had* such and such a thing for 10F.

Trades for money are often cheap, depending on the immediate needs of the seller. The boy who has no money or any hope of having some soon may trade his lighter for a pack of cigarettes, or his phonograph for 10F. Those who have a feel for profiteering exploit the others, but few of them realize it because they are only interested in the immediate pleasure the transaction brings them.

Once the desire is satisfied, things previously acquired at great cost may be lost, forgotten, given or thrown away and have no further importance after some time. The exchanged item may be returned to its owner but for an object of greater value. Some items keep a subjective, personal value; watches, for instance, are never traded.

The item may be tainted. After a bad deal, the object itself is considered guilty of being crooked, and then it may lose all value. The example of the unfortunate trading of a jacket shows both how fast the operation takes place and this kind of projection of subject on object.

> Henri bought a navy nylon jacket. René offered him 20F for it right away. Sale completed. Henri puts the jacket on the bed and goes away. Henri's brother, who didn't know about it, comes in and says, "What a nice jacket! I'll give you 50F." Sale completed; 30F profit for René in ten minutes. Disgusted by this losing bargain, the buyer no longer wanted the jacket, which disappeared. [Reported by Cecile.]

In this society where nothing is very important and yet where nothing is free, a loan may be just a tacit short- or long-term exchange. Thus, cigarettes are not shared but loaned. The boy who has none smokes the others' until the day when he will offer his open pack even if the unscrupulous boys quickly take them away.

Every gift calls for a countergift. Every loan must be paid back, and this may include some notion of interest if the possession is invested with unusual value or great prestige. A car may be loaned for a little money, for example, and a room in town was loaned to a boy to "bring girls up" in exchange for canceling a debt and then in exchange for a small sum of money.

Spiritual as well as material goods are exchanged. The boys teach each other the new dances and choose songs for each other that "they'd get a kick out of." The girls teach each other beauty tricks. There are loans of hospitality and food between friends. It is strange to see one person going to sleep at another's, a stairway away. The Mediterraneans especially carry on this exchanging of places to sleep as a consecration of friendship. They give each other advice on how to act with the opposite sex, and they exchange confidences, troubles, and windfalls. Everyone knows everything—worries, thefts, sweethearts—about the others. "We tell each other everything; we can't talk to anyone else but us," says Ahmed. Addresses and places to go are communicated without delay to the "pals." Blows as well as insults and rough words are traded when they have a scuffle, from which they often keep a dazzling reminder of the other's strength.

In La Halle's society of pals, there is neither completely equal sharing, complete pooling, nor completely individual property. Everything is loaned and traded, and goods circulate according to an unformulated rule that is very close to being an obligation to give, receive, and pay back.

System of Values

NOTION OF MONEY

Money is used principally for fun and is considered only secondarily as a means of acquisition. It is the sign of immense prestige, and there is a sensual pleasure in the act of holding out a bill to the barman, thus making it an instrument of pleasure in two ways.

Money is needed to pay for what they cannot get free. We have already spoken of the popularity of the traveling fair, the bar with its slot machines and juke boxes, and candy and sweets. The boys are willing to pay admission to the dance halls, but it must still correspond to their scale of values. As Ahmed puts it,

> We don't go to those trashy town dances unless we're flat broke or have nothing to do that night, but we never pay. We go to the movies first, and around midnight, when the cashier is gone, we get in free. We only pay in the popular night spots.

Pocket money is passed around, and there is no difference between money from wages and that obtained by some kind of trafficking. In a gang of close friends, those who have nothing are not left out. It seems natural for the boy who has money to pay for the others at the café or the movies. Those who pay for the others never talk about it; it is perfectly in order and is done on the condition of being paid back.

An hour of pool costs 3.5F, a rate they are willing to accept because the game is coin-operated. They also spend a lot on cigarettes, usually regular ones but deluxe when they want to impress the girls, but they hate to use their own money for utilitarian purposes like paying the cleaner or buying underwear. If their mothers do not see to it, they quite often do not have much left to buy clothes or useful things, and they get them in other ways.

Clothes from the American surplus stores are very popular, and the adolescents like to shop at the flea market or at the hand-me-down markets—places full of people where the atmosphere is not entirely legal. Besides, it is easy to buy one and steal two in the anonymity of the crowd. Everything bought in the flea market—spare parts, pants, pea coats—may be meant for trading, for cash or not.

For the project adolescents, money is less of a commodity necessary for subsistence than the symbol of man's omnipotence. "Money is for having fun; things you steal," says Cecile.

THEFT

There is great ambiguity in the notion of theft, residing in the fact that what is normally considered theft in society is considered legitimate appropriation in La Halle, the just revenge of the poor against the rich. Do our young thieves intend to take a thing for themselves or to give it away, for its cash value or for the benefit of the group? Moreover, their misdemeanors must include group destruction of property, where the same playful element as in theft and the insignificance of the notion of property enter in. We shall not make our brief analysis of the adolescents' stealing from the penal point of view, therefore, but rather try to see what the hierarchy of thefts is from the boys' perspective, beginning with the least important.

The children of La Halle are petty thieves who do not know the techniques of the professionals so their thefts are more in the nature of scrounging. They live cut off from the world, example is contagious, and the desire to make an impression makes it advisable to steal like a hoodlum. Ahmed says, "There's not one guy here who can brag that he hasn't stolen, and if you stop you lose your touch. That's when you get caught."

The hierarchy of thefts is organized on the basis of the difference between appropriating something and stealing it from someone. As long as the person robbed is anonymous, the act is unimportant. In their eyes, there is no theft as a result of keeping something because anything found rightfully belongs to the finder, so briefcases and cameras found on public transportation are legitimate property.

Scrounging is legion. We shall mention for the record the "borrowing," of motorbikes on public thoroughfares and all thefts of records, clothing, and various other things from display cases, a practice at which the girls excel. Stealing from vans, which consists of appropriating anything in a vehicle, proceeds in the same spirit. Railway cars are robbed with glee; this is like hitchhiking. Siphoning gas from a car is also scrounging, unless they know who owns the vehicle, in which case it is an act of revenge.

Stealing from their employer is also normal because it is not the owner's person that is robbed. There are so many materials laid out that it is only logical to sneak off with some of them. Moreover, the role of the foreman is important; underpaid himself, he closes his eyes to petty thefts, and the adolescents wrongly feel tacitly covered up. The girls are more prudent than the boys, whose behavior sometimes gets out of control (one of them took twenty-seven amplifiers from his employer).

The cellars are continually examined and ransacked but even though this robbing of project residents is anonymous, it does not find support among all the adolescents.

Stealing a car is in a separate class. It is more than a show of prowess, an exploit, or a theft. The adolescents unconsciously perceive it as self-affirmation, and it enables them to satisfy a long-suppressed desire. Besides, it is thought of as just borrowing, and it entails many more risks. The adventure often ends swiftly and brutally: "I really just stole the gas," says Baba, getting out of a car between two policemen.

Stealing money is more serious in their eyes: "That's real stealing." They have to have courage to rob someone or to stage a burglary. The boys make no distinction between premeditation and taking advantage of an opportunity. "Real stealing" also means stealing from someone they know, so they thought Baba did something wrong in the following instance:

> He wanted a [motor] bike and couldn't find one anywhere. There was one downstairs of Daniel's that belonged to a visiting pal from X——. He took it up to the bathroom in his house and spent the whole day doctoring[6] it with chrome he had saved up.

This does not prevent the adolescents from stealing from each other occasionally. They hate to be robbed but do not attach great importance to the loss of an object. If the victim is particularly attached to it, he will make a search for it and steal it back. If it is impossible for him to find it again, he will get one like it by any means. He will never lodge a complaint.

Theft is almost general to various degrees among the project youths and is void of any moral content. It entails the risk of being caught and punished, and those who indulge in it

respect the rules of the game and accept this risk, so there
is no dishonesty involved (this is a concept also held by the
parents).

MUTUAL HELP

If a problem arises between an adolescent and the adult world
—parents, employers, or representatives of authority—he is
sure to find refuge and comfort among his peers. There are
numerous mutual services rendered in connection with finding
a job, and the others bring food and clothing to any adolescent
temporarily on the outs with his parents. Furthermore, there
is a tacit but absolute league against authority within the group,
aimed at protecting the youths who have run away from foster
homes or penal institutions. Everyone knows how hard it is
to find an adolescent on the loose if he has had time to reach
the protection of the group. Food, secret lodging, hiding places,
and addresses are provided, at least temporarily.

> One night they went through all the cellars with torches of twisted
> paper set on fire, looking for a sixteen-year-old girl on the loose.
> They didn't find anything but a little red couch that had been
> carried into our own cellar. The girl slept there several nights.
> Then the boys brought their girlfriends there . . . and all the runaway
> boys slept there. It was for guests. [Related by Cecile.]

While some act upon it more frequently than others, opposition to society finds support among all of them and violation
of the law is not a negligible element in prestige; the members
of the gang are welded together as long as its consequences
last.

AESTHETICS

We have already alluded to this, especially in regard to clothing, where we have seen that the adolescents are not slaves
to fashion and show a certain amount of individuality. They
consider art to be exclusively reserved for the middle class,
but they show an appreciable poetic sense. They know an
infinite number of songs whose words they copy in a notebook,
and they often sing in their own group, appositely choosing

the songs suited to their voices. They are not captivated by the popular idols, whose lack of talent they criticize, but the stars' fulgurating success tempts them (about ten boys had an audition in a studio in the city). While they like to dance to rock, they also sing the songs of Aznavour and Jean Ferrat.

Self-expression has not dried up in them. They have the art of telling stories and all night long they embellish, dramatize, and act them out to the laughter of their audience. They love making sometimes mean jokes, and their arguments and fights are at times played out like medieval farces. Some of them write poetry in secret, and others try to compose songs [see appendix], but none of them plays an instrument except one or two who play the harmonica. Both girls and boys draw naive pictures designed as wall decorations, and they ingeniously manufacture objects of their very own. They have the potential for all modes of self-expression but these remain embryonic because the ever-present expressions of the surrounding culture prevent them from developing.

Changes in the Gangs

The life span of subgangs is conditioned by two factors: how long the leaders are around and how quickly the boys grow up and change their age group and personalities. If no one leaves because of eviction or relocation, the life of a gang is about two years, that is, until the leaders disappear or change their behavior as they become adults.

This is why the look of La Halle's group of young people has changed in two years. The warrior class was dismembered and has not yet been re-formed. "The biggest kids moved—we really miss them—and the guys who were the biggest hoodlums before have turned into big snobs," says Robert. Henri is married; Baba is in jail. This was a large gang two years ago, and it set the tone and led the way for the others. Now the youths seem more peaceful and go in for dancing more, under the aegis of a gang led by Mediterraneans. But they are eighteen or older and will soon disappear from the scene.

Another phenomenon comes into play too: the aging of the

project. Two years ago, we were told that the Europeans "don't like the wogs very much." The more time passes, the more leveling occurs among ethnic groups, and if there was segregation two years ago, it no longer exists. One can even foresee the rise of Arab and Jewish leaders. But the twelve to fifteen age group is large, and we cannot tell how it will be organized. Just recently we noted the appearance of a new gang of warriors in the same age bracket as the previous gang, which tends to prove that there is a two-year cycle.

The End of Adolescence

Army service and marriage traditionally put an end to adolescence. At nineteen, the boys àre called up and more than one girl is already married. Military service is met with great reluctance at La Halle. Some boys use any means to get out of it, such as getting discharged for personality problems, while the others wait resignedly until it is time to go. None of them goes before he is called. Those who are on leave report sick. The regiment does not have the meaning for them that it had for their fathers.

In fact, military service comes too late. Seventeen is the optimum age for adolescence in the project. At eighteen, the boys feel completely like men; by nineteen, they are "old" and want to settle down, and the regiment upsets their plans.

They marry early, to a mate met outside La Halle. The boys generally disappear from the project between nineteen and twenty-two, unless they stay and live temporarily in their parents' homes with their wives and children. Except for the Moslems and Jews, the girls leave even sooner (between seventeen and eighteen) and sometimes live alone before setting up housekeeping or marrying.

In conclusion, the adolescents' informal group shows a kind of solidarity based on coexistence. It is not to be confused with a "mechanical solidarity" of the kind found in military society where all the segments of the group are articulated with each other, nor an "organic solidarity" based on division of labor. It would seem to be solidarity of a cultural nature to the extent that there is a temporary community of mentality, customs, beliefs, and reference-models that unite the adolescents of a single age group. This division by age is conceived and intended as such by the adolescents themselves, and they support their age group as though they had a membership card in it. This cultural kind of solidarity seems to make it clear that, for each adolescent, it is more a matter of "being with" such-and-such a leader having the desired characteristics than of being all together. They are all together only at special times, for example, when the boys feel threatened as members of the project by an outside gang.

Homogeneity within the informal group, between gang members and between gangs themselves, comes about in the realm of values. The forms of solidarity that appear are always the same, for example, helping the runaway. The aesthetic experience is the same, whatever the gang. As far as it goes until the end of adolescence, opposition to society seems to be structured in the same way by every individual: defiance of adults and homosexuals, attempted misdemeanors, and fighting.

Nevertheless, this almost homogeneous system of values remains out of line with the informal organization of the adolescent group. This would be another subject, but it would be interesting to know whether a system of values of this type but with more compelling force than this one would result in a truly structured social organization. An investigator like J. Monod attempted a primarily structural analysis of gangs rather than elaborating conceptually the social organization to which it might lead, and elsewhere, Ph. Robert gave just a critical picture of the gangs from a more philosophical perspective.[7]

Conclusion

As we have already shown, children of all ages in the La Halle project, from babies to young adults, enjoy a freedom always accepted by the parents (except most notably for the Moslem girls). There are no strict limits on this freedom, owing to the lack of a formalized system of discipline, so children and adolescents will try to win maximum freedom. This desire, common to all young people, is more easily satisfied in the project. For school-age children, it is the result of a lack of parental supervision, for which the parents would not think of blaming themselves. For the adolescents, it is because, having acquired a certain amount of financial independence, they have a means of bargaining with their mother and also with their father, who always plays a somewhat retiring role and who is in competition with them.

The notion of time and space consequently seems to be characterized in a special way for the project children as compared to other urban groups.

Time. The time of the preschool child is not segmented by the rhythms of tasks or strict obligations. He does not put away his things at a set time, mealtime is not a ritual, and playtime separated from the rhythm of family life is practically unlimited. Time is quite indeterminate.

School-age children submit to the temporal constraint of school, but this is offset by a constant desire to run away from it. After class, they have all the leeway they want to live in the lax rhythm of the project, and let us remember that no one makes them do their homework.

For the adolescents, whose childhood has been conditioned by this primary rhythm of the project and by schooldays viewed as a temporal constraint, the strictness of time spent in an apprenticeship or on a job cannot be accepted easily. This is a partial cause of the frequent individual breaks in the rhythm of work through partial idleness and unemployment. We must remember that the adults live from day to day and that this concept of time is very likely a reference-model for the adolescents, who all live in the moment. (This is not peculiar to La Halle adolescents, but we can account for it more coherently in the project.) Leisure time is seen as unlimited until military service comes along, and the usual eight-hour day is not a unit of measure.

Space. We note that the three age groups mentioned above take possession of three concentric zones: the inner courtyard for the little children, the vacant lots and their environs for the school-age children, and the commune, the department, and the city for the adolescents. All three of these are much more vast than the play areas usually available in an urban setting.

This concept of freedom in time and space, acquired early and lasting until age twenty, is perhaps a reciprocal of the values of individual freedom and opposition to society. These values, drawn from the adult subculture, are influenced by the concept of freedom in time and space, but when they become stronger they affect this concept of freedom. This would explain the adolescents' becoming "better organized" as they grow older.

NOTES

[1]Some children do not understand the mechanism of the monthly rating. We were present at an argument between ten- and eleven-year-old boys about "what makes you first or last." Some chose grammar, others thought arithmetic was most important, but no one considered the importance of the whole of school work. If a child has been marked "excellent" on an arithmetic paper and then finds he is fifteenth in the general rating, he thinks an injustice has been done. The teachers are not fully aware of their students' ignorance about this.

[2]The project harbors a large number of stray cats. Some articles were published in the paper denouncing the children's mistreatment of the cats, but nothing was proven.

[3]Vocational training for adults from age seventeen: six-month practical courses for which the student receives the minimum wage, leading to a diploma highly valued on the job market. The range of trades offered is quite varied and help in finding jobs is guaranteed.

[4]Cf. Dr. Fombastie, "Barlu, Rodeo ou Complot," *Le Monde*, September 1, 1966.

[5]Proudhon, *Qu'est-ce que la Propriété?* Ange Laribé edition, p. 245.

[6]They have boxes full of steel numbers that they use to doctor the motors. They buy the registration of an old, worn-out motor at a scrapyard and stamp the registration number on the stolen motor after patiently filing off the old one.

[7]Ph. Robert, *Les Bandes d'Adolescents* Editions Ouvrières, 1965; "Evolution de la Vie Sociale," series ed. by Ph. Chombard de Lauwe.

Part III

THE NORMS OF SOCIAL LIFE

We have seen how the residents of La Halle live in the family cell and the project, but it would be a mistake to conclude that we are dealing with a closed world that is entirely marginal to society. In the study of individual, family, and social life in the project, we have in fact been continually confronted with a dialectic between the "closed" and the "open." The lives of the children, the adults, and (in part) the adolescents—their activities, leisure time, and games—are subject to specific rhythms and are set on a territory divided according to the various functions it has to accommodate. But at certain times in daily life, these rhythms and organization of space are broken up to mesh with those of the surrounding environment. For instance, school life appears as a compulsory temporal relationship of the child with another system having fixed class hours and an institutionalized space that the children of La Halle must share with others. In such an example, we can really see the dialectical relationship between the time–space experienced in the project and the time–space of the school. In fact, as we have shown before, while the children attend school under compulsion, they willingly turn back to the closed system of the project, which they consider their own. They refuse to participate in a time and space that might offer them a life more dependent on the school, for instance.

Here is another example. For those women who do not work outside, life is restricted to the limits of the project (even for daily errands) and to the rhythm of household tasks. They find this life as much a constraint as a factual condition to which they try to adjust. If we talk about constraint, it is because we have noted that all of them conceive of real leisure as something only outside the project. When they can get away for a distant errand, they do not hesitate to do so, and they really consider this moment spent elsewhere as an escape. Thus here again there is a dialectic between a closed system of time and space accepted half out of obligation and half out of habit, and an open system appearing as participation in life outside.

Compared to the attitudes of the children and the women, the behavior of the adolescents illustrates this dialectic still more perfectly, because they live in both systems at once. Their daily rhythms unfold inside the project for those who are unemployed and outside it, as with the men, for those who work. But when night comes, these rhythms are broken, and it is the relationship with the outside that dominates, with the adolescents leaving for the city or other places by means of transportation they have provided for that purpose.

These notations do not give sufficient account of one aspect of the dialectic, that is, that it no longer impregnates just the rhythms and space they live in but also the concept of the norms of social life. In this third part, we should like to show that there is an alternating predominance of the closed and the open, depending on whether it is a matter of social relations, time and space, or information, and that they both coexist in the system of values. In fact, as we shall show in our last chapter, the closed comes into play in the formation of certain values peculiar to the project, and the open in bringing in outside values.

9

Social Relations

This subject has been taken up several times in preceding chapters. We shall analyze here the relationship with outsiders, and how relations with neighbors are perceived as compared to observed reality.

Relationships with Outsiders

We compared the project to a village but it has the special geographic feature that, unlike a village, it is built at a dead end. You do not go through it to go somewhere else, no crossroads bring passersby to it, and you would never expect to meet a lost traveler there. The project suffers from isolation, and so all those who do not live in it are strangers to it.

Who, then, are the outsiders who penetrate this closed world? They come here as part of their jobs, with a very precise objective that rarely concerns the whole group. They are relatively numerous compared to those who enter an isolated village and are totally different from them.

In a village, two kinds of visitors could be taken into consideration: nomads who earn their living by amusing the fixed population, and regular tradesmen who come by at set times. Continuing relationships are formed around simple commerce and, depending on the personality of the visitor, exchanges may take place that go beyond simple conversation.[1]

No outsider comes to La Halle to amuse the population. A small circus was set up for an evening just once in the four years, but it has never been seen again.[2] There is no playing field on which an outside athletic team could be accommodated.

The Arab butcher is the only tradesman who visits regularly. The ice cream vendor appears almost every day, but only in summer and for a clientele made up exclusively of children. The paper-seller, the nougat vendor, and the blind peddlers who visit the neighboring HLM's do not come into La Halle.

One of the characteristics of the project is that the outsiders' faces are always unfamiliar, as if they were taking turns carrying on the same function, and those who would logically be expected to visit do not come. For instance, the priest, whose parish is in the town and who might be expected to come to the project, admits that he never calls any more than the minister or the rabbi.

The outsiders who visit the project do so in the line of duty, and their occupations represent society at various levels: commerce, authority, social services, and health.

Commerce

While the usual tradesmen do not pass by, the project is not forgotten by the canvassers from big companies but the game of commercial relations is not played according to the usual rules. Unlike the itinerant grocer who sets up shop in the center of the community and waits to serve his customers, who remain relatively free, the canvasser addresses himself to the individual and forces himself on the customer's home and will. Moreover, buyers from the project are treated as an anonymous clientele because the businesses that offer goods for sale and the faces of their salesmen change from year to year. For the residents of La Halle, each canvasser is a new, continually changing intruder to be combatted. And even if they write and ask the salesman to call, the man who comes is rarely the one with whom they dealt previously. As for those who spread their piles of linens on the courtyard pavement, they sell "on the run," then disappear, and do not come back. The people of La Halle are not customers in the usual sense, and no warm or lasting relationship is established between buyer and seller, who always remains an unfamiliar stranger.

Authority

The representatives of authority are many and their visits are frequent. They address themselves to the individual and not the group, and their arrival is generally a sign that someone has committed an act judged reprehensible by society or that he is being put under surveillance. They appear in the recognizable form of the policeman, the gendarme, the foot patrolman and the process-server, or in the more equivocal form of men or women not in uniform whose exact role or whose ultimate authority is not well known. These are the social-service workers, the family allowance tutors, the project manager, and even the school official who comes to get absent children.

The uniformed police represent the law and public power. They are a necessary institution that is both hated and accepted as eternal; the residents run away from them but they also call upon them as need be. Those who have given way to violent behavior, those who are delirious or drunk with anger or liquor, those who refuse to return to the psychiatric hospital at the end of their "leave," those who have attempted suicide, and those for whom the time has come to serve a prison term decreed long ago are all hoisted into the patrol wagon.

Even if they are unbearable, policemen are part of the normal order. Much more disturbing are the plainclothes detectives who make investigations, or the commissioner himself, who has the tenants' goods repossessed while they are away. It is he who forces open the door, and he is also there when occupants are evicted.

The policemen's faces change too, depending on whether they belong to the central police station in the canton capital, the substation at the project up the road, or some other police unit. La Halle is known as the "souses' project" at all the police stations in neighboring localities.

From time to time, the gendarmes arrive in force looking for an adolescent evading military service, or holding a motorbike thief by the collar. They rummage through the cellars and empty their contents. They keep an eye on the boys and harass them. They are hated and feared even more than the police.

The patrolman acts as a watchman. He is a more familiar figure and an anachronism of whom the children make fun. His kepi distinguishes him from afar, and he is carefully avoided.

No sound accompanies the process-server, who comes to deliver the inexorable, incomprehensible blue paper signifying a court order for debts. Defenseless in the face of this threat, the person concerned goes around showing the document to sympathetic neighbors. The process-server is regarded fatalistically like a plague, as is the Treasury agent whose mission it is to recover unpaid rents and furniture taxes.

For the project people, these roles are lumped together as one threat. Police and justice have the same meaning.

The lone women who pass through the project doors can only be social workers or, worse still, police assistants.[3] Their visits provide a source of worry or distress because they may result in one or more children being taken away, or even in the forfeiture of parental authority, so strange and unfamiliar social workers are greatly feared. The police assistant may come back some morning at 7:00 with two detectives, as she has done before, to take the child away to a foster home. That is why project residents are on the lookout behind the curtains and watch these strange assistants, whom they consider dangerous, to see where they go; it is important to know into which stairwell they are going. At the thought of a visit from an unfamiliar social worker, some women panic, cry, or become truly ill or very depressed.

The tutor from the family allowances, who helps the household manage its unbalanced budget, was appointed with the family's agreement. He nonetheless represents judicial authority, and residents cannot be sure to what extent his role is peaceful. Perhaps he will be severe if the budget is not reorganized quickly enough. Even though he takes over all the money worries, he remains somewhat of an intruder for the families in his charge, and for the others he is a stranger, perhaps an enemy, with whom it is better not to commit oneself. This is why we have classified him among the representatives of authority despite his helping role.

There are different degrees of being a stranger. The manager, who comes once a week, is least so. They fear him because they do not know if he is a friend or an enemy, but they do not run away from him. They try instead to get into his good graces by offering him a drink. In fact, all complaints must be submitted to him because he is the residents' spokesman to the public authorities. On the other hand, he plays the policeman, scolding those who are negligent and threatening those who do not pay the rent promptly, and they never know what he might betray about secrets he hears of.

Social Services

Another, more familiar outsider frequents the project. These are the people more specifically in charge of social services provided as such, with the repressive side blurred. They are in the project regularly or almost all the time.

First come the instructors from the youth club who keep the children busy every night with games or group activities. They moved in at the same time as the residents. They no longer arouse distrust but they meet with resistance as soon as they try to exercise any authority.

The district social worker's office in the project is open once a week. Everyone knows her and her activities are generally tolerated because they are in response to voluntary requests by the interested parties. Yet she remains an outsider whose opinion is feared and whose domination must be accepted in order to get something.

Supervised Training set up an office in the project a year and a half ago. In the minds of the adults, the instructors are primarily representatives of judicial authority.

Common to these three types of social workers is the fact that they have offices in the project. They are no longer unfamiliar, and the residents do not feel they have to keep an eye on them any more. Yet they remain unassimilable outsiders, as we shall see further on.

The agent who pays out the family allowances plays somewhat the same role as the village mailman. He is subjected to extortion by some of the men who intend to appropriate the whole allowance, and he innocently becomes the cause of arguments in the home. He is the only outsider we know of whose arrival is greeted with joy, but the mailman is really a relatively anonymous and unimportant person.

We have yet to mention some charity women who always come in pairs, carrying a sack of clothing. They make infrequent visits to just a few families, and they cross the courtyard amid general indifference.

Health

Many ambulances are used in La Halle. They are almost never the same ones, and the orderlies are anonymous, but the ambulance must be mentioned as a frequent strange intruder and a cause for curiosity.

The PMI is set up in the project and is open once a week. A doctor and three nurses work there but hardly anyone knows them except mothers of children under six.

Four or five doctors share the clientele from the project. All but one live in town or in the apartment complex. When the project opened, one doctor moved into an apartment made available by the government to the medical society. This created confusion in people's minds. They were misinformed and thought this doctor had been put at their disposal by the public authorities, so they refused to pay for their visits or else paid for only one visit after having the whole family examined. In his desire to help *"those* people," the doctor added to the confusion by distributing free samples and answering all calls. Later, tired of an "impossible clientele," he refused to take care of them and kept only about ten families whom he considered "normal clients."

Another doctor, who looks after fifty families, says it is easy to make contacts in La Halle, but they remain superficial and the doctor remains an outsider. The women do not trust him and they are cautious in their confidences, which are always oriented around their sex lives. As an example, Dr. B. cites a woman who, after complaining to him about her husband's impotence and telling him how unhappy and dissatisfied she was, got into his car on the pretext that she was going in the same direction and openly propositioned him on the way. He says the men never volunteer anything during the consultations, to which they come infrequently.

Beginning with the foregoing list of outsiders, we must try to analyze what confers this status. The teacher, the priest, and the doctor are not considered outsiders in a village even though they come from elsewhere on a particular mission. They may not live in the village and yet be part of it, because they are partly blended into the community life. In La Halle, on the contrary, the outsider is never assimilated or integrated even if he establishes quarters in the project.

The first reason, which cannot be overemphasized, is that one or several of the following characteristics or facts is common to all visitors:

They are there for a reason;
They do not have a choice of place;
Their identities change over time;
They represent authority and public power;
They intervene on someone's orders;
They have the right to look around, pass judgment, and supervise;

They want to get something;
They force themselves on the home.

Why should we be surprised, then, that every outsider represents a threat a priori? The residents defend themselves against the intruder with bad temper and aggressiveness.

Second, each outsider addresses himself to the individual or at best to a limited group, never to the whole group. It is true that this is difficult in a place devoid of community life, but the fact that the exchanges always take place without witnesses reinforces distrust and fear, isolates the outsider, and helps make the individual feel attacked.

Finally, the residents are aware that they do not belong to the same social class as the visitor, especially those who have the right to pass judgment on them. One woman said to this observer, "You can say what you like; you're not like us, you're rich." Mrs. H. corroborated this remark by saying, "You're the only woman we know" (that is, the only one outside our class). But is this not because the visitor coming into the project feels right away that he is different? Does not every visitor have some preconceptions before entering this seemingly hostile world?

"They're savages, those people," says the manager. It is true that you can pass someone close enough to touch on the stairs and greet him without receiving any response. It is true that doors may be slammed in your face; that you have to call out your name and the object of your visit before someone will open the door; that the ground floor windows shut in front of you; that the curtains hide curious glances; and that those who usually come knock in a certain way so the stranger is always discovered. He is not always invited in; sometimes the visit is conducted through a narrowly opened door. All the rules of courtesy may be neglected in regard to him. It is also true that once their distrust is overcome, the people of La Halle are capable of the warmest hospitality and the greatest courtesy, whether this is part of their tradition or not.

The outsider is anyone not brought in by someone they know, and he generates fear. In contrast, the arrival of a mass of outside people causes no excitement if they are relatives or friends of a resident. The residents simply say, "Look, the Untels are having company." When there is a warranted invasion of relatives among the Arabs of thirty people a day for six days, as happened when three brothers were circumcised, nobody thinks of these arrivals as outsiders because the Arabs, like the Spaniards or Italians, are part of the project.

The concept of nationality does not have any great meaning in La Halle. Only Mr. M., a Pied-Noir, expressed disappointment at not finding only Frenchmen where he lived. The French residents do not use the word "foreigner"; they always designate a neighbor by his name and not by his nationality. They admire and greatly envy the minority groups' cohesion and the spirit of mutual help that they see in the hospital, at construction projects where they have met some of them, or in the project. All of them are used to the mixing of different populations, and the most important thing for them is to be able to communicate in the same language, which is French in this case.

For the project people, the outsider is primarily someone who is not part of the family. "I've found more affection among strangers than in my own family. Georges prefers his family; he's a racist," says Mrs. V. And disunited though it is, the project is like one big family, so outsiders include all those who have no connection, either close or distant, through some bond of physical or social relationship.

Relationships with Neighbors

We are struck by two apparently opposite reactions when chatting with the project residents. In any kind of conversation, with anyone except the traditional Arabs, we quite commonly hear generalized complaints about the neighbors: "No one gets along; the neighbors aren't nice; everyone fights." But when we ask them to be specific about the relationships, we run into an unconscious refusal: "I don't see anyone; I don't know anyone." Moreover, this answer may come from a woman who is having someone in for coffee at that very moment, and who the day before told the inquirer about the latest incidents concerning the neighbors. So there is a difference between how they see the relationships and how these really appear.

Everyone agrees that relationships are difficult in the project. First, each one interjects an opinion about the others, without any amenities, in regard to the past, present, and future: "Do you know what she used to be? Those women can never hold up their heads"; "He's from Algeria but he's half black. He likes blood, like all the people of that race; he goes to the slaughterhouse just for the fun of seeing blood" (this is a Kabyle speaking); "She wears her dresses too low-cut; her kid will turn out bad." These opinions establish reputations and set off behavior that is curious, jealous, and fearful on one hand, and self-justifying and competitive on the other. Each person's insecurity is aggravated by everyone else, and a great deal of emulation comes into play in a climate reflecting this insecurity.

Jealousy and curiosity cannot be separated, and they are exercised in all sorts of places. "When I come back from shopping THEY look to see what I have in my basket," says Mrs. H. The district social worker reports that many people would rather see her at the town hall (a round trip of over a mile and a quarter) than use her office in the project, so the neighbors will not know of their visit to her. The help she can bring one person is cause for quarreling between him and another person who feels hurt. Jealousy reaches its culmination when it is a matter of one's love life. For instance, "I don't talk to her since she told everyone I was nice to the TV repairman," says Mrs. C.

Lasting relationships are rare. They are destroyed by jealousy and also by the betrayal that is part of self-justifying behavior. To say that the other person has done something reprehensible is to say that you deserve a better opinion. Here is an example of self-justifying behavior in regard to neighbors. Mrs. P. knows she has a bad reputation. She is accused of not taking care of her house or children. When she bathed her three children, bought them shoes, and had their hair cut, all on the same day, she went about the courtyard and took them visiting so they could be admired among the people she knew.

The residents never say, "What will the neighbors say?" but rather, "I don't give a darn about the neighbors; they can drop dead." But in reality the opinions the neighbors may possibly express are constantly at the back of their minds. These opinions may be positive or negative, and they may activate emulation and competition, especially in outward signs of wealth. Mr. H. says, "I get a lot of pleasure out of buying something if I'm the first one to have it." And Mrs. N. says, "We absolutely must buy another TV. We're the only ones who don't have it in the whole building."

Relationships in a burdensome and inescapable proximity are found unsatisfactory, difficult, and limited, and there are actually some twenty families, among those who think themselves superior to the others, who live withdrawn to themselves.

On the other hand, the yearnings that follow complaints against the neighbors are on this order: "I'd like to have friends who are trusty, loyal, serious, and intelligent," says Mr. B. "I'd like to see people, but decent and educated people; their race doesn't matter," says Mr. H. "I would like to live somewhere else, in the suburbs, away from all these people," says Mrs. H. "As for me, I'd like to have people over more, but here it degenerates into a fight," says Mrs. D. "What we'd like is to live in peace and friendship with all the neighbors," say Mr. and Mrs. V. "I would like to live on Rue X in the city, for the environment," says Mrs. C.

They nostalgically evoke the old neighborhoods where they lived previously and formed relationships with the merchants and artisans. Uprooted from their old town and street, they have found a sensation of strangeness in the project, and they have lost a feeling of freedom and the illusion of possible choice. It is important to note that these people were not neighbors in the past, and no common memories bring them together. Is it for this reason that relations are difficult between people who yearn for harmonious relationships?

The frequency of fortuitous encounters is favored by the physical arrangement and the fact that all the people shop for food at the same store. But here, unlike a street or a neighborhood, their nearness is imposed, limited, and circumscribed. Choices can be made only within the group, just as in a concentration camp, and the only possible defenses against loneliness are fortuitous encounters or voluntary visits.

The project people all know each other and know everything about each other, even if they do not know each other's names and are known by their peculiarities (the blonde, the fat woman in *L,* the one who drinks, the one who has a Dauphine, etc.). But they know nothing about each other except the present. They did not go to school together, and they do not know each other's families or past histories. There are many gaps in this kind of acquaintance since there is no reference to a common past. They meet only in the present, and maybe that is why constant association quickly degenerates into quarreling.

When relationships go beyond the stage of simple encounters, they are organized in more selective directions. First, they get to know their immediate neighbors on their landing and then in their stairwell. They know their rhythm and standard of living. This acquaintance seems to be extended gradually to the whole bloc, due to convenience of location. We sometimes hear this reflection: "I don't know the people across the way as well."

People of different backgrounds are mixed together since they are distributed at random in all the stairwells, except for one where there are no Arabs. The group formed by a stairwell crosses ethnic lines. Then affinities arise in connection with ethnic or sex group. The women are bound together by mutual tastes or a past that brings them closer together, or simply in order to bear their condition as women. We perceive a multitude of female cells that are shifting and difficult to observe.

Relationships by ethnic group are not impenetrable but are

corrected by the mixing in the stairwell. They are preferential in the case of Jews and Arabs but not restrictively so. The mixed group lives in relative isolation except for its relationships with the husband's ethnic group.

Some families who think themselves superior show a desire to be isolated, avoiding any encounters with neighbors. We find families whose social status is determined by a slightly higher economic level or more demanding aspirations, but we also find the dispersion of these families in different stairwells; the social typology does not coincide with the geographic.

There is a prevailing interest in others, except among the wealthiest. The Arabs and Jews show hospitality and generosity, and encounters with neighbors do not leave the metropolitans indifferent; they are curious and love scandal, but they are also capable of generous impulses. It can be said of all of them that they meet more often in times of misfortune than in times of jealousy-provoking felicity.

The mutual help we have already discussed is practically never carried on except at the level of survival. It is done with discretion and dignity and is never publicized. Its numerous ramifications are difficult to discover.

There is also solidarity of the community as a whole but it comes into play in just two kinds of circumstances. One occurs when the whole community feels wronged. For example, one day the caretaker did not put out the communal garbage cans, and this was interpreted as an aggressive act. All the residents then spread the contents of their individual garbage cans on the sidewalk. The other circumstance is when death strikes one of the residents. Then a neighbor volunteers to collect money in each apartment and records the small contribution opposite the name in a notebook. A wreath of flowers bearing the inscription "Friends and Neighbors" is purchased, and the remainder of the collection is turned over to the family of the deceased.

This chapter shows the project residents' feeling of rejection, their ambivalence in relationships with neighbors, and their awareness of forming a group, all at the same time. The feeling of rejection—marked by their being uprooted from the old town and street, the strangeness they perceive, and the loss of a feeling of freedom and the illusion of possible choice— creates a negative ambivalence in relationships with neighbors. They blame others for being what they themselves are. But this negative aspect is countered by the exchange of services and solidarity and their evident sociability. Negative and positive ambivalence coexist. The residents are capable of both hating and devotedly helping each other, of showing great unselfishness and betraying each other. They are afraid of each other and at the same time they yearn for selectively warmer bonds. Moreover, their attitudes and behavior toward strangers—whom they see as coming from outside, from constraining authority—reinforce their awareness of forming a coherent group, whatever their ethnic differences may be. In fact, except for the Pied-Noirs, they do not show racism.

It is interesting to note that these conclusions about relationships with neighbors are identical to those in the section on adolescent gangs: the lack of structuring in relationships, the importance of mutual exchanges, and the mobility of social connections. Beyond the opposition between the two generations, relationships seem to follow virtually the same type of organization.

NOTES

[1]Cf. the role of the peddler in *Histoire d'un Paysan* by Erckmann-Chatrian.

[2]Perhaps because some adolescents took off with the receipts from the performance.

[3]Name wrongly given to policewomen.

10

Time and Space

In the project as elsewhere, time is manifested as the rhythm of life and is linked to the disposition of space. In this chapter, we shall look first at the rhythms of life and then at the concept of time and space.

The Rhythms of Life

There is no single rhythm in La Halle but rather a sum of individual rhythms subject to different schedules. Yet similarities in the residents' concepts of time, the search for comradeship, and the fact that the great majority of the women are in the project all day bring about a daily rhythm peculiar to La Halle. We shall study this daily rhythm and then try to analyze the seasonal and annual rhythms, with the patterns of each ethnic group and the areas where these overlap.

The Daily Rhythm

The project follows a triple rhythm whose parts are superimposed on each other and coincide only at the evening meal because the children and working people are on strict schedules. But for one thing, this regular rhythm does not involve the whole group, and for another it generates times of social intensity and slackening. The residents are subject to two kinds of rhythms, one precise and imposed, the other lax and individual. In the course of the year, this division into two forms of life is found on workdays as well as on Saturday, and daily as well as seasonally.

The signal for the beginning of the day is given by noise. Everyone complains about it. From 5:00 A.M. it swells and spreads: banging doors, crying babies, swearing, voices, the scraping of metal beds being dragged over tile floors, groaning fuel pumps, and accelerating motorbikes climbing out of the cellar entrances.

Reveille is the point of dispersion. Men, adolescents, and a few women leave at staggered times until 8:00, showing no consideration for the neighbors. They do not all leave at once nor are all the working people away at the same time because not everyone has regular working hours. The laborers on rotating eight-hour shifts[1] and the hospital attendants take turns providing daytime and nighttime services. Similarly, the workmen leave earlier or later depending on the distance of their current construction site from home, and they may or may not come home for lunch. On the whole, however, the morning is marked by the departure of the men.

Most of the children are going to measure time from 8:15 until 4:45. At 8:00 they are ready, and there is an exodus since they all leave in a group at the same time. This movement is as regular as the tide; together with the departure of the men, it represents the only occasion when there is a single rhythm in the project. It is interrupted only on Thursday, which is not a schoolday and which the children organize as they please.

After having been subject to the schedules of the rest of the family, the women are left alone or with their infants.

Some of them feel free while others feel lonely, but in any case they are going to spend the day according to their own cadence. But we shall see how the search for human contact influences the rhythm in which they live.

We have observed two kinds of partially collective behavior. Every morning about ten mothers (almost always the same ones) accompany their children to school. There is no danger on the way, so their presence is of no real use. They wait for each other in pairs at the foot of the stairs and come back in two or three groups of friends after watching from a distance as the children enter the school building. These are the women whose strict (often Moslem) husbands do not let them visit and gossip with the neighbors, who have hardly any friends, or whose apartments are inhospitable—in short, those who suffer most from isolation or who greatly need social life. These women have set up a veritable ritual of encounter each morning, which is the first escape to the first chat of the day. It expresses a need for verbal exchanges and integration into an organized rhythm. These mothers have created a social function for themselves based on a pretext that cannot be questioned by their husbands. The proof that this is just a social function is that if they are busy preparing dinner at noon, or invite a friend in, or have something else to do at 4:30, the women generally do not return to pick up the children.

After the children have left, the time is devoted to household tasks until noon. The lady of the house has a relaxed rhythm that is hardly subject to either her own discipline or one imposed by her activities. What does not get done this morning can wait until the afternoon or tomorrow. If the husband is not working that day, for instance, the wife may go back to bed; a visitor sometimes finds a couple in bed at 10:30, sleeping with all the doors wide open, and calling "come in" from back in the bedroom. However, we can say that on the whole the women tidy up the apartment after its occupants leave.

Then we see the second occasion of the day for recreation (the first for some): the women meet their neighbors and take possession of space. In the deserted project the women take purse in hand; even if the refrigerator is well stocked or the absence of the father and children considerably reduces the needs of the table, they are always short of bread or something else, so they can go to the supermarket. The women meet on the way and dally a while. Some go twice in the morning, but there is no fixed time, and meetings are left to chance. The women leave alone but very often return in pairs, accompany each other home, and invite each other in if the house is aired out and presentable. Between 11:00 and 12:00 one often finds a neighbor sitting down with a cup of coffee or an apéritif. The Moslem women are happy to have friends in at that hour. The visitor is given a taste of the food already prepared, and her youngster accepts a plateful; it will not pay to try to feed him lunch at home afterwards. Instead of coming in, they sometimes gossip on the common landing, which they use as a porch; they can take a look at the stove or the baby through the half-open doors.

To the women who appropriate the project in the morning must be added the men and adolescents who are not working because they are taking a temporary rest, or are convalescing, disabled, or out of work. Their number varies. They all arise rather late, so they appear around noon and wander around the courtyard.

The Arab butcher's delivery van appears at 11:45 in the courtyard now animated by the returning children. It brings together primarily Arab customers and crystallizes that moment of relaxation people take before a meal. No one is in a hurry to be waited on. It is a meeting place for regular customers who stand and talk with meat in hand.

Noon is one of the day's poles of intensity, but the rhythm remains relaxed. The courtyard is not completely emptied; unlike the apartment complexes that are deserted at the sacred mealtime, La Halle has no set hour for dining and the noon meal is not a rite. Adults come and go. The children play in shifts, eating in a short time and returning to the courtyard, even in winter. Boys and girls make last-minute purchases until 12:30, when the supermarket closes. The meal is often served several times as people drift in. There is no rule among the Moslems either; one day the mother may preside over the meal and another have a bite in the kitchen. The adults show even more whimsicality about food and mealtime if they are alone at noon. It is not uncommon to find a woman sitting down with a steak in a friend's kitchen at 2:30 "because [she] did [her] whole wash in the morning," or another eating chocolate pudding at 3:00 "because [she] didn't feel like eating at noon." Nevertheless, the noon hour is a time for at least minimal regouping of the family cell.

The afternoon resembles the morning although there are more men at home because the night workers and the garbage collectors have returned. But they take a nap, so the women are alone again and the time is divided between work and encounters as in the morning. Each task is left up to the individual, with some women organizing their chores and others following the impulse of the moment. Some never go out, while others run their errands in the afternoon. Those who stay home will spend hours at the window or go off to a neighbor's with mending. Still others prefer to dispose of their tasks quickly so they can go visiting here or there and keep a needy neighbor company. They offer each other coffee, sweet white wine, and cookies.

Time has been passing slowly but it accelerates somewhat after the children come back, needing snacks and running in and out. The solitude is broken, and the women go back to their apartments. Relaxation and the arhythmic cadence are over for them, and another time is beginning, parallel to the one in the morning, that will be organized around the regrouping of the family.

The children, on the contrary, are now free of the school bell that has punctuated their whole day. They begin to live in their own rhythm again, the rhythm of the games called for by the season, and again take possession of the project or the vacant lots.

Evening brings the working people back between 6:00 and 8:00. They call to each other and chat a while before going in. Then the family cell closes in again around supper, which brings everyone back together, and the project vibrates with the noise of the separate, adjacent cells. In summer, as we shall see further on, this return of the working people occasions meetings between families and much more intense intercourse with neighbors.

The noise diminishes around 9:30. The windows that stay lit during the night are not always the same ones, and the habits of this or that resident cannot be defined with certitude. Some are reputed to retire early, others late. In general, it can be said that La Halle residents go to bed when they feel like it, on impulse, without obligation or constraint, and regardless of the effort to be put forth the next day. The project's night life is as arhythmic as its daytime life and evinces the same anarchy.

Thus, with variations according to age and sex, the same characteristics are found: a regular and imposed rhythm generally applied to the group, together with a relaxed individual rhythm, and a corresponding dispersion of individuals and regrouping of the family or neighbors.

A more intense sociability accompanies the residents' free rhythm. Saturday is an example of both temporal anarchy and grouping. It is generally not a working day; it is the eve of a holiday and is devoted to preparations for Sunday. The sign of Saturday is the swelling of the shopping bags. An unaccustomed effervescence reigns, with couples coming and going. It is a day of freedom when people can get together in pairs and devote themselves to multifarious activities, especially in the afternoon. The men may be called upon to do some shopping, or they may take their wives out. Between 2:30 and 4:00, they are also to be found watching a game on television, especially in winter, or repairing their cars on the curb, weather permitting. They meet with other men, encountering each other by their cars and coming in and out of the basement. A vacation atmosphere emanates from the project. The evening meal lasts longer, without the adolescents who have slipped away. The girls spend the afternoon setting their hair, while the boys meet here and there, but evening brings them together in the streets. Saturday is a day for assembling in cells or groups.

Saturday is scarcely more marked among the Jews who, dispersed among a different community, put the holiday accent on Friday evening. Once the children are bathed and properly dressed, the Sabbath begins around the apéritif and the traditional meal in a thoroughly cleaned apartment.

Sunday is different. Not a day of work for anyone, regardless of ethnic group, it is a day of family regrouping. Children conform to the parents' rhythm: they sleep in the morning. Everyone holes up at home and no one goes to his neighbor's. Each cell closes in around the father, whether his authority is rejected, submitted to, or accepted. The courtyard is unusually deserted; the children are dressed in their Sunday best, even the Moslems, and they do not play there. The noon meal, more carefully prepared than usual, stretches out. Strange cars are more numerous from noon on. The project no longer suffices unto itself; in the afternoon, the family cells need something brought in from outside, whether in the form of a television program or visiting relatives. The adults go out very little but the adolescents slip away after dinner from this overly restricted world.

Thus, the daily rhythm of the project scarcely differs from that of other social groups.

Seasonal Rhythm

The division into two styles of life—individual dispersion or regrouping in or between families—stays the same whatever the season, but climatic conditions partly determine the intensity of social life, which reaches its apogee in warm weather. It is expressed in both time and space, according to sex, age, and ethnic group, in an atmosphere of freedom. The arythmic way of life reaches its full extent in summer, as will be shown by a brief description of the project and its extension, the vacant lots, in the sunny season.

The heat induces everyone to keep all the windows open and stay outside as long as possible. The old people, who are hidden in winter, appear on the benches. The curb benches are occupied by the idle men who stop to chat after watching the little ones on the playground, and by the nonchalant women sunning half-naked babies. The lightly clad women dally downstairs longer, stopping on the staircase and calling as they pass to neighbors who have stayed home and are peeling their vegetables at the window. People in the courtyard converse with those upstairs. The art of playing hooky has many adepts in June but the schoolboys are not punished for this, and they sprawl on the ground and play marbles in shady corners.

In the afternoon, some women spread out blankets and nap on a patch of grass in the vacant lots, and sometimes they even eat dinner there. The children join them for a snack; the portable ice chest keeps the drinks cool. Some tired, pregnant women and some Moslem women induced by the sun to follow their former ways stretch out on the ground between the building and the enclosure in the shade of an abandoned car. From 5:00 on the boys invade the vacant lots and do not come back until night.

The project's appearance changes little during August because departures for vacation are spread out and few in number. But the height of social intensity is in the evening, when the working people return, calling to each other and stopping to chat on the sidewalks, the women joking with the men from their windows. They eat late in order to take greater advantage of daylight encounters and conversations, and those who are free early come out for a walk until night falls. Inside and out, the project resounds with voices. The boys do stunts on their motorbikes, and the girls walk in pairs along the sidewalk as though it were a boulevard. A young girl passes by with a covered plate, an offering of food destined for a friend of her mother's. Relative calm is established around 10:00, but the adolescents still hang around in bunches and at midnight their loud laughter brings invectives down on them.

Summer Saturdays are like this evening hour of rest in the summer months. Children bring drinks to the men. The project is the scene of slow comings and goings, and every encounter between two people is the occasion for a snatch of conversation. In winter, the glacial draft in the courtyard chases people into the house almost as soon as they come home, whereas the long summer evenings permit the free expression of a slowed rhythm and great sociability.

Annual Rhythm

Because of ethnic differences, the annual rhythm is not measured in the same way for everyone, although there seems to be a certain homogeneity in regard to Saturday and Sunday, as we have already seen. It should also be noted that Moslems do not observe Friday as a day of worship.

The weeks and months follow and resemble one another, and the seasons are differentiated into just two—summer and winter. The return to school is the only occasion that marks the autumn, affecting not only the children but also the parents who compare what they have bought for the children. The year is divided up for the working people by days off and the month of vacation, for the children by Thursdays and school vacations, and for the women who stay home by the cadence of the men and children. The month of paid vacation is not a break for everyone because three-fourths of the adults do not leave the project; but for each it corresponds to the cessation of the imposed rhythm and the opportunity to give free rein to his individual rhythm. Vacations are spread out from June to September so they have no great repercussion on the project's collective life except to add slightly to the impression of nonchalance that emanates from La Halle in the summer.

The national calendar gives everyone just about the same landmarks, but holidays seem like ordinary Sundays to some ethnic groups who preserve their own special reference-times. Holidays will be dealt with in the last chapter but it should be noted here that the Moslems continue to live in the rhythm of the lunar year (the biggest events are the month of Ramadan and the Aïd el Kabir) and that the Jews' time is still cut up by their numerous holidays (of which the most important is Passover) so their year unfolds according to the religious calendar, whose days are counted by seven before or after the holiday. For the other residents, Christmas, New Year's, Easter, Bastille Day, and All Saints' Day provide landmarks for their year.

The parts of this triple rhythm are superimposed and sometimes coincide because of society's pressure on the minority groups, the existence of the mixed group, and the adolescents' desire to conform to ambient rites. For instance, in order that all the children be treated alike, Christmas is celebrated around a standing fir tree in almost all Jewish and Moslem families. The mixed Arab–French group follows both rhythms at once: the Moslem husband observes Christmas and Easter, and the French wife celebrates Arab holidays and knows when Ramadan is even if her husband does not fast. The adolescents avoid the holidays peculiar to their parents' ethnic group as much as they can and conform to the traditions of the majority. When Easter and Passover coincide, the holiday reigns in almost every home, and Jews and Christians mention this coincidence as though it brings them closer together.

Nothing especially different from the rhythms found in the larger society is disclosed in the rhythm of life in La Halle. However, we may note that there is a partial acculturation of the different ethnic groups by the dominant group, beginning with the extension of the Christmas tree custom.

Concept of Space and Time

Space

This simple description of daily life gives us a glimpse of an internal adaptation to the artificially provided space, and a utilization of that space varying by taste, age, and sex. What was once a definite, rectangular space has been given a local color and existence by human beings.

Four years ago the project was just a strange place with no community facilities turned over to deracinated people. They reacted against its prisonlike aspect by annexing the exterior. They responded to its bareness and its impediments to domestic privacy by using those dark and secret places, the basements.

They came into the space provided for them, a strange place with no past. It has one now because the residents have restructured it according to certain traditional themes. They have given it import, and they live in terms of the meanings they have filled it with even though these meanings are unconscious. This sensation of an unfamiliar space that had been tamed prompted us to call the stairwells "streets" and the courtyard "the public square"; we had come to realize that while the artificial regrouping of a whole Kabyle village in Djebabra gradually transforms the peasants into townsfolk,[2] the regrouping of 175 heterogeneous families, mostly from the city, tends to restore a village structure to an artificial urban dwelling place.

Even those apartments turned to the outside have windows overlooking the central interior space. The children call it "the court" because it reminds them of the recreation court below their classroom windows. The adults simply call it "downstairs" if they live on an upper story, or "in front" if they live on the ground floor. It might be the sole public square around which all the houses were built—an unofficial, unsanctified square without a church, but a square just the same.

Stairwells *K* and *L* "down at the end" are considered far off and their residents are less well known. Since it is all relative, it is true that they are not as close and are less directly concerned by the central square.

Outside the square, which is common to all, space is distributed by sex and age group. The women appropriate the landing porches (where they argue and fight) and the school path; there is also the shortcut that, spurning the access road, they have traced along the second building in coming back from shopping. The men are away too much of the time and have hardly appropriated a corner of this world. Those who are free regularly or in the afternoon reign over the benches in the square and lean against the back wall. The basements belong to the men who store their motorbikes and utensils there and to the adolescents who take shelter there from adult control and the unobstructed view from the windows. For this reason, the adolescents have also reserved the corners of the doorways and all the less visible nooks.

The cellars assume great importance. Used not as originally intended but as an esoteric space, they serve each person in secret objectives. They conceal clandestine love affairs, and the common corridor linking them serves as a subterranean passage for the thief who goes in at one end and comes out the other, his deed accomplished. Women who are visiting someone and do not want anyone to know about it take this secret passage, as one of them admitted: "I went through the basement to get to your house. I don't want the others to see me coming so often." Even the little children hide there, and everyone hides objects of varied origin that he would rather not have lying about at home.

The children have an immense space. The youngest share the area set aside for them, sit on the stairs when they have been told to stay close to home, and are allowed to play on the ground-floor landing, a small inner court sheltered from the rain.

The immense stretch of vacant lots, "the field," represents a real privilege for the seven- to fourteen-year-olds. It effectively corresponds to the fields surrounding a village, and it gives the young townsfolk the opportunity for big, free games and an acquaintance, albeit limited, with the earth, plants, and small animal parasites. The children suddenly disappear over the palisades and actually live in "the field" among odd constructions of scrap iron transported with difficulty from a distant dump. First the parents had to go and look for the children, and then they too got into the habit of taking a walk in what they christened "the prairie."

The children have chosen a vocabulary that is more rustic but nonetheless poeticizes that exterior space to whose constant, imperious call they are subject every day. In their "field" they have their "hills" that hide their huts from enemy observation and their "pond" for everyday; the distant "lake" is reserved for summer Thursdays and vacations. There is a clay island in the middle of the "pond" that is hard to reach and stimulates their imaginations; they call it "the planet."

This space—poeticized, esoteric, distributed by age and sex—would have been remodeled despite the strong concrete

walls if the authorities did not watch over it. Starting with
two parallel gray blocks and the annexed vacant lots, the residents have nonetheless rehumanized the space passed on to
them; they have made it a kind of village, built around a public
square and bordered by a vast meadow.

The difference from the apartment complexes is striking.
The tenants in the bedroom communities flee the anonymous,
deserted exterior and take refuge in the limited space of their
apartments, the only part they have personalized. In La Halle,
on the contrary, a kind of projection onto the exterior is quickly
perceptible. Outside is where contacts and meetings occur,
outside is where one likes to be. The residents have taken
joint possession of that exterior space.

We must not carelessly make risky or exaggerated comparisons, and delude ourselves that a village has been realized
on the basis of a dwelling place confined to two buildings.
No village is possible without a town hall, a church, a café,
or the slightest form of community life. Despite the residents'
unconscious efforts to find meeting places, the project still
looks like two long rows of similar, attached cells where no
one really feels at home. It is just a regrouping of people,
all of them fish out of water, torn from the traditional structures
of the city or town, from which it is detached. By upsetting
the organization of space, this regrouping alters the concept
of time.

Time

In La Halle time may be empty, measured, lost, or killed.
First we must remember the feeling of transience and waiting
that weighs on the adults. Of course it is not continually on
their minds, but it is latent and it hinders a valid apprehension
of the future. Whenever someone tries to evaluate his situation
in the project, he feels uneasy. Rumors often arise, spread,
and die on the theme that "the prefecture is going to tear
down the buildings," "We'll all have to be gone in two years,"
or "The mayor is going to put us out next year." These asser-
tions have no official foundation but they are evidence of a

constant uncertainty. The time spent in the project seems long. When we ask someone how long he has been there he always answers, "a long time" or "It's been quite some time." We have to persist to get a specific "since the beginning" or "more than a year."

Time is usually thought of as constituting a long- or short-term program. Looking back, one can see whether or not the program has been carried out, as this verification constitutes a history by establishing landmarks in the time that has elapsed.

For the psychologist Debuyst, "a subject is adapted to duration to the extent that he does not live in the present."[3] It may be said, then, that all La Halle residents are unadapted to duration. Nothing is sacrificed for the indefinite and seemingly threatening future. Time is dislocated and lived from day to day like a simple sequence of moments.

Consequently, it is difficult to remember the landmarks of the past, and the informants have great trouble recounting their lives in chronological order. The listener gets nowhere by trying to calculate the time elapsed, and he must be persistent to get specific information. Then he discovers a curious phenomenon: unlike the peasants who spontaneously reckon backward in time using personal and general events as signposts, the project people, who have no landmarks, remember the exact dates. Instead of measuring a period of time approximately when they have to call it to mind, they say, for instance, "It came to an end on October 4, 1962." Because they are in a shadowy, indefinite, temporary situation, they can use only the official, objective way of dating events.

If duration is not mastered, how is daily time experienced? We have previously described the day's rhythm, which is both measured and lax. The day is cut up into different times by the children's regular departure and return, the morning coffee, the men coming home free in the evening as if they lived in a work camp, and the start of television broadcasting.

The exact time matters only when those who work must leave—just once a day to each of them. Moreover, clocks are considered a luxury and generally are not found among the furnishings; the alarm clock, adopted strictly for its effective ringing, is not always visible in the house because it is permanently enthroned on the nightstand. The men wear wristwatches. Some women do too, because they want to be stylish, but they really do not need them because the rhythm of the children and television are enough to tell time by.

All the television screens are lit at the end of the afternoon, at the approximate time when television programs begin. If no image appears yet, the screen will stay lighted until broadcasting begins. Supper will be taken care of at the end of the serial or another such regular program.

Movement in the project tells time imprecisely but well enough, yet it cannot be said that there is really a collective time. If there were a single rhythm, there would be group cohesion, but this cohesion is prevented by the existence of subgroups and the diversity of separate, individual vocational activities subject to society's schedules and dates. As Pucelle says, "The more structured a society is, the more it concretizes its own time, and conversely, it is more structured if it has been more successful in elaborating its own time, divided by the landmark dates of its history."[4] However, an effort to combat the plurality of rhythms seems to be taking shape. Frequent coopting of workers, for example, would tend to show a desire to follow the same schedules. Also, there are waves of unemployment among the adolescents and then they are almost all working at the same time, and this fact tends to prove that each tries to identify with the rhythm of the group.

In La Halle, time is the coefficient of boredom; it is empty and meaningless, an unlived duration. How can the residents fill these empty moments when nothing is happening? We have seen that the women have no use for time. Tasks are done in any order, according to the desire of the moment. None of the idle men and the women at home know how to occupy their time. Everyone waits for it to pass and tries to kill it if it does not pass quickly.

Residents often had no running water before moving to the project, and the women were tied to the drudgery of carrying it from the street fountain to the sink, and they also had to light the fire with fuel cut up or carted in by the men. The

modern apartment suddenly emptied their time of its substance. Many of them used to have a job but they no longer
have much to do. Some of them wax and polish the floor all
day long and do not know how to create diversions to avoid
being haunted by empty hours. Others drink; still others spend
a great deal of time outside in the courtyard or in town. One
of them bought a sewing machine for "[her] afternoons," but
she quickly tired of it as of a toy that could not cure boredom.
The women are neither more maladroit nor lazier than others,
but they are cut off from the world. Someone would have
to help them not only to keep busy but to devote themselves
to activities that would satisfy them. They simply indulge in
vain, sporadic efforts and no motive force drives their latent
but unexpressed desire to do something.

The Jewish and Moslem women do not organize their time
differently, but they do not suffer through it in anxiety and
boredom. They, at least, enjoy their rest. They are contempla-
tive and are capable by tradition of spending whole afternoons
stretched out on a couch, comfortable and happy to be there.
For those women still attached to their religion, duration is
broken up by the recurrence of the holidays they still observe.
Finally, their past and their old habits make them fill their
days with a host of petty labors. The slow cooking of traditional
foods and homemade pastries, including searching for the
necessary ingredients, demands an enormous amount of time.
They are not gripped by the anxiety that makes some women
kill time, but, like all the others, they are never in a hurry.

The women's time is entirely their own, which means there
is nothing they have to do. Nothing really matters and what
is not done today will be done tomorrow in an unorganized
and amorphous duration. For example, they have to obtain
innumerable documents, and they have infinite difficulty in
undertaking the required bureaucratic procedures. It is especially difficult for them to do so on the day and at the time
that the official wants them to come because they let themselves be distracted by any incident that crops up. On the
other hand, paradoxical as it may seem, the day one of them
decides to settle a matter at the family allowances office in

the city, for instance, she is to be seen—fat, cardiac, struggling against the wind with a one-year-old in her arms—setting out for the church to catch a bus that will not arrive for twenty minutes. Because she has not foreseen how long her errand will take, this same tired woman will come home around noon to take care of the children, only to leave and twice again inflict herself with that long, almost expeditionary trip.

The women never complain because what might be considered time lost (since it could have been utilized better if it had been better anticipated) is in fact just time gained. These tiring, sterile comings and goings have given the illusion of a full day. Time passed all by itself, and they did not have to look for a way to shorten it for once.

The words "kill" and "pass time" recur often. One woman, whose children were taken away and who is trying to get her concubine's daughter, who is also in a charitable institution, projected her time like this in order to fill the emptiness of her life: "When I have the little girl, I'll be busy doing housework in the morning after school starts; in the afternoon I'll straighten up the house; when she comes back I'll look after her; and time will pass!"

The idle men also wait for time to pass. They sleep, listen to their transistor radios, help the women with the housework, do the shopping, take a walk, putter about at home or at the neighbors', and get bored. They make no more provision for activity than the women. Everything is done on the spur of the moment. That is why there is no evidence whatever of shared recreation.

There is no awareness of rest or leisure time as opposed to work time. The notion of leisure is implicit in every act of a day in which—you never know—the passing time may bring some small, unusual event. If an unexpected visitor comes along, he will immediately find his host completely at his disposal. The host will cling happily to those moments that a working man would consider lost but that have taken on another quality for the project resident and are subtracted from the usual duration. Thus, the notion of free time is unknown in the project.

No one is ever bothered by interruptions. When people get together—a time stamped with joy, pleasure, leisure, celebration—it is a privileged time compared to that amorphous duration, culminating in the holidays and what may still remain of ceremonies. Saturday is an example of this: by putting everyone in the situation of those who are not working, it has the effect of blending the different rhythms in these privileged moments, making possible a common experience; but curiously this experience is of amorphous duration.

Time is not money in La Halle. We have seen that there is no notion of productiveness or of time wasted, poorly used, or lost. Lack of planning is shown in the way expenses are anticipated, and there is a consistent connection between this disregard and the notions of time and duration.

For example, one couple let itself be tempted by a salesman selling on credit and bought four warm, expensive quilts in the middle of April, even though they have just two beds. When asked, "Why?!" this couple answers, "It doesn't matter if we give them back if we can't pay; the first installment isn't due until July." Not right away, that is; and only the present moment counts, in which they can play the game of showing off the quilts to the neighbors. They are put on the floor and are not used, but "maybe some day we'll have some beds." It is the unreality of the distant future that is involved because they do not plan to buy any beds in the near future.

But could not this lack of organization in time be interpreted instead as a yearning for an original kind of freedom? They do not rebel against every constraint and against all the usual rules of society; they just disregard them and quite simply deny their existence.

For example, work does not seem to be an imperative for everyone. When some of them become tired of the monotony of workdays, they stop and "go on Social Security"; they have themselves listed as ill and get along on the daily benefits, which are less than wages. They do not refuse to give their sons a start, but they do not take any steps in connection with the school, the employer, or the crafts guild. They start to open an account but do not follow through even though they know they will not get what they wanted it for. Vocational, political, or religious commitments mean nothing to them. They buy things without taking into account their real needs and budget. They are capable of cheerfully spending a month's wages in a day, loaning a large sum on a generous impulse to someone who is insolvent, stealing casually, and conceiving legitimate or illegitimate children, without worrying about the next day.

Is this not, in short, the kind of freedom to which artists and nonconformists are commonly conceded to have a right? But in La Halle there is a certain, almost Islamic fatalism underlying it. Used to being beggars in a society that wants it that way, they cannot help but be aware that "someone will provide," to some extent in any case.

It must be said that they are under continual government pressure in exchange for the charity they are used to getting. They must fill out applications, compile records, and fill out a large number of forms within the required time before foreclosure.[5] Even paying is complicated because of the effort of going to the post office and sending a money order. The court (they do not know which one) keeps an eye on them, and all the information concerning them goes through the police station, which summons the interested parties.

They receive all kinds of help but they feel insecure because every unfamiliar paper throws them into a panic and they are harassed by the courts and threatened by the public authorities, so they have gotten into a vicious circle and take unfair advantage of every kind of begging.

Legal and financial language is incomprehensible to them, and their badly worded letters, having fallen into the pits of blind and omnipotent officialdom, remain unanswered.

They react against this guardianship, which sustains them but assails them on every side, by denying that there are any rules; and it is just one step from denying their existence to refusing to follow them.

Their attempt at autonomy is expressed by a rejection of schedules and precise appointments. Since the struggle is too unequal, they opt for a certain philosophy: to let themselves be carried along, denying all constraint, living from day to day and almost according to the season. In short, they want to be free to organize their work, activities, and movements as they please, and to regulate their own speed even though they beat time out of step.

To choose a kind of refusal on the time level is to try to organize a time based on nothing, because adjusting to the future requires an effort to anticipate in the present and any kind of commitment requires perseverance, which the people of La Halle refuse to put forth. We can almost say that their need to be inscribed in duration is satisfied by fortune-telling and the magical kind of thinking that governs their choice of horses for betting.

Their aspirations arise in reaction to their neglected state and the resulting official obligations and summonses (the poorer they are, the more papers they have to fill out just to live). Their kind of freedom is an attempt at autonomy in the Kantian sense, but the effort remains anarchic and unrealizable, and they are punished for it.

If we try to define the concept of space and time, we come to the conclusion that for the people of La Halle space is a closed space belonging to them and engendering a special vocabulary, a delimitation fantastic in the very terms used for it (for example, "field," "plain," or "prairie" for vacant lots). In the same way, the concept of time is specific to the social group of the project, marked by economic conditioning and by relations with the outside. Its indefiniteness about the future is its essential characteristic. This indefiniteness, which is an individual trait in the larger society, is here socialized by the group.

There is thus a striking paradox between the daily, seasonal, and annual rhythm, which reproduces that of other social groups in the larger society except for a few details, and the concept of time and space precisely specific to life in La Halle and its relative isolation. Here again we find that "ideology" does not mesh with how the people represent their life to the observer.

NOTES

[1]The men work from 6 A.M. to 2 P.M. the first week, from 2 P.M. to 10 P.M. the second week, and from 10 P.M. to 6 A.M. the third week.

[2]P. Bourdieu and A. Sayad, *Le Déracinement*, p. 156.

[3]Personal interview with Mr. Debuyst, who is studying the underprivileged classes in Belgium and France.

[4]Pucelle, statement at Bergson conference, Société de Langue Française de Philosophie, 1959.

[5]To obtain a divorce, for instance, they must request free legal help, but first they must gather together certain documents.

11

Information

We shall consider these different kinds of information in turn: information previously acquired at school, while traveling, or through various experiences; external information received through modern media; and internal information.

Previously Acquired Information

The level of education is just about the same for all and is low on the whole, rarely going beyond primary and elementary grades, with the Arabs considerably increasing the proportion of illiterates in the project. Table 11 gives an estimate of the level of education based on responses from thirty men and thirty women.

What has become of the ideas learned at school? They have often been profoundly altered by being forgotten or not being used. For instance, unsupported by actual sight and experience, the knowledge of geography has foundered. They own neither maps nor globes where they can look for landmarks,

Table 11
Level of Education

Level of Education	ARABS Men	ARABS Women	JEWS Men	JEWS Women	METROPOLITANS Men	METROPOLITANS Women
Cannot read	90%	100%	0%	50%	2%	1%
Can read only	8	0	0	0	2	0
Can read and write	2	0	50	45	65	65
Has CEP	0	0	50	5	31	34
Higher level	0	0	0	0	0	0

and they hardly know the location of places where they have been or where people they know live. Seas, oceans, and mountains exist only in imaginary locations. One woman refused to look on a map to see where her children were placed, saying, "It's not worth the trouble because I don't know the place."

French history is summed up in a few dates (such as 1515) remembered automatically and out of context, and a few kings' names (for example, Louis XIV). They know almost nothing about the French Revolution except that there was one, and they do not always know if Napoleon lived before or after it. There is no chronology in what they remember.

In the natural sciences, the people know only what life shows them; for example, they learn some rough anatomy through their illnesses.

The women who hold the CEP have kept the ability to express themselves legibly and comprehensibly in writing. They take care of the family's mail and official business so they keep the habit of writing to some extent. They benevolently act as public scribes for their illiterate neighbors; there is approximately one public scribe per stairway–street, who is always a woman. On the other hand, if they have never left the area as is most generally the case, these same women are as lost in cosmic space as the Kabyle who, holding out a box of matches as a tangible example, begged someone to explain who lived on top and who on the bottom, the Chinese or the Americans, and where was the beginning and the end. The women who have the CEP seem to consider their educa-

tion an end and not a means. An attempt to get three intelligent
women to read some easy novels was doomed to total failure.

In contrast, those men and women who did not go far enough
in school as children want to raise their level of education.
They do it by patiently working to correct themselves, without
outside help.

Although the men have not received any real technical training for the most part, they place less importance on their
elementary level of education than on the knowledge they
have gleaned in the course of travels provided by military
service and various occupational experiences (some of them
have some idea of several trades even if they do not use them).
Many of the men between thirty-five and forty participated
in the war in Indochina. Yet even if they have more experience
than the average project resident, they do not seem to be consulted or invested with any special prestige. The original
source of information they represent cannot be used in La
Halle. They are not set apart but they have a slightly different
status than the others with whom they cannot communicate;
lacking common reference points with the others, they prefer
to remain silent about their past experiences.

The following case is typical. Illiterate at eighteen, this man
went into the parachute corps, going first to Japan, where his
commanding officer taught him to read, then to Saigon, Cambodia, and Djibouti. He crashed during a jump (he had 663
to his credit). He is an excellent bridge and poker player.
He has a profound nostalgia for Cambodia, where he would
like to live, but he says he "can't talk about all that here;
I keep my memories to myself."

M.K., a Tunisian Jew, can hardly have a conversation with
his neighbors either. He was the electrician for the bey of
Tunis and was a sailor for years. Along with the Arabs and
foreigners, the Jews represent knowledge of other cultures
but they cannot speak of it to the uninitiated, out of modesty.
But the Jewish and foreign men have former occupations and
an education equal to those of the metropolitans, while the
Arabs, who cannot write, hope that the gaps left by a partly
rejected oral tradition will be filled by their present technical–

vocational experiences and external information, to which they try to be receptive.

In short, the residents can be divided into several groups in regard to information previously acquired: those whose knowledge is limited to a normal primary education, the unsupported memory of which is slowly being changed; those whose low level of education is compensated by technical knowledge and various experiences; those who are illiterate and who participate in another culture and yearn to accumulate new knowledge; those who have the benefit of both education and technical knowledge and more or less first-hand acquaintance with other cultures but who are isolated by being unable to pass on any of it; and finally the very small proportion of those who have received almost no kind of information.

Such as it is, this varied knowledge is relative, and the rich and varied information coming from outside must constitute booty from a higher level. But such information is not always comprehensible, so it is either accepted without possible criticism, rejected, distorted, or misinterpreted.

External Information

Newspapers and Books

The people of La Halle buy few newspapers, although it is true that there is no nearby newsstand to induce them to buy. The caretaker keeps a stock of about fifty *France-Soir* and also has ten *Aurore* on order for both projects. This number obviously does not take into account a few people who buy one daily or another on their way to work, and we must also not neglect the fact that papers are loaned among neighbors. The *Huma-Dimanche* is read in almost all homes because, they say, "They deliver it to your house and it has the TV program." *Equipe* finds a small number of sports enthusiasts; we would estimate that there are about ten of them in La Halle.

No resident that we know of subscribes to a newspaper, and no one buys or receives a trade or union paper. Political papers are almost never read, at least at home, because a few co-workers orally transmit political information from a morning paper. The priest distributes the parish bulletin only to those children who are going to catechism class (50 percent of La Halle's children). An annual municipal bulletin is distributed in the mailboxes.

The La Halle reader looks in the daily or weekly only for current events and most often reads just the headlines, the athletic results, the news items, a documentary article, the classified advertisements for jobs, and the list of horses for the races.

The television weeklies are too expensive to find customers in the project, and those with numerous photographs illustrating the news (like *Paris-Match* or *Noir et Blanc*) are familiar only to those who frequent waiting rooms. The popular women's weeklies also are rarely bought or read, any more than popular-science magazines, but *Femme d'Aujourd'hui* has a few readers who loan it to others.

The residents do not limit themselves to reading newspapers. They also read books, but this term may be confusing because a book for the people of La Halle is anything bought at a newsstand that has a cover and a smaller format than a newspaper; for example, it may be a periodical. These "books" are composed solely of comic strips or photo-stories published monthly by the standard romance magazines such as *The Two of Us, Intimacy,* or *Secrets.* They bear prominent titles like "monthly magazine of teen-age photo-stories" or "the great photo-stories of love," and cost 1.5F. The young women bring them into the house and put them in the cabinet, but the whole family reads them. The women do not like stories "to be continued," and these publications are generally chosen because they contain a complete story. They circulate in small piles through the stairwells. You always hear them say, "I'm going to so-and-so's to borrow some books." The boys' "comics" are also read by the adults.

When they are asked, "Why don't you read other novels?" the women especially reply, "Because there are no pictures in the big books." Written letters no longer conjure up anything and only the visual image is accessible. However, a few men read cheap, short detective novels that they buy and resell secondhand, and a few women read short love stories. One man boasts that he only reads the "Serie Noire" [detective stories] "because it has better novels than the others." One woman admits that the love stories are "crap" but she cannot read anything else.

The few authors they remember (especially Victor Hugo) were taught to them at school, and they consider them reserved for scholars. Only the municipal library is available to them but they do not go there and their patronage is not solicited by any other library from a school or in a book bus. In their minds, "library books" are reserved for educated people because they are too difficult to understand. "Real books" or "big books" should be "instructive" and therefore hard to read. If by chance a mother buys her son a book, it can only be an encyclopedia.

Practically no books get into the project, even channeled through the children. If the observer says that libraries have easy and pleasant books, he just meets with amused skepticism because his assertion runs counter to their concept of the Book.

Content and form in books must be considered. For the project people, content may be of two kinds: a display of knowledge superior to theirs and therefore not meant for them, or a story of love and violence whose function is relaxation. The form is thought in letters written close together, and this form is no longer accessible to them. It can no longer conjure up concrete situations in their imaginations through abstract signs. They will choose easy stories "written" in "books" where the signs are replaced with pictures barely elucidated by captions. This regression to pictures and abandoning of the translation of signs is becoming a generalized phenomenon that is not special to the project, but it seems to be reaching its full extent there because the residents confess they *cannot* read without pictures.

We must yield to the evidence that the twenty or so people still capable of absorbing short novels represent (in inverse relation to education, moreover) the elite who can still deal with abstractions, the elite of a group of people almost unable to write. Knowing how to read is reduced to a simple commodity of daily life, somewhat in the way a tourist is more comfortable in Greece if he can read Greek letters.

You may reply that the project people still read the newspapers a little, but actually they just skim the headlines and the paragraphs under the photographs, shrinking from the effort to pay the attention required to understand an article and getting only a rough idea of the facts. They have replaced the serial stories of the previous generation with comic strips. This is why they do not read the political papers that discuss and interpret the news, not, as they wrongly claim, because they are not interested.

This rejection of written thought abolishes the difference between the illiterates and the others. They all receive their information from the same source: television. However, two similar comments show a deep persistent difference: "Why should I read when I have TV?" said so often by the French, becomes "Fortunately I have TV, since I don't know how to read," among the Arabs.

Unlike those who are free to do so but refuse to, the Arab endlessly deplores his inability to understand written letters. For him, writing has a sacred character and contains all knowledge. Those married to Frenchwomen require their wives to read them the newspaper, and they can guess the value of the illustrated papers in which their wives seek escape, saying, "If I knew how to read, I'd read books that just have writing."

Because of this detachment and distance from discursive thought, purposeful or not, printing has lost its power and everyone receives most of his information orally through radio, television, and public report.

Radio

Radio has taken a back seat in its shape and its influence. The big "set" anchored in the dining room that brought the family together for a program has disappeared, replaced by the small transistor radio that goes from kitchen to dining room. Listening is completely modified for the ear is no longer attentive. In most cases, no one has seen to the quality of the set, which is usually small and modestly priced. There are no plug-in radios anymore except for those usually found in the garbage cans and now stuck up in the closet awaiting amateur repairs and possible resale.

The reason for choosing a cheap transistor radio is not solely economic but is a matter of the form of attention being displaced. The radio keeps the woman company in the deserted apartment, staving off silence and emptiness, but she does not choose particular programs. The voice of radio has hardly any authority anymore and the role conceded to it is that of music box, alarm clock, and broadcaster of news during the hours when television is not on. It must be movable in order to follow the user around.

Since it has become of minor usefulness, very high audio quality is not required except in special, exceptional cases, as is shown in the example of one Arab. Uneasy at the thought that he might have to return to his own country, he wanted to follow Algeria's social development. For this reason he felt the need to listen attentively to several Algerian programs so he bought a quality transistor set for the sum of 1,800F, which makes it very convenient for him to pick up African stations. This set does not compete with television at all; its owner uses it for a very precise purpose.

Radio, therefore, is just an accessory. The people hardly ever look for anything but singing, and, although they most often listen to Europe I, they do so only inattentively. Moreover, they do not try to learn anything from it that they do not already know; it provides only a minor kind of information. Residents rarely mention the names of the announcers whose voices by themselves, detached from any corporeal presence, are of diminished interest and lessened authority.

Recordings of music or speech are not popular and phonographs are rare, belonging mostly to adolescents who use them for dancing and Arabs who want to listen to Andalusian music.

Television

Television exercises an almost absolute attraction in La Halle. Every home has a television set; it is missing only temporarily in case of repossession, and those who have none watch their neighbors'. All the television sets are equipped with the second channel, with few exceptions. They are always in working order and are replaced when they wear out; they are expensive and are bought on credit and never secondhand. In short, anyone who is not a television viewer is ill-adapted to modern society. The project people, so often rejected, want to be placed in the same rank as everyone else and, thanks to their television set, they think they are. The announcer says "Good evening" to them as well as to the others, and there are only two stations on television, offering the same mass culture to everyone.

The second reason for this lasting infatuation is that shows have now come into the home. Certainly it is not only in La Halle that people wait for night and the surprise of "what's on TV." But here, where they "can't read when there are no pictures" and where they have lost the faculty for paying attention to the radio, this mode of audiovisual transmission of information is the only suitable one. The image draws the eye and commands attention without any personal effort. Television offers a tangible reality, and we must not minimize the importance of the sudden bringing in of the whole outside world, from the Vatican to the Elysée, into the lives of the project residents.

CHOICE OF SHOWS

We must try to study how shows are chosen and whether they are subject to criticism.

It is difficult to know what the project residents select, and even if they do, because their answers do not correspond exactly to direct observation. Adolescents and adults give the same quick, spontaneous replies to the question, "What do you like to watch?" Everyone prefers "movies, variety shows, singing, and sports" regardless of sex; they pause a moment and then give more diversified answers depending more on their personality than on sex or age. A certain modesty or reticence about making much of one's own tastes is observed. Husband and wife spontaneously give identical answers. A list of preferences has been set up for nine households (Table 12).

Table 12
Favorite Television Programs

Family	First Choice	Second Choice
1	Movies, sports, variety shows, singing	Scientific programs, ballet, dance programs
2	Movies, variety shows, sports, Panorama [weekly news special]	Scientific programs, animal life
3	Detective movies, variety shows, sports	Newscasts, scientific programs
4	Movies, serials, Five Columns in One [monthly news special]	Medical programs, Explorers' Magazine [wildlife]
5	Movies, singing, detective stories, variety shows	Circus, games
6	Singing, movies, serials, variety shows	Scientific programs, newscasts
7	Movies, variety shows, sports	Thursday show [for children]
8	News, detective movies, singing	Stairway to the Stars [circus], medical programs
9	Movies, sports, singing	Five Columns in One, newscasts

We should not be surprised that we do not see televised news mentioned more often. This does not mean it is spurned; quite the contrary. The 8:00 P.M. televised newspaper is followed so regularly that it did not seem necessary to the informants to mention it as a choice.

The table expresses a classification according to taste, but it should not induce the reader to think that the people of La Halle limit themselves to watching what they like. The show "Readings for Everyone," although it comes on late and might not be thought amusing for those who do not read, is never mentioned but is not unknown to them, and the plays passed over in silence are watched whenever a movie on the other channel is not competing with them. The answers concerning programs have never been negative except for one—"The opera is awful!"—but this does not necessarily mean that the television set will be turned off in that home on opera nights. Actually, all the television sets are turned on in the evening when programs begin and are shut off sooner or later depending on how tired people are. In between, every-thing presented on television is absorbed. Preferences are not exhaustive and choices depend more on one's state of fatigue than on taste. On nights when they are not sleepy, they wait until broadcasting is over.

Yet we must not minimize these preferences reflected rather accurately in the table, which particularly reveals the enthusiasm for scientific discoveries. One woman said about this kind of program: "We listen to them even if we're ready to drop," and a man said, "It's too bad they're so late"; these are the only two allusions to a real choice that we have collected.

If choice enters in little over time, then does the fact that there are two channels let it be expressed? It seems not. The second channel complicates matters. The viewers would like to see everything and feel cheated because part of the show is going on without them, so they will check quite often during the evening to see whether they have made the right choice and the other program does not interest them. They will keep listening from a few seconds to a few minutes before going back to the first program.

This changing of programs during a show is a factor in family arguments when tastes are not alike; this is the case particularly in North African families with adolescent children. The choice is then within one person's jurisdiction; only the person in authority is entitled to impose the program. If the father is weak, he complains that he always has to suffer through his older children's movies and favorite singers and cannot listen at leisure to something else, because his sons take charge of turning the knob.

The younger children watch attentively on Thursday, when it is raining, and during the serial; the rest of the time they watch what they like until they go to bed.

Programs forbidden to children attract the adults.

We could say a lot about how the residents listen. Television is a presence they cannot get along without, but it in no way stops anyone from attending to various occupations. They watch from the corner of an eye amid the general hubbub, and silence is imposed only if the program excites attention. Television is in the way if an important visitor comes along, and then the sound is turned down or all the way off but the picture stays on. It presides over all the noisy holiday meals while no one is listening; it is better not to listen than not to see. There is no television without a picture so none of the television sets are turned on when music is broadcast without any picture in the afternoon. The same people may listen sporadically, irregularly, and over the children's noise, but also very attentively and for a very long time.

The picture sustains and fixes attention. This is what causes the popularity of the news shown and reported every day by someone who is not anonymous. The appearance of politicians on the screen certainly brought about the interest that the project people, who are usually not political, entertained for each candidate in the December 5, 1965, presidential election, and the attention with which the adults listened to each speech.

We may wonder what comes of this access to all sorts of knowledge and how they see this enlarging of their world view. Most of the newly received knowledge is laid over deficient foundations of which they are not even aware, and they cannot refer back to even a partly forgotten knowledge. This is why historic programs are not mentioned; they have no other value than momentary amusement. On the other hand, everything concerning the news, referring to current or very recent events, finds an echo in their memories and is of enhanced interest. Landscapes have the attraction of picture postcards but it is impossible to reconstruct the geographic puzzle. Classical works in theater or music are assuredly recognized as intended for a different public.

It is not the same with scientific programs because they do not refer back to a "culture." Everything concerning the cosmos, interplanetary rockets, and nuclear physics brings in the marvels of the modern world, but at the same time the project viewer is no more ignorant at the outset than most other viewers, except for the specialists. Because there are no such references, he is free to become enthusiastic and apply his intelligence in order to understand.

Medicine seen through the eyes of the surgeon with his instruments, and seeing the sleeping patient and the bared organs, are exalting for the same reason, but to this must be added the magical element and the ascendancy over ignorant people always enjoyed by the person who can cure without your understanding how. In addition, the distant reference points you may have are not theoretical but from your own body.

CRITICISM

The people of La Halle do not criticize television. Their judgment of it is most succinct ("It was good" or "It was ok"), and they do not express themselves or compare opinions when the program is over. Their difficulty in analyzing and synthesizing and the absence of judgments and discussion have two consequences. The first is that they cannot "get their bearings" and put the new ideas in context and so get everything they might out of the program. The second is that they unconsciously consider television as education, so no criticism of this dangerous, didactic role is possible. "It's so, they said it on TV," is often heard, and "We saw it on TV" is a peremptory remark used to support a statement. Gingerbread or apple juice is found on the tables at times "because it's good for the children; they said so on TV." Advertising has not been taken as such but is now a sacred truth, believed by everyone and replacing the former power of the written word. Paradoxically, programs conceived for educational purposes, in household arts for example, are hardly ever watched and have no influence.

Television is a center of attraction whose importance in La Halle cannot be denied. Being audiovisual, it magnetizes the attention, creates a feeling of intimacy, offers amusement, and measures off time. It gives everyone the same opening onto the world and as such exercises a fascination that the residents can no longer do without.

Movies and Other Shows

There are few project people who still go to the movies but this is not because television has replaced them. The fact that the city is far off and difficult to get to without a car and the never-ending furnishing of their apartments provide the psychological and economic reasons for their having stopped going out.

Movies have kept the prestige of the large screen, the darkened room, and paid seating. The adolescents go to many of them. The adults like to go "for a change," and those who do meet one of these three conditions: they have no children, their children are old enough to stay alone, or they have a car (their own or a neighbor's). For all of them, it represents a means of combating boredom. The important thing about movies is not the film they are going to see but the special outing in town or elsewhere. This is leisure activity par excellence. The choice of films is determined by the reason for going out. Those who go out because they "get fed up" make do with whatever happens to be available, but those who have decided to have a "big night out" go to the city to a theater that shows the spectacular movies.

Recently released films are not generally sought, and televised information about them does not seem to influence the adults. If a choice is made, it is based more on the favorite stars or the romantic or melodramatic content of the film.

Going to the movies is a reason for getting out of the project much more than a means of obtaining information. It is something exceptional connected with the idea of festive occasions, bright lights, and night life. It is becoming a more and more unusual entertainment in La Halle, where we can estimate that about twenty couples still go to the movies, with a frequency ranging from once a week to once a year. Three-fourths of the adults have never gone again since they moved into the project.

Other shows are mentioned only as stray whims: "I'd kind of like to go to the circus," or "If I went out, I'd go see an operetta." As television opens up new horizons on the entertainment world, it creates desires but cancels them at the same time: "It's not worth going because we can see it on TV."

Project residents are particularly well informed about the entertainment world; they know the music hall and singing stars and talk about them as if they were close personal friends.

There is practically no reading, people do not go to shows, and only songs (the popular expression of poetry) are listened to on the radio, so external information comes into La Halle in a special way and almost exclusively from television. Through it, the residents have access to the surrounding national culture. It is impossible to know exactly what the viewer registers and retains, but the fact that there is no weakening of enthusiasm is closely connected to a need to know that is partly satisfied by television.

Internal Information

There is no means of spreading information or news about the project. No place was provided for a bulletin board, and the infrequent little sheets pinned up in the caretaker's office are put up on individual initiative or concern the rent. The neighborhood policeman, who still exists but who is limited to a repressive role, does not spread information about municipal decisions. No conferences or meetings take place because no facilities were provided for that purpose. Since no information is given out publicly, there is no assembling to allow discussion of a notice.

All information, whatever it may be, is received individually. Consequently, the only means of spreading information must be individually by the grapevine, going by word of mouth through a whole group with nothing showing on the outside. The caretaker is part of this circuit, representing a privileged source of information because he is particularly well informed about everyone's doings and private life. The grapevine functions along preferential distribution lines—limited to a subgroup or a fraction thereof, extending to a whole group and even overflowing its edges, or covering the whole population, depending on the importance of the news or those it concerns—as shown in the following examples.

Example 1. Two children were severely punished at school for breaking a window during recess. Their mothers advised a few other mothers next door of the aggressive procedure they were going to try with the principal. Then the news was carried from neighbor to neighbor but limited to just the residents of three stairwells, and comments on the slap resulting from the proceeding were also passed along that line.

Example 2. A newspaper published an article in 1964 denouncing the overly large number of North African working people in the overcrowded hospitals. This article provoked the anger of an Algerian (the only one who had the newspaper that night) and the whole Arab community, including the mixed subgroup, was immediately informed and commented on the fact that "the French refuse to take care of the Arabs."

Example 3. A newspaper published an article in 1966, which was maladroit to say the least, on the project itself, in which it said that the residents were social problems under court surveillance and the children were dirty and unloved. This news, which spread chagrin and consternation, was passed along, always from neighbor to neighbor and without any reaction showing on the outside. All the members of every home, from youngest to oldest, were alerted and that evening there was not a resident left who did not know all about it.

The subject of the grapevine is an event, whether it relates to an individual, a small number of people, or all the residents. A fictive element almost always enters in, added to the facts. A fact exists and then its distortion prolongs its existence. The event produces a secretion, as is shown in the following exam-

ple. An adolescent has just died; the fact is plain and undeni-
able. The news circulates and then two women visit each apartment to take up a collection and make the death official by
telling people when the funeral will be. But how did he die?
The truth no longer matters and cannot change the facts, so
interpretation has free rein. Suicide is the first version: some
say the boy poisoned himself with sleeping pills, some claim
they have it from the mother herself that he hung himself
from the window latch. But others whisper behind their hands
that this is far from the truth, which it is not nice to talk about:
"He burst the veins in his head while masturbating." Probably
very few know the exact cause of death.

What is important is that an event has provided a topic of conversation for several hours or days. Events have the life-span
and consistency of a rubber balloon in the project, swelling
inordinately and dying without leaving a trace.

All information does not necessarily come from facts and
much room must be left for internal and external rumors.
Unsubstantiated reports or news of unknown origin, reason-
able or not, circulate in the project at times. They are dealt
out like truths, leaving out even the eternal "It seems" or
"I've heard" that usually announces this kind of report. The
rumors reflect concern or uneasiness; most of the time they
are pure inventions and circulate at the same rate as gossip.

It would be useless to try to evaluate the density of gossip
in La Halle for it always exceeds all estimates. Everything
is known about everyone. Not only is everyone's family history
known, but the slightest details, the smallest doings are commented on, interpreted, and distorted. If the ambulance comes,
for instance, someone is there to say that it is for Mrs. So-
and-so's fourth miscarriage and to construct a comparative
theory of abortion techniques based on named examples.

Some ill will often presides over the transmission and exag-
geration of this kind of information: the value judgments that
flow from it are accepted and lead to the typing of individuals
and the establishing of reputations. There are "nice" and "not
nice" people in the project but their classification is changeable, and reputations built on fragile foundations are frequently

called into question. For instance, a certain couple may enjoy general respect but when the neighbors find out that these two struck each other, they are put back down to the status of everyone else and everyone is informed of this revision of the social scale. On the other hand, there were few comments when a woman was taken away at dawn to carry out a jail sentence even though the reason for her leaving was known, because the established order was not disturbed.

News items and value judgments do not form the sole content of internal information, and an economic and social column must be added. There is a whole web of knowledge woven from neighbor to neighbor, based on official information learned by individuals or obtained at the town hall, that is not theoretical but is based on concrete cases, like a kind of jurisprudence. There are "technical advisers" on all the possibilities of Social Security who are asked to help fill out forms. An element of interpretation comes into play, so these advisers can tell or teach someone what he would have difficulty finding out from Social Security personnel—everything bordering on illegality. Certain women know well the deficiencies in Social Security operations that make deceit possible and how far such deceit can go.

Medical knowledge is transmitted in the same way. Before calling the doctor for a sick child, residents ask the opinion of the "neighbor who is an expert on it." The women make the diagnosis, prescribe treatment, and even furnish the medicines if they have some left over from previous illnesses. This does not prevent calling the doctor but is basically a game of gaining and comparing knowledge. "I'm very good at medicine; I never make a mistake. Everything the doctor says, I've already discovered," says Mrs. H.

There is always an interpretive element added to real or erroneous knowledge, a need for spreading information, and a deviation toward illegality, whether it involves the medical or economic area.

In economics itself, we note that the people learn nothing from financially disastrous experiences and that no information is circulated concerning bad businessmen, for example. On the other hand, addresses considered good are communicated to the inquirer. In addition, all secondhand buying and selling operations, everything concerning any kind of trafficking, and everything more or less set apart from usual commerce is one of the privileged domains of internal information.

This information is relatively abundant. It is conveyed by public report and gossip, has a quick run, and is quickly forgotten. It forms a compost of knowledge in socioeconomic matters and even tries its hand at a kind of ineffective self-correction. It is rarely connected to the multiple external pieces of information received through television.

In short, information is circulated in La Halle as it is everywhere else—through education and socialization on one hand and through the mass media and finally rumor on the other. It is only in the perception of information that a cleavage occurs between the project and other social groups: the distortion or nonabsorption of elementary-school knowledge, the importance of the televised image (and not of the raw content of the information), and the power of rumors. These rumors initiate a more real communication that may be translated into an exchange of information and lead to mutual aid.

12

The System of Values

We have tried to transcribe certain aspects of the project residents' lives in the preceding chapters. In order to complete their view of the world, there remains the consideration of their concept of authority and justice, their ethics, and their religion.

Prestige and Authority

The two essential components of relational values in La Halle are "nice people" and prestige on one side and authority and the hierarchy on the other.

"Nice People"

We have tried to get the residents to define this oft-repeated term in order to find out to which individuals or social classes it was applicable and to what it was connected in their minds. But while we customarily heard this qualification conferred affirmatively or negatively on project residents in general conversation, the answers to "Who do you think are 'nice people'?" were theoretical and did not name names.

Couple 1

Man: "Someone who is clean, who works, who loves his wife and sticks to her."

Woman: "People who have a good mind, who don't criticize others; it doesn't matter if they get money wherever they happen to find it."

Couple 2

Man: "Intelligent people who have a trade, who are polite, and don't ask anyone for anything."

Woman: "Educated people. They can get in anywhere, they earn a good living, and don't worry about other people."

Couple 3

Man: "Understanding, intelligent people who don't argue; it doesn't make any difference whether or not they have money."

Woman: "Nice people get in everywhere; they do as many dirty things as we do but they hide it. They have money and the whole world at their feet. They don't call attention to themselves, and they only mix with important people."

To the question, "Is the parish priest one of the 'nice people'?" they answered, "No, the priests are like everyone else; there are some nice ones; it depends." And the mayor? "He's a politician, it's not the same thing; ours isn't nice, he doesn't like poor people." On the other hand, when they learned that a social worker they knew had divorced his wife, they exclaimed. "So, that happens to nice people too!"

It follows from these answers that "nice people" may be completely separate from those representing some degree of authority. They must not have faults or perform acts bearing some moral disapproval. We note some agreement, here as elsewhere, in their respect for intelligence and education, as well as for the power of money. But this latter condition is mentioned but little compared to the emphasis on the individual's moral worth, which is not so much traditional as it is relative to the social condition of the La Halle residents.

The nice people are those who "don't call attention to themselves" and who "understand other people." The people of La Halle, we must say once more, are in a humbled position, but in answering these questions they reverse roles, pass judgment on themselves, and look for a definition outside themselves. This is striking in Woman 3's reply above that "they do as many dirty things as we do." So nice people are not "we"; nor can they be the representatives of authority who do not meet the above-mentioned criteria. They sense that nice people have a body of qualities that are precisely those not attributed to the people of La Halle.[1] That is why they did not spontaneously name a neighbor, and why we had to insist before they would give an example. The example the residents did give was an Arab couple with many children. The husband was a very steady worker. No one has ever complained about this couple, who fits their definition of "nice people": "Starting from zero, they've become very well off, with all the comforts. Their oldest son has just made a good marriage. They steer a steady ship." Starting with this description, we shall try to analyze the assets that yield prestige.

The Notion of Prestige

The attitude toward those who may be admired is almost always ambivalent, split between criticism and respect. They therefore admire the Arab couple but they add that this couple knows how to steer its ship. Success is recognized but not effort.

External signs of wealth are a source of prestige but these are relative to the residents' income scale. Furniture has a high value, as do lamps and curtains. A car excites covetousness but only a new one is surrounded with prestige. Those who own an automobile are not exempt from criticism or mockery if owning it is deemed out of keeping with their way of life;

for example, one man was criticized for buying a new car when he owed money to all his neighbors. An Arab who cleans the motor and body of his car every day is openly made fun of: "He sits on the bench looking at it. He hardly ever uses it; he drives around the courtyard and puts it back in the garage because it's not fit to stay outside overnight."

Ostentatious expenditures for a ceremonial occasion also arouse admiration and envy. On the other hand, the rich are hated on the whole as the owning class: "People with dough run everything; it's not fair."

Kindness, self-sacrifice and qualities of the heart, cleanliness, and courtesy also yield prestige but, unlike the economic sources of prestige, models for everything concerning human qualities are not taken from inside the project. Television offers people another system of references, and they are quick to hero worship, although that word was never used in the course of the interviews.

We have classified the examples and definitions of prestige that we gathered under four headings, and have written them in the order in which they were given to us.

(1) "Those who are committed to their work."
Example: Those who teach retarded children, surgeons.
(2) "Those who are better than others."
"Those who have talent."
"Those who are honored everywhere."
"Those who have really earned their success."
Example: Several sports champions, and movie actors.
(3) "Those who are very well educated, who do scientific research."
(4) "Those who make beautiful things, like painters, sculptors, dancers."

Heroes, who are primarily masculine, are therefore esteemed for their unselfishness and their exploits, and the better established their success, the more prestige they have.

In regard to the respect for higher education, it is interesting to note an ambivalent attitude again revealed by one informant: "We have to be afraid of people more qualified than us—doctors, professors, teachers—because we have to accept what they say since we can't check on it." And this restriction raises the question of authority.

Authority and the Hierarchy

People invested with prestige are rarely connected with authority. We have seen how much the outsider representing authority is feared.

The mayor, the priest, and the teacher are not looked upon with respect, and these examples are significant of the general attitude of the people of La Halle. They totally reject any authority exercised over them, perhaps because they have too often felt that it is coercive and that it emanates from invisible and almost occult governmental powers.

The authority of the "boss" (or employer), the only person who has direct command over them, is no better accepted. They generally fear him and do not like to argue with him. They tolerate his existence and submit to his orders on the job, but if they think his criticisms are unjustified they simply leave the job: "One boss is as good as another."

In order to explain the project residents' attitude, we must talk about the system of authority in which they live. First, we must not overlook the fact that unlike a village, the La Halle community is not run by anyone. It is directly subject to the laws and the authority representing them; this authority is concretized not by the men invested with it, but by multiple intermediaries who may intervene in anyone's life.

The residents continually have only the relationship of inferiors to superiors, without ever coming in contact with the important people in politics and government. The long hierarchy is not next to but always above them, so their reaction is the same as in previously described areas, such as financial limitations. They reject every constraint, they deny the hierarchy, and they do not accept the authority of the inter-mediaries or, by extension, of anyone they have not called upon. All of them, except the Arabs, go directly to a relatively high level in the hierarchy for every ordinary procedure, such as the elementary-school superintendent [in the Ministry of

Education] for affairs concerning the school or the Attorney General for dealings with the court.[2] But when the affair seems more important to them, they address themselves directly to a higher or supreme authority. It is not surprising to hear statements similar to the following: "If the principal keeps bothering me, I'll write to Christian Fouchet [Minister of Education]." This is not an empty threat or a boast.

The "authorities" are two in number: the prefect and General de Gaulle. (We must also mention the Pope, "who can do anything, even stop the war; he's omnipotent.") The prefect represents the administrative side and General de Gaulle the government. They cannot see these high personnages but they write to them. Moreover, since General de Gaulle is considered the supreme leader, in a situation believed to be dangerous, they bypass the prefect (the last intermediate echelon) and write directly to the chief of state. "You always have to go straight to the big brains" is frequently heard.

Of ten people questioned, all had written at least once to General de Gaulle, most often to obtain housing. "I asked the mayor and the prefect for ten years about my housing. Eight days after my letter to de Gaulle I had an answer: I was to go in his behalf and see a gentleman at the Prefecture. I was greeted at the Prefecture like a great lady: 'Please sit down,' etc. . . . Two hours later I had the keys to the apartment." They also write to the President for other reasons, especially to beg for a reprieve after receiving a minor conviction or an eviction notice.[3]

The President is well known, people know where he lives, and he, more than the government, represents parental authority. They rarely have any interest in the deputies, however, and never call upon them. The project residents do not get excited over elections for the legislature. The only opinion we heard about the ministers is that they "line their own pockets."

The people of La Halle only accept the authority of the men who are in top positions of command. They see these

personages or write to them on their own because they
believe that "these people, who are more intelligent and
all-powerful will understand" them. And they send long mis-
sives full of hope and trust to General de Gaulle, who seems
to represent an absolute paternal power that is all the more
mythical for having no relation to the image of their own father.

Ethics

By ethics we mean the whole composite of manifestations
of cultural and moral values: aesthetics, material and moral
ideals, religion, and celebrations.

Aesthetics

The differences between the various ethnic groups in regard
to aesthetic feelings will be diminished by the severance from
traditional values among the Jews and Arabs, the fairly similar
economic conditions for all, information on aesthetic matters
derived from furniture and clothing handbills, and the emulation operating between neighbors. Rather than examining the
ethnic variants, which we shall point out as need be, we shall
try to analyze how aesthetics are considered in interior decoration and in connection with eating patterns.

INTERIOR DECORATION

When we visit several apartments at random, we are at first
struck by the colorful walls and the similarity of the furniture.
We must not forget that this is the first time that this population
has really furnished a home, except for those who had a house
in French North Africa, and they had only the bare necessities
for eating and sleeping when they came here. We must also
remember that when the apartments were originally turned
over to them, the walls were simply covered with a coat of
plaster.

All the Mediterraneans, including the Italians, as well as
the poorest metropolitans, paint the walls. The others, who

want to give the impression that they are financially comfortable to some extent, prefer to use wallpaper. There is a surprising luxuriousness and diversity of colors in all the apartments.

The living room and adjoining bedroom at Noufissa's have
orange ceilings and green walls and doors. The Keltoums have
decided in favor of sea-blue on the ceiling and shocking pink
on the walls, which are broken up by green doors. Green,
blue, pink, and orange are the traditional colors of the Magrab
spreads hung on the walls. Pink coupled with a lilac called
parme is found at the D.'s (French). The lilac is combined
with blue and green at the I.'s (Jews). The colors are red and
green at Mrs. A.'s, and pink, green, and blue again at the
H.'s, but the hues are toned down. The apartments with the
least furniture are the ones bursting with color, while these
same colors pale into pastels among the most financially comfortable residents. At still another home, four different
shades and patterns of imitation cretonne wallpaper were
chosen for the living room.

The poorest people do not paint the dilapidated walls still
sometimes covered only by their first coat of plaster, but most
of the project residents (especially the Jewish women) repaint
or repaper their walls frequently, as often as once a year. They
follow certain fashions, such as the current ones of using *parme*
and wallpaper with imitation stones like those seen in the
hallway. They do not like yellow.[4] The people focus their
creativity on the walls; those who are unsure copy the others
(the flowering of green doors and many colors of paint began
with the Arabs).

Furniture everywhere consists of a dining set, more or less
shiny new or rickety depending on finances, and bedroom
furniture. A satin pajama case won at the fair is often found
on the double bed, while the children's bedrooms are the
most summarily furnished. For about three years, the custom
has been spreading of sitting on a couch while watching television; there is a matching armchair, and both are covered in
synthetic plush or expanded vinyl. A narrow bed covered with
fringed rayon recalls traditional furnishings in some Jewish
homes.

We know of just one metropolitan who designed an original

interior. He transformed a corner of the living room into an aviary where a throng of birds revel from floor to ceiling and two or three cages hold others, including a crow. (Parakeets have appeared in other apartments since this family moved in.) He separated the hallway from the living room with a gate and a framework for climbing plants. But here again this decoration is addressed to the wall, and the furniture is as functional as elsewhere.

Pieces of furniture are chosen in terms of their intended use, and this is a controlling function. That is to say, no one would put a spare bed in the dining room, for example, and convert it into a place to relax by putting cushions on the bed. If someone sleeps in this family room, they use a convertible armchair bought for that purpose, so that no trace of sleeping will be visible in a place set aside for eating.

Attempts at lighting effects are unknown but the electric bulbs are generally covered with small cheap lampshades. Project residents might like to buy a chandelier but it is considered of only minor utility so it is a luxury. Lamps are practically nonexistent but we note a growing fashion for night lamps in the bedroom.

Even the Arabs do not have rugs, but they are sometimes found in Jewish homes.

Objects with particular uses cannot be converted to decorative purposes so what is left of Arab and Jewish traditional objects (decorated glasses, bottles, perfume containers) are all shut up in the buffet. But knickknacks, irregularly scattered about, serve only as decoration because they are not used; these include little copper pots, tiny plastic flower pots, scale models of a street lamp with a drunk clinging to it, bouquets of pink feathers won in the lottery, souvenirs, and gifts.

We do find doilies and vases that are both functional and decorative. The vases are usually filled with artificial flowers. This does not stop residents from liking cut flowers, but they are expensive and fade quickly. To alleviate this inconvenience, almost all the European housewives keep potted plants.

Except among the Arabs who have a few naive pictures from Cairo, there are almost no cheap pictures. These are replaced by the falsely exotic wallpaper (with camels and palm trees) first found in Arab homes and now spreading to their neighbors, and by pictures of "real painting"* that take their place in the center of the middle wall. These paintings, depicting deer in the undergrowth and sunsets on the sea, show how far emulation and lack of reference points come into play. When a picture-seller invaded the courtyard one day, two or three of the most well-to-do residents rushed to buy his wares at 80F, and he sold twenty-five in an hour.

Plastic flowers hung in a garland around the room at the ceiling are also found in one Arab home, but in general the walls are quite bare except for the examples mentioned above. There are no framed family portraits, except at homes of the Pied-Noirs, and rarely any holy pictures. A few baby photos find room on the buffet.

A lack of curtains is considered a great mark of poverty and ugliness. The ideal is materialized by large pieces of printed cretonne falling to the floor on either side of the window and sometimes acting as a portiere in the living room. Curtains, like wall colors, are changed as often as possible.

The people are probably not satisfied with their aesthetic efforts because they frequently rearrange the furniture; this phenomenon is common to every group. The buffet moves from right to left and the table that was pushed back returns to the middle the following week, as though they wanted something new or found it impossible to achieve a harmonious arrangement.

The reference system within the project follows this circuit: the Arabs get their criteria for furnishing from the Jews, who have previously gotten them from the richest metropolitans, and pass on their colors and a certain exotic flavor to the poorest metropolitans.

EATING PATTERNS

Eating patterns are subject to the same financial injunctions, but they are modified by the rhythm of complex interrelations

---

*Cheap reproductions that are hand-painted but mass-produced.—R.S.

within groups. We shall look first at how the meal is served and then at its content.

Serving

We know that no one has table linens in La Halle, but these do appear among the things they want to buy whereas neither china nor silver, which are unknown here, were mentioned.

Each family has the minimum in cooking utensils, odd plates, aluminum flatware, and glasses that most often were originally mustard containers and were chosen for their decorative design. Unlike the middle class, the project people did not receive a "complete service" or a chest of silverware when they were married. They bought dishes as they needed them and so have a very limited supply.

Moreover, no one taught any of them how to set the table, so it is set much the same by all. The Jews put on a cloth tablecloth on Sunday and Friday, and get along with an oilcloth or nylon one the other days. The most comfortable mixed and Arab families use a cloth tablecloth every day.

Among the Europeans and the mixed group, each person has flatware placed at one side and one plate that will not be changed during the meal. When the investigator is invited to dinner, only her plate is changed. The food is placed in the center of the table, often in the cooking utensils. Everyone serves himself or gives his plate to the mother.

The Arabs and Jews sit around the table in any order, with the master of the house sitting down first. The flatware is piled up, and everyone takes some or passes out spoons and forks to the others. There are generally not enough knives; they are not usually used since the food is well-done. The wife fills the plates in the kitchen and brings the full plate to each one at the table, with the best piece going to the guest and the next best to the father. Portions are not distributed equally this way, but this is a European adaptation of the old way of eating from a common plate; if too much is left in a plate, it will be kept in the pan and reheated the next day.

Bread and fruit are also distributed from hand to hand. Appetizers, which are kept for Friday or prepared in the guest's honor or when the wife feels like it, are picked up here and there on the end of one's fork from two or three saucers put where everyone can reach them. Chicken is eaten with the fingers.

When the portions of the main dish have been distributed, the children may eat theirs where they like—for example, sitting on the floor—or leave their plate half full.

The appetizers, which are not served every day but occasionally mark an improvement in the menu, reflect an effort in all groups to serve well and decoratively.

There are no napkins or not enough of them; they are shared by several members of the family and are replaced by used cloths or even by towels (among the Arabs) or handkerchiefs. There is always one for the guest.

The Menus

The Arabs and the Jews remain attached to culinary traditions but it is materially inconvenient to prepare traditional dishes because their success depends on exotic ingredients that are more expensive than in Africa or are difficult to procure. Saffron has disappeared, green tea has been abandoned in favor of coffee, and the couscous [a North African stew] lacks the tart taste of home-style butter. This is why truly traditional food is reserved for holidays and is adapted to local foodstuffs and cooking methods for everyday.

Table 13 shows some sample menus popular in the four groups. We see that all groups have dessert, as well as appetizers; when there is none, it is because of a lack of money. Dessert most often consists of cheese and fruit in the French and mixed households and fruit and pastry in the others. A taste for pastry has survived among the Arabs and Jews and is passed on to the second generation; it is easy to make and anise and sesame seeds keep a long time in the house.

While the popularity of fried steak has spread, couscous has also gained adepts. Semolina is easy to buy, and because of the resemblance of couscous to pot-au-feu [a typical French stew], all the metropolitans who have relations with Arabs, Jews, or Pied-Noirs have adopted it. Some Frenchwomen even ask Arab women to make them some and they will pay for it, and the supermarket also carries some in cans.

Real mechoui [skewered lamb] has been given up for lack of utensils because no family has a brazier, but it has reappeared in the mixed households because the women know how to make good use of the stove burners and grill for this purpose. They have learned to like broiled lamb and are in the process of acclimatizing their Moslem friends to this version of mechoui.

The Arabs and Jews eat a great deal of fried potatoes and have adopted all the European fried foods. Spaghetti is served more often, a result of the influence of the Italians and Tunisians.

The Frenchwomen have never learned much about the refinements of cooking and often serve cold cuts and canned foods, but the others have not adopted this habit. Salad is generally served at all tables.

They all have the same drinks: wine or beer for the adults (except the Arab women) and soft drinks for the children. Anisette is the favorite apéritif. After-dinner drinks (like cognac and rum), as well as liqueurs (like creme de banane) especially favored by the women, are bought on payday in small flasks because of the price.

Because they all like fried foods and they all shop in the same place, their cooking methods tend to become the same.[5] Since they have taken up the Arab custom of bringing each other food offerings, the metropolitans may get to like cooking again because the Arab women's cooking skill is more developed. Jewish pastry and kemia[6] are much enjoyed. A mutual influence may operate over time that will reduce the amount of time spent over the stove for some and increase it for others.

DRESS

We shall say just a few words about dress because the project hardly differs from other working-class milieus.

The men generally do not change from their work clothes during the week except when they go out, for example, on Saturday, even to go shopping. They have a business suit or

Table 13
Sample Menus

Mixed Household	Arab Household	Jewish Household	Metropolitan Household
APPETIZER			
Tomato salad	None or small	None or	Tomato salad
Hard-boiled eggs	shredded salad	Kemia-brik[1]	Mixed cold cuts
Sardines or soup			or soup
MAIN DISH			
Broiled lamb	Fried mackerel and	Stewed chicken with	Fried chicken
Green beans or	fried potatoes	rice and salad	Fried steak
pork and beans	Lamb stew	Fried potatoes and	Cube steak and canned
Steak and fried	Stewed chicken and	salad	vegetables
potatoes	fried potatoes	Vegetable fritters	Spaghetti
Sausages and mashed	Lamb couscous	Meatballs	Canned cassoulet
potatoes	Pâté à la arissa [a	Stuffed peppers with	[bean stew]
Lamb couscous	Tunisian spaghetti]	rice	Pot-au-feu (occasionally
Lamb leg or shoulder	Fried steak	Couscous with tripe	couscous)
with kidney beans	Fried meatballs	and eggs	Game stew
		Fried steak	Roast (beef, horsemeat,
			pork, lamb) and mashed
			potatoes
			Pork and beans
			Canned tripe
			Sausages and mashed
			potatoes

Salad
Camembert
Fruit
Coffee

Bananas, fruit,
  or cake
Coffee

Braided anise bread
Cake or fruit
Coffee

Salad, cheese
Fruit
Coffee

SABBATH OR HOLIDAY

Appetizer
Poultry or roast
Couscous
Cake (from a bakery)

Couscous
Several kinds of
  meat with gravy
Homemade pastry

Apéritif
Mixed appetizers
Couscous
Homemade pastry

Appetizer
Roast or poultry
Pastry (from a bakery)

[1]See *n* 6.

jacket and pants and prefer to wear a white shirt with it. During
the week, they like to wear checked or print shirts. The Arabs
are no different from the others except that they take off their
shoes at home or wear sandals.

The women are different. Those who have lost their shape
due to age, pregnancy, or privation wear run-down shoes and
anklets in every season or stockings held up by garters. When
they go out, they put on a coat of nondescript shape and color
over a blouse. They never put on make-up and do not take
care of their hair, which is curled once a year or not at all.

Those who are younger or less worn out pay more attention to
their appearance when they leave the project. Then they put on
their make-up carefully and dress in bright colors, especially on
the upper part of their bodies. They like fake fur or synthetic
jersey coats; they think cloth coats are too severely styled and
too expensive. They do not have clothes reserved for Sunday
and they put on the best they have to go out during the week,
but they do not dress up for themselves. At home or in the project they wear worn skirts and sweaters or stay in blouses and
housecoats for hours at a time.

When the Jewish women go to a party, their transformation
is amazing. Usually inclined to be negligent, they take from
their closet some formal gown or even an astrakhan coat in
winter, and make themselves up with skill.

Some of the Arab women still bear tattoos on the forehead
and chin that they do not try to eradicate (unlike the big-city
women in the Magrab); their clothing becomes European in
inverse proportion to their age. They generally wear a wide,
colorful skirt down to midcalf, a nylon blouse, a wool vest,
and flat heels, and they do not fail to cover their heads when
they go out. The youngest Moslem woman in the project
dresses and uses make-up like the European women, according
to the fashion standards spread by the Prisunics, while some
women in mixed households become Arab in dress, tying a
scarf under their chin and showing a fondness for overly long
skirts. The Arab women have continued to wear gold bracelets,
to henna their long hair (as do the Jewish women), and to

use kohl on the edge of their lower eyelids. No one comments
on their style of dressing.

The children generally have a Sunday outfit. From age seven
or eight, the boys' is the same as the men's: white shirt, tie,
jacket, and pants. The girls have a special dress or skirt.

The adolescents do not follow fashion closely, and the girls
do not know how to dress like "teens." They prefer ordinary
nylon stockings, even in summer, to print stockings or the
socks now in style, and even keep them when they have runs
in them. They like high-heeled shoes. They take good care
of their hair, changing shades often, and use make-up abun-
dantly.

It is hard to talk about the "dress" of people who have trouble
clothing themselves; the word seems inappropriate and tends
to be reduced to "clothing."

SELF-EXPRESSION

We know little about self-expression because it is especially
hard to break down people's modesty to get some information,
and direct observation cannot be carried on. Nonetheless, we
must report that it exists because some residents are reputed
to have good voices and it seems there is much singing on
holidays. In addition, some would seem to have talent as song
writers, poets, and public entertainers at big celebrations: they
tell and act out stories, present plays, and make up songs.

They all like dance music and songs, but no one plays an
instrument. Sometimes, though not often, the Arab women
dance when their husbands are not home, beating time on
a pan. The French also dance among themselves on holidays.
We have not seen any expression of the plastic arts but we
know at least two women who keep their husbands' poems
in the dresser. The modes of expression do not seem to have
undergone any alteration or change from those of adolescence
alluded to in chapter 8.

We discover nothing very special in the area of aesthetics,
compared to the rest of society, except that economic condi-

248 *The Norms of Social Life*

tions limit the possibilities and mutual influence operates more
than in an apartment complex, for instance.

Ideals

We shall deal with the material ideal and then consider moral
ideals as expressed through the notion of good and bad.

All the ideas about the material ideal have been brought
out in previous chapters. We know that because of their past,
which has not equipped them for it, and their present, which
is taken up with material problems, the people of La Halle
cannot really build a future. All their energy is mobilized for
survival, so they take refuge in dreams, and their ideals refer
to nostalgic notions, advertising, and "fashions." These ideals
are unrealistic plans and hopes:

"To earn a good living."
"To find a good job."
"To have a house with a garage."
"To set up a small shop and be in charge."
"To buy a farm in Dordogne."

They all long to leave the project and find security, and they
escape by identifying with the heroes on television.

This sort of utopian ideal is held especially by the French.
It is not found among the Arabs and Italians, who think they
already have gained something compared to their previous
economic situation and therefore keep up their efforts and
rather realistically count on their children for a constant
improvement in their standard of living. For the Jews, their
ideal is linked above all to their religion, which they try to
maintain in its entirety despite the loss of community. Some
try to make a small place for themselves in the society around
them and others turn toward Israel, the Promised Land, knowing full well they will not go there.

The notion of good and bad emerged at the beginning of
this chapter when we defined "nice people" and is present
in the section on relations with neighbors. It is justified by
referring to oneself rather than to traditional norms, so we

might arrive at a morality unique to La Halle; but since the rupture with tradition takes place unevenly, differences still subsist despite the appearance of constants that are partly a result of living in the project. It should be noted that the residents are made to feel collectively guilty through the occasional blows to their self-esteem. This collective culpability does not engender individual culpability but it partly determines the prevalent notion of good and bad, which is closely related to their social life.

The similarity of responses is symptomatic. Says one woman, "What's bad is to be too nosy, to dislike each other, to criticize people without knowing them," and then adds, perhaps for the benefit of the investigator who in her eyes is probably the bearer of a different morality, "and stealing and all those whatchamacallits, naturally." The other answers are the same: "Good and bad is love and hate," or "Bad is disrespect of others, vengeance, betrayal."

The notion of transgression or sin does not exist for the people of La Halle. Abortions, stealing, and drunkenness are not considered reprehensible; "That's life." Evil is incarnated exclusively in not "liking each other," which is an essential principle of charity in the original meaning of the term. This choice is the exact reflection of their deep longing in reaction to a seemingly hostile world, and the projection of their own impotence to realize this inaccessible ideal.

Imprisoned in the same community, the Arabs and Jews tend to give the same definition as the others but add, "Good is to raise your children as best you can," implying that this is without the support of your original community. This comes from the same inner attitude of uncertainty and insecurity in the absence of a coherent system of references.

The material ideal connected to their economic condition is similar to that found among all economically underprivileged people, but the notion of good and bad comprises a particularly strong, utopian value of comradeship. This value seems to be found in other "subcultures of poverty." Among those he studied in Mexico, Oscar Lewis notes "a strong sense of individuality . . . a desire for understanding and love."[7]

Religion and Celebrations

Religion

It is appropriate to make a clear distinction in religion between the three ethnic groups. All three are moving away from religious observances to various degrees. We shall begin our study with the Jews, who seem to be the most "religious," then the Moslems, and then the Christians. We shall also look at some aspects of superstition.

THE JEWS

In the case of the Jews, it is impossible to distinguish belief from religious practice for they are intimately commingled in Judaism. The duties in practice as prescribed by the Talmud and the additional rites introduced since it was written closely overlap everyday life. However, we observe a decrease in religious practice brought about by two factors: the loss of the Jewish community because of the distance from the synagogue, and the diminishing degree of religious instruction received by the project Jews.

Previously, even if their knowledge of Judaism was insufficient, they complied with the prescriptions of the community and attended synagogue services regularly. They do not have this support in La Halle, so they have to advise each other, and those who pass for masters were probably just among the humble faithful before. Three women are religious advisers, and one of them claims that only six families practice the religion correctly and the others "do what they can because they don't know any better."

We shall take a brief look at how the Jewish religion is observed through prayer and worship, rites and symbols, sacraments and holidays.

The Talmud requires three prayers daily, to be said in a group of at least ten men, so it is easiest to go to the synagogue to pray, but this is impossible for the project Jews to do, at least every day. Another element in their creed is the public reading of the Torah three times a week, and they cannot comply with this either. In addition to the daily prayers, blessings must be recited on various occasions; for example, saying grace before and after meals is obligatory. A different service and prayers are dedicated to the Sabbath. All the obligatory prayers must be recited in Hebrew, with the head covered, but the father's and son's black skullcaps, as well as the prayer shawls they all own, remain in the bottom of the dresser. Once a daily practice, the prayers are now reserved for holidays.

On the other hand, the consecration rites attached to meals are largely maintained despite economic difficulties. Meat is separated from milk in cooking and in the diet, which is set by law, and Jewish residents take every opportunity to go to the city to buy kosher meats, which they then carefully rinse. Outward symbols, such as the box mounted on the doorjamb, have disappeared, except for the oil lamp burning on the Sabbath in the husband and wife's bedroom.

We know nothing of the marriage ceremony, but the sacred and holy character of the marriage bonds is preserved. Jewish unions are absolutely stable no matter what sexual games the husband and wife indulge in.

Circumcision generally takes place at the prescribed time—seven days after birth. Although at the beginning it was a simple "sign of alliance" in the Bible, circumcision is acquiring the value of a sacrament in their minds by assimilation to Christian baptism.

Although Jewish children in La Halle avoid religious instruction,[8] when they attain their majority according to the law at the end of their thirteenth year, they must carry out a ceremony confirming them in their duties of religious obedience, which consists of reading the Torah in public, and they are usually willing to go along with this. This ceremony is commonly called communion in La Halle.

The "appointed times"—days of feasting or fasting—constitute an original feature of Jewish life. The first such time is the Sabbath, a day of rest, during which Jews must abstain from any kind of work or occupation. The Sabbath is commonly observed in La Halle as a day of rest and joy. Richer meals and loaves of braided bread, symbolizing the wedding band, are eaten that day. The father goes to the synagogue in the afternoon but the women are torn between their housewifely concerns and the obligation not to do anything. Some are tormented by the prohibition against lighting a fire, on which they infringe in order not to "constantly bother a non-Jewish neighbor every time we need to turn on the gas." The women therefore prepare the meals and clean the apartment the day before in order to work as little as possible on the Sabbath, leaving God to judge their good intentions.

According to the rabbis, there are three principal holidays and the most important is Passover (in March or April). It lasts seven days and its observance consists of eating unleavened bread. The women clean the house from top to bottom before Passover in order to remove any trace of leavened bread. They also buy new dishes; the old ones are given away or put aside to be used again later, depending on available finances. The men go to the synagogue every day after work and stay late, but the family service with psalms and hymns is being curtailed more and more.

Seven weeks after Passover, the Jews celebrate the festival of weeks (Shavuoth), which lasts forty-eight hours. Shopping and traveling are prohibited during that time. The men go to the synagogue where they must spend the whole night studying the Torah. Depending on their state of fatigue, their work for the next day, and their piety, the men from La Halle stay just a few hours or go to sleep at dawn at a coreligionist's home.

The third holiday (in October) is called the holiday of huts (Sukkoth in Hebrew), and this is the one the project people find impossible to celebrate properly because each family is supposed to build its reed hut on the roof or in the yard and eat its meals there for seven days. The importance of this holiday has therefore diminished.

Thus, out of the three principal holidays, only one is celebrated according to the law. But others are strictly observed, especially Rosh Hashanah, the New Year (in September or October), which inaugurates ten days of penitence. On Yom Kippur, when penitence culminates in total fast, all the adults abstain from food, the father goes to' the synagogue to make public confession, and the children are kept home.

In addition to these "appointed times," there are a certain number of less important feast- and fast-days. The most joyous is Purim (in February or March), when cakes and sweets are distributed. It has fallen more or less into disuse because it is mixed up with the Christian Mardi Gras, but it is preceded by a fast that is observed seven days before. Another fast is observed in August, followed by nine days of semimourning.

Finally, another minor Jewish holiday has gained importance in La Halle. This is the Shechinah Rabbi, which consists of "shunning hard work and having a good meal."[9]

The way Jewish holidays are celebrated in the project is summed up like this by one informant: "When you have the means you do all the holidays and even take a taxi to go to Saint-Georges to buy everything you need. The years when you don't have the money, you particularly celebrate Passover, Yom Kippur and Shechinah Rabbi." In short, just observance of the holiday of Passover, the great pardoning of sins, and a minor gay holiday remain.

The Jewish women, who are not required to attend synagogue services, have a dominant role when there is a funeral in the family. They scratch their faces and rend the tops of their dresses and then they go and weep together. They wash the body if it is a woman. They supervise the period of mourning, which lasts a year, and tint their hair black if they had hennaed it before the death. They stay at the home of the deceased and take charge of preparing meals for the near relatives, who gather for seven days devoted to prayers. Then they gather the family together again for four consecutive Sabbaths. On the fourth Saturday, the meal is composed of the deceased's favorite foods and the house is open to all who wish to come in and eat. They repeat this again in the eleventh month after the death, and then again on each anniversary. Meat is not eaten for the seven preceding days.

The Jews' insufficient Hebrew instruction has economic consequences. They cannot pray because they do not know how, but since they have remained very pious and wish to comply with religious precepts in important circumstances, especially in time of death, this leads them to pay ten strangers to pray during the seven ritual days if the family has no men capable of doing so.

The son or daughter of the deceased must also ritually attend public worship daily for the eleven months following death to pray for the defunct. La Halle Jews contract with the rabbi to light a lamp and pray for the defunct himself.

It is also symptomatic that, although no member of the clergy is necessary to pay respects to a dead Jew, the project Jews insist that a rabbi be present at the washing of the body (if it is a man) and pray over the body. They claim they pay a lot for this (700F, by their report). They also express great admiration for the Jews who can send their dead by airplane for burial in Israel.

Although their beliefs are very hardy and all the principal rites are preserved in spite of material difficulties and social pressure, the Jewish religion seems to be dying in La Halle despite outward appearances and the men's efforts to find communal support in the synagogue. The home is in fact the most eminent institution in Judaism and that is where a life of devotion must be taught. The disappearance of prayer in the home and of instruction in Hebrew and Talmud keeps the second generation from the knowledge and practice of Judaism. Only one family in La Halle is capable of passing on all the religious observances.

THE MOSLEMS

The Moslems are further along the road to effacing their religion than the Jews. We should distinguish between those who married even a distant cousin, according to tradition, and those who live with a Christian and have given up religious practices more rapidly. Along with the Jews, however, they share that common characteristic of a surviving belief in God, and even among the most acculturated of them, God is mixed in with daily life and conversation.

But since God rightly allows those who are traveling not to comply with the essential rites, the project Moslems, who are living abroad, tend to consider themselves excused from certain observances and to allow individual freedom of choice. This is not to deny that the Moslems are more influenced by the lack of community and social pressure than the Jews.

Let us recall that Islam requires the believer to say five prayers every day, while turned to the east, after making ritual ablutions. These prayers may be said at the mosque or wherever one happens to be when their hour strikes. The Moslems are also bound to fast from sunrise to sunset during the month of Ramadan. Finally, they must go on a pilgrimage to Mecca at least once. In addition, the Koran proscribes eating "dead animals," blood, and the meat of pigs, and prohibits wine and games of chance. It prescribes giving charity to the poor, orphans, and travelers. A Moslem must sacrifice a sheep on the holidays of Mouloud, Aïd Seghir, and Aïd el Kebir, and must circumcise his son at about age three.

What is left of these religious practices in La Halle? Many of those who emigrated when they were young have never known anything about the verses to be recited in prayers. And what working man would be willing to leave his place in the production line to prostrate himself in front of the Christians in the shop? Finally, since five prayers are required, it does not suffice to say just one (for example, the evening prayer), so prayer is completely forsaken. For this reason, they do not frequent the mosque although they are happy to make it the goal of an outing. No one carries out the pilgrimage.

Fasting remains. The men in mixed households do not, but the traditional households still practice it. We note that the observance is diminishing, however. In one family, for instance, the mother complains that she was the only one who fasted this year. The grandmother is getting too old and the older children, who used to fast at least part of the time in previous years, as well as the father, who usually fasted, ate every day.[10] The older the children grow, the less willing they are to submit and the less strict the family becomes. However, the women are anxious for the religion to survive and will be the last to give up the effort enjoined by Ramadan.

The women also see to it that observances in connection with food are respected. They do not drink alcohol, and we know at least two men who do not allow wine to be brought into the house; wine is also proscribed for holiday meals. The same thing happens with pork: the men eat whatever they are served in the company cafeteria or accept a ham sandwich for morning snack, but a woman would not prepare pork in the house.

The Moslems married to Frenchwomen do not observe the food prohibitions, but the others still buy live poultry and wring the necks themselves so as not to eat blood or "dead animals." The religious Moslems buy meat from the Arab butcher because he lets them think that he slaughters the animals ritually himself, but he buys them at the slaughterhouse like all the other butchers.

Food regulations are strictly observed on holidays. Until 1963, the sacrifice of sheep for Aïd el Kebir took place in the form of a secret slaughter behind the wall by the vacant lots, with several men putting their funds and skill together. If they are watched too closely to do this, they bring back a quarter of a ritually slaughtered sheep from M—— or another community.

Aïd Seghir and Aïd el Kebir are still celebrated, the one minimally just after the end of Ramadan, the other as ostentatiously as possible in the form of a traditional banquet to which all the project Moslems invite each other. A few mixed households receive part of the food or are invited to the meal. Only Aïd el Kebir shows signs of being perpetuated; it goes far beyond the limits of the family.

Circumcision provides an occasion for one or several banquets to which project neighbors and friends are invited, either separately or at the same time as the relatives who come from all over the area. While prayers have disappeared and fasting is becoming less strict, circumcision has kept its value intact. Called baptism out of modesty by the women in mixed households, circumcision is really the sign that makes the child a Moslem. While the isolated man in mixed households in other localities has given in to his wife, the Moslem fathers in La Halle, drawing their persuasive force from the example of their coreligionists, have all had their sons circumcised regardless of their wife's heritage. Just one Frenchwoman won her case by promising that if her children were not circumcised they would not be baptized as Christians either.

Certain aspects of Koran morality are also preserved, for example charity to the poor and the rule of retaliation. Financial aid and hospitality are as real in the project as avenging one's honor with a knife.

Religious practices among the Moslems are thus diminished to a very considerable extent, being reduced to nothing for some and to imperfect observance of fasting and food prohibitions for others. Verses from the Koran are being completely forgotten, but belief remains nearly intact in everyone, as concretized by the application of the morality of the Koran and the absolute insistence, even by the least pious, on passing on Moslem status through the tangible bodily mark of circumcision.

THE CHRISTIANS

All the project Christians are Catholics, if we are to believe the minister, who asserts that he does not have any parishioners in the project. Individual interviews closely corroborate what the priest says. If the estimate of the amount of belief is based on the observance of liturgical rites, one may think at first that belief is disappearing, but this is not so. It is only that belief and practice are dissociated. The priest estimates that the proportion of believers in La Halle is not below that commonly counted in the city's working-class population—65 percent. He bases this estimate on the number of children going to catechism classes—at least 50 percent—because he claims that none of the adults go to mass on Sunday. Project Catholics do not observe obligatory holidays either, except for Easter communion, to which the women of Spanish and Italian background go. The other holidays (Christmas, Ascension, and Pentecost) have completely fallen into disuse.

We can say then that the project Catholics have given up community religious practices, although half of them still impose them on their children. According to the priest, who teaches them catechism himself because of their backwardness and lack of discipline, these children show great sincerity and go to mass until they have made their solemn communion. It is striking that parents very rarely accompany their children even for this ceremony, and it is the older sisters or invited relatives who take on this role.

But if religious practices are disappearing, gestures and rites count much more than they do elsewhere. The priest tells how one woman came and made a noisy scene because no altar boy served a mass for the dead. It is because of the population from La Halle that the priest refuses to modernize his church by taking out the statues. He thinks he would lose his child clientele if he complied with the present severity of the church. The people would not stand for changes in their usual surroundings.

In fact, individual practices have replaced the formal community rites. "It is not unusual," says the priest, "to find a woman kneeling before a statue or a man sitting with a cigarette butt in the corner of his mouth, in the empty church during the week." They have a religious sense that they express as best as they can and they manufacture a religion for their own use, with special hours or moments and informal prayers.

The interviews with the adults reveal that they "don't go to church because the priests are asking for money all the time" but that they "have a religious temperament and respect the things of the church." Some men admit that they "say a prayer at home" or "go into church sometimes, just like that, when I'm passing by" or "think about God sometimes." The women, whether raised religiously or not, "want to go to church, but don't dare," or go and pray, burn a candle before a statue, or present a bouquet to St. Thérèse when they are "having trouble."

Their prayers always express a request in special circumstances. For instance, one woman went to ask St. Thérèse to grant her wish (that the doctor give her an ovariotomy), but once she got what she wanted she did not go to give thanks. Time has passed and she no longer dares to enter the church. She tried once but had to leave, seized by a laughing fit. The cathedral is on the way to the courthouse, and we know two women who lit a candle before an altar before going to a hearing.

One woman confesses, "I only think about God when I need to." All of them, men and women, wonder sometimes "if there really is someone, seeing there's so much misery," but none of them are avowed atheists. As this comment puts it, "We don't go to church but we're not against it."

A still greater respect is observed in regard to the sacraments but it is addressed to the rites surrounding them rather than to the sacraments themselves. We shall look at them in chronological order.

All the children are baptized sooner or later depending on economic and social difficulties—two or three at a time or on the oldest child's communion day if need be in order to reduce expenses. Baptism has kept its essential meaning since it consists of "bringing the children into something"; "You can't let them be nothing."

Communion, on the other hand, is losing its sacred character and is no longer anything but a rite of passage that is becoming less necessary. Some parents send their children to catechism class because they themselves received instruction in it and they care about passing on religious values; others hope to provide against some danger in this way, for example, "spoiling a marriage because of some business about communion"; and finally others let their children have free choice after they are eight even though they were baptized.

On the contrary, marriage, or at least the first union between two young people, must be blessed by the priest. If they do not just live together in La Halle, they are married in a church. Civil marriage has no value except to legalize an old liaison or a second union.

The sacrament of marriage takes on superstitious import. A union is official and has more chance of lasting if it receives a blessing. Thus it is that a priest is often called upon to marry a pregnant girl to whom he must give religious instruction, baptism, and communion in a week.

The same emphasis on rite is observed in relation to death. The priest says he is never called to the deathbed to bring extreme unction. This may be due to the fact that the sick person dies in the hospital and receives regular visits from the hospital priest, but above all it is because only the funeral rite is important in the eyes of the living. The defunct must be given the proper obsequies.

Now, we know the project people's financial difficulties, and the common burial ground occupies a relatively large space in the town cemetery. However, the family will see most particularly to the quality of the religious service. All the dead are buried "in church," even—or especially—suicides "because we don't tell the priest." "I couldn't have him buried like a dog," says one of the poorest project women who recently became a widow. And behind the coffin, comments are made on how well the priest did: "It was pretty good, after all; there was an organ." This respect for the mortal remains is so general that not a single body has been taken away without an immense wreath of fresh flowers presented by the La Halle community fastened to the hearse. The obsequies could not be solemn if there were no religious office, and this dignity of the interment has infinitely more importance than the last sacraments.

Among the Christians, therefore, there is a very strong religious feeling and respect for the sacred behind an apparent detachment. We have never heard the slightest ironic or irreverent reflection about religion or a profession of atheism even among the men. The belief in God remains but it is detached from community practices, which are abandoned except in the case of particular ceremonies like those surrounding marriage and death.

Superstition

Superstition—pagan survivals or rituals whose meaning has been forgotten—is quite prevalent in the project. It is associated with religious life among the Jews and Moslems and is very widespread; it is very easily discovered by direct observation, and the women talk about it willingly. We shall simply mention a few examples by way of information because a list of all those we know of would be long and tedious.

Moslem babies wear amulets (especially gold fish) to ward off the evil eye. The Jews keep a lamb shoulder bone from one Passover to another in order to have good luck all year.

A Jewish woman holds the fact that she combined the "communion of my two sons" responsible for her financial disappointments. Another threw a handful of salt on the courtroom floor before the trial. Among the Jews, the dead person lies on the ground completely wrapped in a shroud with a knife on his chest before the arrival of those who will cleanse him. It is difficult to obtain precise information about superstition from the Christians, however, because the people refuse to admit they are superstitious, probably out of vanity. Yet practices connected with religion, like the candle or flowers offered to a statue, are readily mentioned as specifically religious acts.

But there are other practices spreading contagiously through the project. Five women we questioned stated that they had each gone twice to the fortune-teller at the saddest times of their lives when the future seemed most uncertain. One claims she does not believe in fortune-telling, but the others assert that the fortune-teller's predictions came true, notably those about a remarriage and a suicide attempt. One of them believes so much in what was predicted to her that she makes no effort because "my wheel won't turn until I'm fifty." The same informants assure us that all the La Halle women have consulted the fortune-teller at least once.

One of them keeps a close watch over everything she does during May ("It's my unlucky month"), and she points out that carnations are not allowed into the house on any pretext ("It's a flower that brings bad luck"). This fear of carnations seems prevalent throughout the project and if a bouquet of them were given to someone, it would be promptly thrown in the garbage.

An umbrella must not be opened in the house nor must shoes be put on the table, on pain of catastrophe. Singing a hymn in the house is the sign of someone's departure; "That's true; it's been proven," says one informant. In order to have money, one must fold the bills lengthwise. Examples of these domestic protective rites against occult dangers could be multiplied many times.

The doctor has not discovered any "old wives' remedies" because traditions about them are lacking, but the women themselves alluded to the faith healer and laying on of hands

that was supposed to have put an end to toothaches for two
of them.

All residents use a magical mode of thought in choosing
horses for the races. The numbers in the birth date of a child
or visitor are added, divided by seven, subjected to complicated calculations or used as they are if the bearer is innocent
(a newborn child, for instance). One woman thinks fate is
against her husband, who never wins, because he will not
let her make up the bet herself. National lottery tickets are
bought on favorable days, for example, when some lucky incident has just happened.

Finally, superstitions specific to the ethnic groups have a
tendency to interpenetrate. It is not unusual to see the
Frenchwomen in mixed households wearing an Arab talisman
(such as a golden hand) around their necks. Following a death,
all the neighbors file through the house of the deceased, regardless of ethnic distinctions, so everyone becomes familiar with
each other's funeral rites, among others. A Jewish woman,
stricken by the death of her daughter and touched by the support of her Christian neighbors, lit oil lamps at home and in
the synagogue and also lit candles in the church in order
to entreat all the gods.

In short, the Christian religion and religious practices seem
to look the same as in other social groups (with the exception
of the belief about carnations), with diminishing observance
and recourse to the same magical procedures (fortune-teller,
lottery, horse races). But the Jewish and Moslem religions,
which are religions of strict observance, are no longer completely followed because of distance from the community,
social pressure in La Halle, and the discontinuance of religious
instruction. This decrease in practice for these two religions
thus appears to be linked to the subculture gradually taking
shape in the project.

Celebrations

Religious holidays are already beginning to become a relic
among the Jews and Moslems and are losing their sacred
character among the Christians. The two most important

holidays, Christmas and Easter, are now solely holidays for
children, with Christmas symbolized by the fir tree and toys
and Easter by candy eggs. Having become profane, these
holidays have now spread to all the groups because of social
pressure operating in the project. The Moslems and Jews do
not want to incur the criticism of their children, who would
otherwise not have any toys on the day when the others are
loaded with them, and the number of Christmas trees is increasing every year. The Easter egg rite is becoming generalized;
a good number of Christians did not know about it before
they came to La Halle but they have since adapted to it. Mardi
Gras barely survives in the form of masks bought for a few
children but All Saints' Day remains a holy day, and all those
who can do so go to the cemetery.

Of the profane national holidays, Bastille Day, a popular
day of gaiety, is loved by all and is greatly prized by the Moslems. They scorn Armistice Day, which they label "crap,"
and celebrate the first of May like a Sunday, not neglecting
to buy a sprig of lily-of-the-valley or to go and pick some and
sell it.

The "Huma Fair" [sponsored by *L'Humanité*, the Commun-
ist party newspaper] or the popular entertainments given by
neighboring municipalities have never been mentioned as
celebrations by the project people although we know they
go to them. On the other hand, they have all talked about
birthdays, which give them an occasion for giving gifts and
"eating some cake with a good bottle of wine," and Mother's
Day, to which they also look forward.[11]

Realizing that some festive events were looked upon as
celebrations, while others were not, the observer was
prompted to ask, "What do you call a celebration?" in order
to see what that concept covers for the people of La Halle.
The answers are very clear. Several general ideas emerge,
and the three principal ones, which are all connected, will
serve to define celebrations in La Halle from three points
of view.

"A celebration is when you drink well, more and better
than usual, and eat well with friends or family, to have a lot
of people, to laugh and talk and tell jokes, sing, dance, not

go to bed, forget your worries, flirt, be petted, have some fun between men and women, kiss whoever you want to."

A celebration is carousing, teasing, even exchanging wives. One cannot help thinking of Flemish paintings or Roman orgies or even the feasts that the peasants have after the toil of the harvest is over. The type of celebration described here is in fact the folk festival on which Varagnac commented at length in *Civilisation Traditionelle et Genres de Vie*, summed up in that statement so applicable to the project:

> We have to enclose too much of ourselves in political and social views now to have the profound enjoyment of those festivities of late when, after having toiled mightily without thinking, our fathers simply yearned to laugh with all their being.[12]

In a society that no longer allows people to be excited and boisterous and that has diluted, dimmed, and almost put an end to festivals, the people of La Halle have rediscovered the old rule that makes it possible for men to last and not wear out, by contrasting the monotony of everyday life and constant worries with the prodigality, squandering, and debauchery of celebrations. After, they will live in the memory of the past festivity and in wait for the next one. It matters little that it took months to accumulate the necessary funds or rather that it takes months of privation to repair the hole in the budget created by the sumptuous expenditures.[13]

The people of La Halle could not live if they did not have festivities from time to time, and since the Jews and Moslems eat enormous amounts of food, the Christians feel abetted in their own excesses. They have such a good time that violence and scuffles break out. Does that mean that festivity in the project means total excess in everything? The answer is given in the definition by another informant: "A celebration is a success when it ends well, when you don't fight, when there is no jealousy between men and women." The project people are afraid of their own behavior because the social organism keeping watch around their enclave does not allow disturbances to go on for days at a time. So there is a limit: sexuality may not be pushed to extremes, and there is a code of the proper use of excess.

The first rule resulting from the definition of celebrations given by the residents themselves is excess in expenditures for food and drink and sexual excess that is still limited and codified. The second rule, to which we have not yet alluded, is contained in the words, "to have a lot of people with friends or family." The notion of festivity contains a value of comradeship, and no celebration is conceivable in La Halle without togetherness in the family or with neighbors. A couple does not have a good time alone, and every good fortune is shared with neighbors or friends. When there is a big Moslem celebration, all the neighbors can come in or, if they do not dare to come in, they receive gifts of food. During preparations for the celebration, which are already part of the festivities, the women quite often help each other in cooking and washing dishes, without regard to ethnic lines.

It should not be thought that festivity in La Halle represents just a vital need for excessive eating. The third rule, like the two others, is given by a resident: "For a celebration to be really beautiful, there has to be a ceremony, like a formal wedding, a communion, or a baptism." In other words, it must follow a ritual, but this ritual may retain more or less of its sacred character. For example, we have remarked that parents do not generally accompany their children on the day of their first communion, but this does not prevent the children from being dressed in the proper clothes. So there is really no celebration without ceremony, even if the adults are not present. This is why they participate in national holidays that have some symbols and ceremonies but fail to mention popular entertainments; while these are accepted as enjoyable occasions, they are not viewed as celebrations.

Celebrations are therefore characterized by three things in the project: by the notion of more marked excess than in the working class, where it is disappearing; by the value of comradeship; and by keeping a ritual that has more or less lost its sacred character. Since this aspect of celebrations is identical for each ethnic group, it seems to be specific to the subculture of La Halle.

In concluding this chapter, we may ask whether all the project people have a common system of values or whether the differences in religion and cultural background constitute a hindrance to the creation of this system of values. It seems that the partly utopian value of comradeship due to living together is an essential moral reference point for all the residents even if it is not always put into actual practice. Moreover, all the negative values connected with authority and positive values connected with prestige seem to be the same.

Similarly, while the material ideal may vary with the individual or more often with the family, the moral ideal (the notion of good and bad) seems to be identical for all. Celebrations are also seen in a similar way, as relics of "traditional civilization."

The important differentiations begin at the level of religious practices and experiences. In fact, if the religions of strict observance, like the religions of laxer observance, are not complied with more fully, it is not for the same reasons. Reference to religious values is not of the same sort for all the project people, for these values continue to exist and remain essential for the Jews and Moslems and only ignorance or the fact that it is materially impossible keeps them from complete compliance, while the Christians do not find these values compelling. A margin of freedom has been set up between actual practice and "ideology" in regard to belief.

It is probably in relation to the system of values that the gestation of a subculture in La Halle is most advanced.

In this third part, we proposed to show whether the closed or open predominated in social relations, time and space, information, or the system of values. In fact, it seems that the play of social relations goes from a partial opening to the outside (through the almost forcible penetration of outsiders and the nonacceptance of their presence) to a complete closing in on itself of the project population in relations with neighbors. There is a compulsory opening kept to the outside and a withdrawal of the project into its internal life.

Actual time in the project and the daily rhythms of living partake of a system that is both closed and open, depending on the type of individual (working people, housewives, children, working or nonworking adolescents, etc.), while the concept of time and space and the actual space remain closed.

On the other hand, information is circulated almost exclusively on the basis of elements from outside. Television, whose importance in the project we have seen, constantly brings in new knowledge, and only rumors arise, spread, and die in the project.

We no longer find either the closed or the open predominating in the system of values, but rather the coexistence of both. Authority, prestige, the notion of good and bad, and comradeship are seen as values always specific to the project. But correspondingly, values linked to ethnic origin and religious traditions (for example, parental authority in the Jewish and Moslem ethnic groups) are incorporated into life in the project without alteration, although minor transformations due to interethnic mixing are beginning to appear.

Moreover, values connected with aesthetics and political and social models and stereotypes are generally accepted in the project as in the society around it and do not seem distorted. Yet it must be noted that even at this level there is an ambiguity between the closed and the open to the extent that while the image of the chief of state is the same as elsewhere, for instance, the relationship they would like to establish with him is very different in La Halle. We recall, for instance, that they readily write to de Gaulle to request housing or the reparation of an injustice.

This ambiguity brings us back again to the realization that there is a subculture. It is this overlapping of society with life in La Halle, this play of contiguity, opposition, and reciprocity between the larger society and the society of La Halle, that seems to constitute the specific subculture of this project.

NOTES

[1]We shall come back to these moral notions again a bit further on.

[2]The Arabs more easily put up with a single contact with the person designated to them and therefore bear with the hierarchy and accept authority better. They try to follow the advice given them because they want to become acculturated. If they seem undisciplined, this is more out of ignorance than willful refusal.

[3]We have seen three of these letters but we have not dared ask for a copy.

[4]Their dislike has to do with superstition: yellow is the color of betrayed love.

[5]The distance from places carrying North African foodstuffs limits them to just occasional trips there.

[6]An appetizer of olives and a variety of chopped vegetables, or stuffed, fried puff pastry.

[7]Oscar Lewis, *The Children of Sanchez* (Random House, 1961), p. xii.

[8]Only one family sends its children to the synagogue to receive religious instruction. The other children do not want to go.

[9]An interruption in the forty-nine days of semimourning following Passover, in honor of the anniversary of the death of Rabbi Simeon in the sixth century, which is celebrated with gaiety.

[10]The length of the fast the children impose on themselves is proportional to their age.

[11] This custom is generalized among the Christians and is spreading to the Jews and Moslems in mixed households.

[12] André Varagnac, *Civilisation Traditionelle et Genres de Vie,* p. 369.

[13] One Arab family bought 220 pounds of couscous to serve at a circumcision. Public rumor raised the figure to 880, and this expenditure incited the admiration of the French.

13

Conclusion

The hypotheses indicated at the beginning of this work were as follows: The project constitutes a group because of the residents' taking root in the space made available to them, the existence of interpersonal relations, the creation of subgroups, and the experiencing of time and space in terms of the structure of the group and its subgroups. In addition, the La Halle project constitutes a special group in relation to other groups in society because the residents feel they are rejected by society and society feels it must deal with them separately. Beside the constraint exercised on the project, the residents' uncertainty about the future is another element that makes up its specific nature; moreover, the residents are actually put in a provisional situation by the government. Finally, La Halle is a group secreting a subculture in relative isolation from society. Despite the presence of three principal ethnic groups, we find a coherence of group feelings in a time linked to the future and in a common system of values.

These hypotheses seem essentially confirmed. As we have seen, the residents have in effect been implanted in a publicly owned space allotted to them. The only choice they were offered was to live in the project or remain ill-housed, and their relocation was mandatory if they occupied condemned buildings. Living in common on the same territory created particular interpersonal relations among these residents, regardless of ethnic group; at no time did we find that ethnic difference was the basis for formation of an ethnically homogeneous group.[1] Interpersonal relationships were established between people living near each other, and there are also those relationships that seem to initiate the appearance of subgroups, either by age (children's and adolescents' subgroups) or by sex (women's subgroups). The structure of these subgroups and of the group itself condition the residents' lives in time and space. Here we should recall that the daily rhythms are experienced differently by the men (as working people) and women (as housewives) on one hand and by the children and adolescents on the other, while the very structure of the group formed by the project imposes common rhythms on certain special times such as Saturday and Sunday. The disposition of space and the lack of time limitations for the children and adolescents are also instituted by the structure of the group and the subgroups.

At first glance one might think that there is simply a twofold opposition between society and the project: society's rejection is a constraint on the project that puts it in opposition to society, and it reacts by creating a subculture.

Society actually does reject the project. Some teachers do not consider the La Halle children like other children, the doctor who has moved into the project only looks after about ten families that he considers normal, the merchants do not give credit, café owners refuse to allow the adolescents into their establishments, and employers readily turn down an applicant when they learn that the project is his address. In reaction, the project opposes society. Set down on a separate piece of land, the project people do not feel involved in community institutions. The children go to school to learn to read, but the school is not a socializing institution to either them or their parents. Neither adolescents nor parents participate in organizations or occasional meetings at the school, church, or town hall. The parish priest does not come into the project, and the vicar visits just the very few families he knows. The opposition to outside institutions (government agencies and the police) is total and is always manifested in aggressive behavior. The children fight to defend their territory against children from other projects, and they threaten the nomads. The feeling of belonging to the project arises from this constant opposition to the outside world. As a reaction against society, the adolescents oppose it, beginning with the neighboring projects, and it is on the basis of this opposition that they form a *we*, saying, "Us kids from La Halle."

This rejection acts as a constraint on the project residents. Their relocation is governmental "charity" and not an acquired right as in the HLM's. They pay their rent to the caretaker but any delay brings the threat of the tax-collector, and the government keeps a file on each tenant in which any "misbehavior" is noted. It is this governmental distraint that contributes a provisional and uncertain tonality to the individual and collective future in the project. If the future is indeterminate for individuals and families in society generally, it is usually for economic reasons or because of personal difficulties, but in La Halle the threat of eviction for nonpayment of rent or for what the government defines as "misbehavior" particularizes the uncertainty of the future. The appearance of a subculture seems to result from the population's reaction to this rejection by the society around it and the constraint it is under.

In fact, we find a common system of values based on solidarity from living together that is really manifested on the level of survival but otherwise remains utopian in aspirations that are never completely realized. This system of values includes a common notion of good and bad and identical values in relation to authority and prestige.

The concept of a closed space belonging to life in the project and of a time measured off by seeking solutions for daily economic constraints, lived from day to day and, we repeat, indeterminate as to the future, is also interethnic and specific to life in La Halle. Moreover, modes of thought, living habits, and nascent traditions are becoming uniform. Ethnic differences seem to be nothing more than relics, and some of them are tending to become generalized or at least to be called the same thing. The traditions of Christmas trees and Easter eggs are admitted into practically every home, circumcision is called baptism by the Jews and Arabs, and there are common clothing fashions and ways of decorating the apartment. There is a tendency toward homogenization.

But the problem is not only one of a twofold opposition between society and the project; we must not forget that there is constant interaction between this group and the society around it. The twofold opposition is just one aspect of this interaction which, as we have shown, also comprises coming together, being involved with each other, and carrying on analogous activities. La Halle does not in fact constitute an administrative unit, it is not under any separate management by the central government, and it is administered directly by the various levels of government. In addition, the project has been formed into a specific group by a constraint to which it reacts, and this reaction itself is a constant relationship with society, in modes of thought as much as in practical life. Moreover, although the original cultures of each ethnic group are being progressively obliterated, they continue to play a role, as we have indicated, to the extent that they fade into the subculture being formed (in some aspects of holidays, for example).

Among other things, we have noted that economic conditions are the same as in other categories of people and are even better than in some, and that the rhythms of life scarcely differ from those in the surrounding society. Moreover, the subculture takes the national culture as its reference to such an extent that the ethnic groups' original cultures are disappearing.

We shall take the liberty here of very tentatively suggesting two questions for future research on this type of problem.

First, is the La Halle project not like a prison? In other words, because of bureaucratic and psychological constraints exerted by society, the always unfavorable economic conditions among this population, and the distance from the traditional areas of residence, plus a material, moral, and cultural life consequently different in many respects from the social life around it, the project people are enclosed in a mode of existence that is almost compulsory. At the very least they live under such strict conditions that La Halle might be compared to hospitals, prisons, and boarding schools, which are created out of nothing by society for its marginal members to live in.

Second, would not this environment of prisonlike propensities be strongly inclined to make the people of La Halle into what J. R. Pitts elsewhere calls a "delinquent community"?[2] Pitts speaks of a "delinquent community" in connection with students in an educational institution. He believes that the rigid system of instruction, in which the students participate only by submission and therefore negatively, leads them to form groups united by the awareness of their common condition. From then on, their only way of affirming their existence consists of being rowdy, an embryonic form of revolt.

The problem is slightly different in La Halle to the extent that the intention of the external social system is only partly the socialization of these people and it seems principally a system of rejection to the residents. But its rigidity is comparable to the boarding school and doubtlessly conditions group behavior, which is always aggressive toward the outside world.

But—and here is the real problem—what would make the project a specific social and cultural group? Would it not be the fact that it is a group marginal to the society around it even though it is constantly interacting with that society? The dialectic between the closed and the open that we have tried to develop in these last chapters seems to us to be at the heart of the project's specific subculture. It also leaves its mark on social relations to the extent that, although they are of the same type as in the rest of society, these relations take a special form in both the old and new generations because they belong to a marginal group.

In the introduction to his book, *The Children of Sanchez,* we recall that Oscar Lewis develops the concept of the "culture of poverty," which he also sometimes calls a subculture to the extent that it seems to be in a first stage and will then form a real culture. He gives it essentially the same characteristics we have attributed to the La Halle project:

> The economic traits which are most characteristic of the culture of poverty include the constant struggle for survival, unemployment and underemployment, low wages, a miscellany of unskilled occupations, child labor, the absence of savings, a chronic shortage of cash, the absence of food reserves in the home. . . . the pawning of personal goods, borrowing from local money lenders at usurious rates of interest, spontaneous informal credit devices . . . organized by neighbors, and the use of second-hand clothing and furniture.
>
> Some of the social and psychological characteristics include . . . a lack of privacy, gregariousness, a high incidence of alcoholism, frequent resort to violence in the training of children, wife beating, early initiation into sex.[3]

On the cultural level, Lewis adds:

> A critical attitude toward some of the values and institutions of the dominant classes, hatred of the police . . . gives the culture of poverty a counter quality. . . . Finally, the sub-culture of poverty also has a residual quality in the sense that its members are attempting to utilize and integrate into a workable way of life the remnants of beliefs and customs of diverse origins.[4]

We seem to find here the essential social and cultural characteristics of La Halle's life and culture. They are largely the same as those indicated by Proudhon in *La Guerre et la Paix,* if one is careful to remove all pejorative nuances from the terms he uses. As for the rejection on society's part, the description Louis Chevalier gives of the "dangerous classes" in the nineteenth century also corresponds to society's present attitude toward the transitional housing projects.

But for Proudhon and nineteenth-century society, as well as for Oscar Lewis, there is a cultural tradition of poverty transmitted as a heritage from generation to generation. It is on this point that our hypotheses differ. In fact, the population we have studied is by no means the heir of their nineteenth-century predecessors, either by the type of territory it occupies, material conditions (those of industrial society), or beliefs and modes of thought. It really seems that due to transformations in society, the lumpenproletariat described by Proudhon and Chevalier have as their heirs the modern working class. In the La Halle project, we have become acquainted with a population composed of individuals of different ethnic backgrounds and equipped with different original cultures, assembled fortuitously and not by choice, and tending (according to the hypothesis we have tried to prove) to constitute a subculture of society. We admit that such a social group forms a neo-proletariat, if you like, but without any continuity with the old one.

Moreover, it has not been proved that the adults transmit their poverty to the coming generation. In fact it must be noted that while the adolescents' aspirations remain specific to the material and cultural life of La Halle because of endogenous socialization and the unity of the system of values, they nevertheless tend constantly toward an integration with society.

This is where we are furthest from Oscar Lewis. As we have already said, in the type of social and cultural group we have studied, we think the characteristic quality of the subculture it constitutes comes from its marginality and its interaction with society at the same time. Such groups are not involved with society, but they interact with it. Moreover, in a letter he sent us dated February 20, 1967, Lewis qualifies his notion of the "culture of poverty," defined in his introduction as transcending "regional, rural–urban, and even national differences." Now he seems to want to link it much more to national culture:

> In my new book, *La Vida* (Random House, 1966) I have described some variations on the culture of poverty which have led me to suggest that the sub-culture of poverty has some distinctive national characteristics in addition to the universal ones. Perhaps this is something you should give some thought to.[5]

The question has been raised. We cannot begin to find an answer to it in France on the basis of a single study such as we have just made or some parallel works previously mentioned. Long comparative studies are necessary. For our part, we propose to continue our research on the subculture of marginal groups on the outskirts of large cities in underdeveloped countries or in the ghettos and shantytowns of our urban society, whether or not these groups include different ethnic groups.

NOTES

[1]We have sometimes used the word "group" to designate people of the same ethnic background, but it is quite clear that this term is taken in its popularly accepted meaning and not in its sociological sense.

[2]J. R. Pitts, *The Bourgeois Family and French Economic Retardation"* (Ph. D. diss., Harvard University, 1957), cited by Crozier in *Le Phénomène Bureaucratique.*

[3]Oscar Lewis, *The Children of Sanchez,* p. xxvi.

[4]Ibid., p. xxvii.

[5]Cf. Lenin: "Proletarian culture does not do away with national culture . . ." (Quoted by Roger Bastide in his 1958–1959 course.)

Appendix

Case Histories

Mr. S., Algerian, age thirty-eight

I am from a village on the Algerian-Moroccan border, but I'm an Algerian, an Arab. It was just half an hour's taxi ride from Oujda. My father worked fifteen years for Renault. He left his wife over there in the country, in the house of our grandfather, who kept sheep. His wife wasn't my mother—she died when I was little—and she didn't like me. I had just two sisters. I was raised over there and since I was the only boy, I had to help my grandfather on the land. My father lived in Meudon with a Breton whom he called his fiancée, Mrs. Jeanne. One time in about 1949 he came back to the country; he was big and fat because they ate well at Mrs. Jeanne's: paté, chicken, meat; they had wine; it was great. He stayed a year on his land to help Grandfather and when he went back Mrs. Jeanne didn't like it because he was all black and thin. I said, "Father, I want to go to France too." He didn't

277

want me to, but I left just the same. I lived in Clichy in a home for North Africans, and I went to work for Renault. Then I left because my father sent me back, and then I came back. At that time I was living in a hotel on Rue Vaugirard in the 15th [arrondissement], yes it was the 15th; I stayed there four years. I had gotten married meanwhile, and I left my wife over there. My father, who had left and come back, ordered me to go back to Grandfather, who was getting too old to take care of the land. I refused; I told him, "I'll never go back home to Algeria." What bothered him was that my uncle had come to France too. My uncle is with the electric company—that's the government, there's nothing better than the government. He married a Frenchwoman. My uncle came to Meudon one dày, just like that, with my father's wife and the two girls: he knocked in the night and said, "I've brought you your wife." Mrs. Jeanne didn't like that, but they stayed several months anyhow. My father's wife wasn't jealous; she knew about it. My father went out to the movies with Mrs. Jeanne. His wife lived downstairs. Then the mayor of Meudon promised my father housing but he didn't want it. He preferred to go back to Algeria; but he came smack up against the war over there and he couldn't come back, and then the Harkis killed him in 1956. Afterwards, I went into a sanatorium for eight months, in the mountains—I had my wife come in '59—while my right leg was hurting me. It's my hip that's bad; I've been operated on twice. I went on vacation [in a rest home] through the hospital's social worker. I've had a lot of trouble with this leg. Since I'm an invalid, I don't work anymore; I don't do anything; I go downstairs a little. We lived at my uncle's while I was sick; afterwards we got the place here, and we're quite happy. My wife doesn't say anything but I know she'd rather live in M—— because it's like home. But I would rather be here. My daughter is in sixth grade; we're not savages any more.

Mr. K., Tunisian Jew, age fifty

I was born in Tunis; I know every street and corner of it. I'm from a family of twelve; nine boys and three girls. My

father sold cloth in the Moslem quarter. I was the oldest. I
have my elementary school diploma. I supervised my brothers'
and sisters' homework. There's one who has his supervisor's
certificate, thanks to me. In those days they gave a lot of
homework in school. My brothers were afraid of me; I gave
it to them if they wouldn't work. My sisters married well.
My brothers all moved around Paris, one after the other; they're
all well fixed. There's one at the post office, a mailman, the
youngest, who earns a lot of money; another works in insurance; another is a typographer; and another is in printing too.
Everyone's made out well. They came on my advice; I had
foreseen for a long time that we'd have to leave Tunisia. I
came to work in France ten years ago but I left my wife and
kids over there. We had a house at La Goulette, near the casino,
you know, near the beach; it's a very gay neighborhood in
Tunis, there's lots of people in the summer, you have a good
time, everyone lives outdoors. I went back every year. I hoped
some day we could sell the house in La Goulette, which
belonged to me, but we couldn't take a penny out of Tunisia.
Then when I found a two-room place in Saint-Georges, I had
my wife come five years ago. We piled in as best we could;
we had a hotel room, and besides that we had a kid living
here or there from time to time. The Jewish social fund gave
us money and we got blankets and clothes; they came just
like that. And then we were relocated here, but I managed
to keep the two-room flat where my two working daughters
live.

When I come home at night I want peace and quiet; I don't
pay enough attention to the kids, who are doing badly in school.
I've really done all kinds of things in my lifetime, I've knocked
around a lot. I was the bey's electrician. I spent seven years
in the navy, where I was an officer [sic]. Now I work on the
high-tension wires; it's dangerous and tiring. I have a stomach
ulcer but I don't want to stop working because then I get
bored and go to the bar. The apartment is nice here, we have
six rooms, it's comfortable, and all that, but I've had enough
of living with other people on top of me all the time, and
the caretaker who lays down the law, and you can't do this

and that. I have ten kids at home, or rather, eleven, because we're raising a grandchild; they've got to make noise.

It doesn't pay to leave the project to go into an HLM. It's the same thing—they're still big buildings. I want to buy a house so I can do what I want. It's well worth pulling in your belt a little to pay for it. I've found one in V——; it's closer to Saint-Georges. I think I'll buy it; the kids will help me pay for it.

Mrs. W., French, born in the neighboring commune of parents from the same locality, age twenty-nine, three children

We lived in Marseilles because of the evacuation; I was seven when we came back. My father rented three apartments in an old tenement. It was nice; there was a bit of a yard. But the neighbors in the other wing stank. They had a lot of children, the wife was a drunkard, and so was her husband. What struck me as a kid was that she had lots of varicose veins and her legs used to bleed when he hit her. I still think about it sometimes. She slept with her son-in-law, who also beat her, and when she was tired she'd say, "I'm too done in; take the kid." She was fourteen, the girl. You could hear everything, and we got sick of it. Those people went to jail later on. And upstairs there was another awful couple who yelled and hit each other with a knife in the yard. We were kids, we were scared; we never forgot those images.

I was the oldest; then there was my sister and four brothers. My father wasn't my father. I didn't find out until I was nineteen but I had a suspicion. He didn't like me and, besides, my mother didn't either. Both of them took it out on me; I got beaten up for every little thing. I was scared to death of him; I used to shake when I saw him turn up even when I was sure I hadn't done anything.

My father had a cabinet-making shop right near X——. When he hadn't finished his work, he used to bring corner tables, chair legs, tables into the shed downstairs to be varnished. My sister and I varnished almost every night. We did our homework after, at 11:00 or 12:00. First we sanded, then we put on the varnish, then a light alcohol rub; you had to do

it fast and not let the wad of cloth draggle. If we pressed
too hard, he clouted us one. He hit us for nothing. My sister
and I stuck together and made up a lot of crap about him.
My brother pissed in his boots one day; what a beating he
got that day! We didn't give a darn because he hit us anyway.

We had an obsession about going home after school, because
of him and his varnishing. Nauseated, we were. He went to
soccer games on Sunday when he was young, and fishing after.
We took a deep breath when we saw him leaving. He wasn't
happy either. My mother didn't like him; I don't know why
she married him, maybe because she had me on her hands.
He was a responsible person, though, that I'm sure of, responsible and hard-working. She went running around in the afternoon and even at night; I've seen all kinds of guys at the
house. Anyway, now he lives alone; he's raising the last two,
who are thirteen and fifteen. She wound up getting locked
out and now she's a whore.

As soon as I left school (I never liked school either) I went
to work to get away from the varnishing. I've been at several
factories; I stayed three years at the electrical assembly plant.
Later I met Robert. At first we went out for two years, then
we got together and made an arrangement with my mother,
who gave us a room. I didn't want to get married; I was afraid;
I had seen too much. I would rather have stayed like that;
it seemed like I was more secure. But after three years I got
pregnant so we got married anyhow. And then it started. He
who had always been so nice to me, sweet, polite, and everything, he started going out like a kid and leaving me home
alone. I wasn't working anymore since the baby was born.
He used to go out at night with his boss, whom he liked very
much, to take a ride in the car or go dancing. He talked bad
to me; he said, "Kept women are supposed to slave." And
I, like an idiot, used to watch for him at the window at
lunchtime and iron his shirts. I was bored to death, especially
when we came to live here. If I asked to go out with him,
he'd say, "You can go out with your brat." I didn't understand
why he hurt me. All those dirty words, it was like blows.
Honestly, I'd rather he'd smack me one. He used to tell me,

"You have a puss like a mackerel," or "With your ugly puss you'll wind up like your whore of a mother." But I behaved myself, I didn't do anything, I didn't go out. But a lot of good it did to forgive him each time; in the end I wound up so's I couldn't stand him. And then he was burned in a gas explosion, and it took him three weeks to die in the hospital. I'm the one he called for. Since then I've been living with Michel, who is much younger. For a long time I had an aversion to men. I didn't want to see anyone, I didn't know what to do any more, I let myself go. And then the young people came at night to talk and drink coffee. I kept Michel—I don't know why, maybe because he was still almost a kid. And then he knows if he insults me once, he won't get through the door again. He never talks bad to me.

Poems by a Resident of La Halle for His Wife

New Year's Day–Happy Day

'Tis the end of the year. Soon New Year's Day
Christmas will pass, and then we may
Rejoice with Patricia. For that, 'tis true,
First of January, we waited for you.

We'll set out to see our dear girl, we two
New Year's Day, our thanks to you
You bring a great joy for us this year,
Of holding at last our child so dear.

Would you run a bit, the sooner to come,
To make your visit tomorrow? And from
The door we would our arms hold out,
Hearts filled with joy, together set out.

And you can be sure, in the following year
The day you come we'll all four be here
In our hearts no trace of care you'll see
Reunited forever we four shall be.

Moral

Twenty-six months of woe I've had to take, but then
All that will be blotted out when I am free again.

Your husband (Fernand)

Spring

Like a clock set endlessly marking the hours
Spring comes to warm these hearts of ours
After a hard winter's suffering
'Neath the sky of France, here comes the spring
The birds in the branches sing all their delight
And fly joyously off, on the roofs to alight
And on the bare ground, the grass so sweet
Also comes up, this new spring to greet
The buds 'way up in the branches too
Put forth their first flowers for this spring so new
In the sky a return of the swallows we find
Now it is time to leave flannels behind
In the meadows and woods the first flowers start
Making us happy and warming our heart
The strolls in the woods again are starting
And the joy of the children in frisking and darting
All turns so lovely that charming day
That young and old find joy come their way
And I cannot but send, on this day so fine,
To this great renewal, these good wishes of mine.

For you (Fernand)

Refrain of a Song Composed by an Adolescent Gang Leader (Henri)

I have given up everything, Father and Mother,
For a black leather jacket
Shiny as the night (repeat)
But you know, fine people,
Black jackets
Go to jail, fine people,
At age sixteen (repeat).

Bibliography

Books

Bachelard, G. *La Poétique de l'Espace* (Paris: Presses Universitaires de France, 1967).

Balandier, G. *Afrique Ambiguë* (Paris: Plon, 1957).

Bastide, R. *Sociologie des Maladies Mentales* (Paris: Flamarion, 1965).

Bernot, L., and Blanchard, R. *Nouville–Village Français* (Paris: Institut d'Ethnologie, 1953).

Bloch, H., and Niederhoffer, A. *Les Bandes d'Adolescents* (Paris: Petite bibliothèque Payot #49, 1963).

Bourdieu, P., and Sayad, A. *Le Déracinement* (Paris: Editions de Minuit, 1964).

Caillois, R. *L'Homme et le Sacré* (Paris: Gallimard, Nouvelle revue française [N.R.F.], Idées series, 1950).

Chevalier, L. *Classes Laborieuses et Classes Dangereuses* (Paris: Plon, 1958).

Chombard de Lauwe, Ph. *Des Hommes et des Villes* (Paris: Payot, 1965).

————. *Famille et Habitation* (Paris: Centre National de la Recherche Scientifique edition, 1956). 2 vols.

Epstein, J. *Le Judaïsme* (Paris: Petite bibliothèque Payot #19, 1959).

Fau, R. *Les Groupes d'Enfants et d'Adolescents* (Paris: Presses Universitaires de France, Collection Paideia, 1952).

Friedlander, K. *La Délinquance Juvénile* (Paris: Presses Universitaires de France, 1951).

Friedman, G. *Sept Etudes sur l'Homme et la Technique* (Paris: Bibliothèque Méditations, Gonthier, 1966).

George, P. *Géographie de Consommation* (Paris: Presses Universitaires de France. Que Sais-je? series #1062, new edition, 1964).

————. *Géographie Sociale du Monde* (Paris: Que Sais-je? series #197, new edition, 1964).

Guy-Grand, G. *Pour Connaître la Pensée de Proud'hon* (Paris: Bordas, 1947).

Halbwachs, M. *La Mémoire Collective* (Paris: Presses Universitaires de France, 1947).

Herskovits, M.J. *Les Bases de l'Anthropologie Culturelle* (Paris: Payot).

Hossenlopp, M. *Essai Psychologique sur les Bandes de Jeunes Voleurs* (Paris: Clermont-Ferrand, Imprimerie Générale, 1944).

Huizinga, L. *Homo Ludens* (Paris: Gallimard, N.R.F., 1951).

Laignel-Lavastine, P. M., and Stanciu, V. V. *Précis de Criminologie* (Paris: Payot, 1950).

Le Corbusier. *Manière de Penser l'Urbanisme* (Paris: Gonthier, 1946).

Leroi-Gourhan, A. *Le Geste et la Parole* (Paris: Albin Michel, 1965).

Lewis, O. *Les Enfants de Sanchez* (Paris: Gallimard, N.R.F., 1963; French translation).

Mauss, M. *Sociologie et Anthropologie*, 2d ed. (Paris: Presses Universitaires de France, 1960).

Michel, A. *Famille, Industrialisation, Logement* (Paris: Centre National de la Recherche Scientifique, 1959).

Parrot, Ph., and Gueneau, M. *Les Gangs d'Adolescents* (Paris: Presses Universitaires de France, 1959).

Robert, Ph. *Les Bandes d'Adolescents* (Paris: Editions Ouvrières).

Varagnac, A. *Civilisation Traditionelle et Genres de Vie* (Paris: Albin Michel, 1948).

Periodicals

Brochon, Pierre. "La Littérature Populaire et son Public." *Communications* 1 (Paris: Editions du Seuil, 1961): pp. 70–80.

Coing, H. "Attitudes Devant le Relogement." *Projet,* March 1966, pp. 276–290.

Colin, Armand, George, P., and others. "Etudes sur la Banlieu de Paris." *Cahiers de la Fondation Nationale des Sciences Politiques,* no. 12.

Friedmann, G. "La Télévision Vécue." *Communications* 3 (Paris: Editions du Seuil, 1964): pp. 48–63.

George, P. "Présent et Avenir des Grands Ensembles." *Cahiers Internationaux de Sociologie* 35 (Paris: Presses Universitaires de France, 1963): pp. 25–42.

Grégoire, Menie. "Le Camp de Noisy-le -Grand." *Esprit,* November 1964, pp. 858–868.

Hazemann, R. "L'Humanisation des Grands Ensembles." *Revue d'Hygiène et de Médecine Sociale* (Masson, March 1976), pp. 159–174.

"L'Immigration Portugaise." *Hommes et Migrations* (Paris: Esna No. 105).

Institut National de la Statistique et des Etudes Economiques. *Bulletin Mensuel de la Statistique* (Paris: Presses Universitaires de France, new series, no. 1).

Institut National d'Etudes Démographiques [Census Bureau] *Travaux et Documents,* Book No. 24, "Les Algeriens en France."

Janowitz, Morris, and Schulze, Robert. "Tendances de la Recherche dans le Domaine des Communications de Masse." *Communications* 1 (Paris: Editions du Seuil, 1961): pp. 16–37.

LeBras, G. "Mesure de la Vitalité Sociale du Catholicisme en France." *Cahiers Internationaux de Sociologie* 8 (Paris: Presses Universitaires de France, 1950): pp. 3–39.

Memmi, A., and Zoberman, N. S. "Recherche sur la Judéité en

France." *Revue Française de Sociologie* 6 (January-March 1965): pp. 68–76.

Parrot, P. "Les Vols de Voitures chez l'Adolescent." *Sauvegarde de l'Enfance*, May 1957.

"Pauvres et Pauvreté dans les Sociétés Riches." Economie et Humanisme, no. 174 (March-June 1967), especially pp. 2–13 and 54–59.

Roumajon, J. "Comportements Inadaptés de l'Adolescent Normal." *Psychiâtrie de l'Enfant* 4 (Paris: Presses Universitaires de France, 1961), section 1.

Sainsaulieu, R. "Les Classes Sociales Défavorisées et la Télévision." *Revue Française de Sociologie* 7 (April-June 1966): pp. 201–214.

Index

Administration of the project, xix-xx, xxii, 12, 13-16, 271, 272

Adolescence, end of, 142, 170

Adolescent
activities: economic within gang, 157-165; occupations, 134-139; play, 152-154; sexual, 60-61, 65-66, 154-157

gang: activities, 152-154; basis of, 143-144, 148-149, 150, 170-171; changes in, 134, 150, 169-170; leaders, 146-148; relations between gangs, 134, 151; relations with girls, 150, 154-157; sanctions in,

Adolescent (cont.)
149-150, 151; territory, 144-146

language, 151-152

social relations: adults in project, 144; girls, 142, 143, 150, 154-157; parents, 139-143, 222-223; siblings, 140-141; society, 144, 153, 171. *See also* Adolescent gang

values, 253-254; aesthetics, 168-169, 171, 247, 283; attitudes toward parents and work, 141-142; attitudes toward society, 153, 168, 171, 275; money, 164-165; mutual aid, 171; theft, 165-168